Learning Difficulties and Computers

Books of related interest

Children with Special Needs
Assessment, Law and Practice –
Caught in the Act (2nd edition)
Harry Chasty and John Friel
ISBN 1 85302 155 5

Dyslexia: How Would I cope?
Michael Ryden
ISBN 1 85302 026 5

Strategies for Teaching Students with
Mild to Severe Mental Retardation
Edited by Robert A. Gable
ISBN 1 85302 141 5

Learning Difficulties and Computers

Access to the Curriculum

David Hawkridge and Tom Vincent

Jessica Kingsley Publishers

London and Philadelphia

First published in the United Kingdom in 1992 by
Jessica Kingsley Publishers Ltd
118 Pentonville Road
London N1 9JB

Copyright © 1992 David Hawkridge and Tom Vincent

British Library Cataloguing in Publication Data
Hawkridge, David G.
  Learning Difficulties and Computers
  Access to the Curriculum
  I. Title II. Vincent, Tom
  371.92

ISBN 1 85302 132 6

Printed and Bound in Great Britain by
Biddles Ltd, Guildford and King's Lynn

Contents

List of figures

Preface

> Participation in the National Curriculum by pupils with special educational needs is most likely to be achieved by encouraging good practice for all pupils. *A Curriculum for All* (National Curriculum Council, 1989a)

This book is about good practice in giving children and adults with special educational needs access to the curriculum with the aid of computers. For the benefit of teachers, parents and the learners themselves, it tells stories of the best that is happening in the worst of cases.

Good practice includes using computers as aids. In 1990, all the 1117 English primary and secondary schools responding to a survey reported that their pupils with special educational needs were using information technology (Department of Education and Science, 1991a).

Good practice must be spread. Of the primary schools in the 1990 survey, 81 percent said they would welcome more advice on how to use the technology with these pupils. For secondary schools, the figure was 77 percent. This is clear evidence that teachers are not yet well-versed in what is after all a new technology being applied in an exceptionally problematic field.

In this book we analyse use of computers to help children and adult learners with cognitive and emotional difficulties, physical and sensory disabilities. We draw on recent research and development in two leading countries in special education, the United Kingdom and the United States. We incorporate directly the good practice revealed by a 1990–91 collaborative study carried out by teachers and others working under our direction and funded by the Nuffield Foundation, a British body supporting research that advances health, education and social welfare. We combine the expertise of teachers with our own knowledge gained in schools, colleges and research centres.

What is good practice? We selected most of the examples in this book because we had seen them with our own eyes, because they were recommended to us by leaders in the field, or because they had already gained acceptance through publication elsewhere. In education there is no guarantee of success, even in those rare instances when learners using a new technique do much bettter on tests than those taught by traditional means. We looked instead for enthusiasm and interest on the part of teachers and learners, for opportunities for the latter to do what they could not otherwise do, for feelings of achievement and restored self-esteem.

We want to tell these stories, in context, to all engaged in helping children and adults with learning difficulties to access the curriculum: teachers, advisory teachers, advisors and inspectors, parents, policy-makers in education and health services, administrators and principals. We also write for staff and students in teacher training institutions: a 1989 survey of information technology in initial teacher training in England and Wales showed that more than 70 percent of these institutions want to give the technology higher priority, but about 60 percent of the staff do not yet use it in their own teaching (Department of Education and Science, 1991b). Finally, we hope that this book will be read by some adult students, too, and will help them to overcome their learning difficulties.

The Nuffield Foundation generously funded our first study (Hawkridge, Vincent and Hales, 1985), which was well received by reviewers in educational, medical, nursing, social welfare and disability journals, but is now out of print in the UK and the US. A few other books are available on special education and computers. Any published before 1988 seems very dated, including our own! First in the US was Goldenberg's (1979) pre-microcomputer analysis of special needs and technological possibilities. Then, the possibilities did not seem nearly as great as the needs. Taber's (1983) booklet for the US Council for Exceptional Children also drew attention to the potential of microcomputers for special education.

Perhaps the best illustrated and most readable volume published before 1985 was Goldenberg's (1984) second book, aimed at US student teachers and teachers, but it contained very little on theory and its long lists of resources rapidly became obsolete. Another interesting US book was Hagen's (1984), of which half was devoted to resource lists, unfortunately out-of-date by the time they were published. Rostron and Sewell (1985), British psychology lecturers, dealt particularly with profoundly deaf children and computers and offered a theoretical basis for their research. Behrmann (1985, 1988) edited papers by US academics and education officials involved in special education. In the UK, Hope (1986) edited papers written by special education teachers, mainly but not solely on using micros with children with moderate learning difficulties. Her book dealt with improving self-esteem and motivation; language skills; reading, writing and spelling; number skills; problem-solving strategies and interpersonal skills.

Hameyer and Waldow (1987) prepared their book, in English, after a 1985 conference in Kiel, Federal Republic of Germany. Most of the papers dealt with general concepts, but a few were reports of small-scale research worth noting. By contrast, Hope (1987) based her second book on what she learned in the UK Microelectronics in Education Programme and later. Written in practical vein for teachers, it dealt especially well with computers and children with cognitive difficulties, trying to use children's needs as the starting point.

Fowler (1988) coordinated a 1985–87 project, funded by the European Social Fund and other bodies, based firmly on classroom practice. The book drew on termly reports written by lecturers at ten colleges and had good examples of Further Education (FE) students enjoying learning with the computer. The tone was practical, with no theory at all, though there were some general observations. The illustrations were frequent and good. It was a book for FE lecturers.

Vincent (1990) drew together the experience of students, staff, and participants in Local Education Authority, regional and national schemes for using new technology to meet special educational needs. He compiled his book from individual articles by 120 authors, as part of the UK contribution to an Organisation for Economic Cooperation and Development (OECD) study of information technology in education. Finally, Singleton (1991) edited conference contributions from British researchers and teachers working on how computers could help those with dyslexia and other language difficulties.

Much can be learned from perusing this literature, but we felt sure the time had come for a book covering recent good practice across the special education field. Our new book is an update for the 1990s. We have not rehearsed yet again all that happened in the 1980s. In Part 1, Chapter 1 looks at the world of students with learning difficulties and the role of computers in that world. Chapters 2–5, making up Part 2, review the needs of learners with cognitive and emotional difficulties, and those with physical and sensory disabilities, in gaining access to the curriculum, and look at recent helpful computer-related technical developments, with many examples. What the teachers and others have told us is the foundation for Part 3, Chapters 6–13, more than half the book. These pages are full of good ideas, examples of how access to the curriculum is achievable with computers. Finally, in Part 4, Chapters 14–16 on policy and practice, we deal with assessing individuals' needs, staff training and the changes still needed during the next decade.

What qualifications do we bring to the task? David Hawkridge is Professor of Applied Educational Sciences in the Open University's Institute of Educational Technology, an important centre for research in this field, not least because the OU has over 3000 disabled students. Before joining the OU, he directed evaluations of educational projects for disadvantaged children in the United States. His PhD at the University of London was on the education of older children with cognitive difficulties, whom he taught for six years. He is the senior author of four other books about computers and education.

Tom Vincent is Senior Lecturer in Educational Technology in the Open University's Institute of Educational Technology. Since joining the OU he has become very well-known for his work with disabled students, particularly through his Computing for Blind People project, and has been awarded the MBE. He was seconded to the Department of Education and Science 1986–88 as an HMI (school inspector) with a national remit for information technology in special education at all levels. He is co-author of two books about computers and education, and editor of another.

David Hawkridge
Tom Vincent
Institute of Educational Technology
The Open University,
Milton Keynes, MK7 6AA

Acknowledgements

Without a grant such as we received from the Nuffield Foundation, this study would have been impossible. We thank the Trustees. We thank the National Council for Educational Technology, Coventry, for agreeing to us drawing on the Council's publications, and for introducing us to teachers and advisors who worked with us: at the Council, Tina Detheridge, Peter Fowler and Richard Poutney were particularly helpful. We would also like to thank the following in the United Kingdom: Joy Bell (Fleming Fulton School, Belfast), Angela Bolton, Helen Dando and Ann Morgan (Ysgol Cefn Glas, Bridgend), Marie Buckland (Kings Weston School, Bristol), Ian Butterworth (Wiltshire Special Needs Computer Centre, St. Peter's School, Devizes), David Calderwood, Giles Clark, Bill Martin and Andrew Wade (The Open University), William Fawkes (formerly at the Mary Hare Grammar School for the Deaf, Newbury), David Haigh (Park Special School, Wakefield), Bill Howard (Boxmoor House School, Hemel Hempstead), Jean Johnston and Katie Pester (Bristol Special Education Microelectronics Resource Centre), Virginia Kelly (School of Education, University of Southampton), Harry McMahon and Bill O'Neill (School of Education, University of Ulster, Coleraine), John Mansfield (London Borough of Sutton), Myles Pilling (St John's School, Bedford), Susie Pinder (Bromley), Roisin Skeffington (St Peter's Primary School, Belfast), Anne Slater (Inner London Educational Computing Centre), Judith Stansfield (Cleveland Educational Computing Centre, Middlesbrough), Jean Tait (Redbridge Special Education Resource Centre), Jean Taylor (Claremont School, Westbury on Trym) and Andrew Wood (Bryncethin Junior School, Bridgend).

In the United States, although we focussed on visiting institutions in California, people elsewhere were also very helpful. We thank: Alan Brightman and Sybil Ellery (Apple Computer, Cupertino, CA), Vicki Casella (San Francisco State University, CA), Lisa Cohen, Anthony Armenta and Heather Walker (Mountain View Special Education Technology Center, CA), Anne Disdier (Trenton State College, NJ), Rona Gertzulin (Santa Cruz Schools, CA), Deborah Gilden (Smith-Kettlewell Foundation, San Francisco), Ronni Griese, Brian Shanner and Wally Manville (Foothill College, Los Altos, CA), David Jaffe (Veterans Administration Medical Center, Palo Alto, CA), Susan Kwock (Special Education, San Francisco Schools, CA), Ann McCormick (Nueva Center for Learning, Hillsborough, CA), Anne Meyer (Center for Applied Special Technology, Peabody, MA), Terry Middleton and Mark Schlafer (SRI International, Menlo Park, CA), Helen Miller (Disabled Children's Computer Group, Berkeley, CA), Benita Rashall (De Anza College, Cupertino, CA), Karen Spychala (McKinley School, San Jose, CA), Sue Swezey (Western

Center for Microcomputers in Special Education, Menlo Park, CA), Joyce Teekell (Mt. Diablo Schools, CA), Decker Walker (Stanford University, CA) and Richard Wanderman (*MacLab MonitorN*, Litchfield, CT). We also thank Veronica James (University of New South Wales, Sydney) and Denise Wood (Crippled Children's Association, Kilkenny).

We thank the publishers and the author for permission to quote from Douglas Biklen's article, 'Communication Unbound: Autism and Praxis', *Harvard Educational Review*, 60, 3, pp.291–314. Copyright © 1990 by the President and Fellows of Harvard College. All rights reserved. We thank the publishers and the principal author for permission to quote from Alan F. Newell, Lynda Booth and William Beattie's article, 'Predictive text entry with *PAL* and children with learning difficulties', *British Journal of Educational Technology*, 22, 1, pp.23–40. Copyright © 1991 by the National Council for Educational Technology. We thank Redwood Publishing Ltd., for permission to quote from Chris Drage's article, 'Taking control', *Educational Computing and Technology*, 11, 7, pp.47–51. Copyright © 1990 by BBC Enterprises Ltd; Sunbird Publishing Ltd., for permission to use two illustrations from *My House Activity Play Book*; Micros And Primary Education (MAPE) and the author, Andrew Wood, for permission to use material from 'Witches With Everything', *Micro-Scope Special*, Summer, 1990; the editor, Mrs Jean Johnston, and Mike Dean, the author, for permission to use material from his article, 'Pupils Take Over the Production of Resources', *PrintRun*, Summer 1990; Macmillan Education Ltd., for permission to quote from Keith Postlethwaite and Ann Hackney's book *Organising A School's Response*; Anne Disdier and Ann Shenkle for 'Zack and the Mac' from *TECH-NJ* (Trenton State College), and the Royal Society for the Prevention of Accidents for permission to reprint in adapted form the poster concerning electricity in the home.

David Hawkridge
Tom Vincent

Part 1

Introduction

1 Learning Difficulties and Computers

In the real world of learners and teachers

We start with the story of a boy who might be doing well at school, had he access to a computer there, and had he teachers with the training and flexibility to bring it into all subjects in his curriculum. The story is told by a US special education lecturer (Shenkle, 1989). But for the context, it could easily be about a British child.

ZACK AND THE MAC

At first glance, Zack looks like a typical twelve-year-old. His sneakers are untied, his sweatshirt baggy, his teeth ringed with braces. He's a friendly guy, looking out on the world with a kind of unsophisticated equanimity.

'How would you like to do an interview?' I ask. 'I think that teachers might be very interested in how well you can use the Mac, and how you feel about using a computer in school.'

Zack isn't sure that teachers would be interested in his point of view, but he lives to talk about what he's working on, so he Saves and turns from the Mac to look at me. 'Will this be in MacUser [a magazine]?' he queries.

From the moment the Mac entered the house five years ago Zack has been at it every bit of time that he can garner.

'How did you happen to get started on the Mac?'

'My dad taught me. Well, not exactly. Mostly I tried things, and if I bombed or needed help, he would help me.'

Zack has been involved in a variety of special education services since kindergarten. His programme has varied from full-time in a special class to full-time in the mainstream, but for the most part both special and mainstream teachers have indicated that he will not involve himself in learning unless instruction is one to one with an adult. In school, Zack does not make sequential responses without intervening cues from a teacher. In other words, he doesn't pay attention, follow along, or complete anything on his own. He doesn't act out, but neither does he go with the flow. In the mainstream, he generates constant concern from teachers who sense that his mind is elsewhere, and who feel he is not keeping up. In the special class he does the minimum.

At home, on the Mac, Zack sets up problems to be solved, pays close attention to what he is doing and what might be required next, keeps all the program limits and parameters in mind, and makes one response after another until he is dragged away.

'What kind of writing do you do on the Mac?' I ask.

'Sometimes I write captions or labels. I mainly use *MacDraw* now for pictures. I can use the mouse and other stuff to copy a cartoon for a magazine. For the play (a community association children's theatre production) I made a lot of stuff. I want to use animation next. In the music program I want to write more music as soon as I get the notes and rhythm the way I want it.'

Zack is characterised in his diagnostic records as having severe auditory and visual sequencing problems, poor attention to figure-ground, poor visual-motor integration and poor visual and auditory memory. But his cartoons on the Mac, particularly those that he has 'copied', are difficult to distinguish from the originals. Every detail is accurate, both in line and scale. He translates from the picture he is using as a model to the Mac screen, using the mouse to draw or select the image he wants. He uses the Mac to enlarge details or to preview the whole.

The music program that he is experimenting with has drawn some really surprising effort from Zack, considering that he has started and quit private lessons on piano, guitar, bass guitar and saxophone! In the past few weeks, he has transposed, figured out chord patterns using accidentals, and written variations that have involved inverting harmonic lines or using fugue forms, all without benefit of formal instruction. He keeps melody lines in mind as he works, or keys in the melody line from a classical tune from memory. His ear tells him if it sounds right.

I put it to him 'If you had a Mac on your desk at school, how would you use it?'

'Well, I couldn't use it for workbooks and stuff. I could use it for reports but I don't know how to type. School work is not really for the computer.'

'You have computers at school, don't you?'

'Yes, but there is only one in the room and you only get to use it when it is your turn and when all your work is done. We have computers once a week.'

'Do you do the same things during computer class that you do at home?'

'No. We have games and math and exercises and we take turns. There are usually four or five of us in each group. We get keyboarding in 7th grade, I think.'

'What if your reading and math assignments were on the computer? Would that work better for you than the books and workbooks you have now?'

'Maybe. But I would have to learn how to type. And I could use the spellchecker too. But we won't be able to do that.'

'Why not?'

'Because nobody has that kind of class in my school.'

Right, Zack. But in special education, the goal is to try to find the 'opening' for special learners. I see a very different boy with a workbook than I do at the Mac. Workbooks and lectures make Zack feel incompetent: using the Mac makes him feel both competent and confident. Zack should learn to touch type, to use the Mac to compose responses to questions and to enter material that will help him, in every subject. He needs frequent access to a computer at school and a supportive teacher who understands how to use the computer as a powerful tool in the classroom.

Zack has real learning difficulties. His teachers say so, and they are in the real world of dealing with children with special educational needs. But what are 'learning difficulties', and what is this business of mainstreaming? What is special education, for that matter? We should define these terms before going on to discuss the potential benefits of using computers.

What are 'learning difficulties'?

Anyone who enters the world of special education for the first time is bound to be struck by the dedicated teachers and carers working with students of all ages who have learning difficulties. Only the number, variety and severity of the problems these helpers face are more striking. In the US, Brightman (1989) suggests that there are nearly 40 million children and adults with disabilities, 85 percent acquired since birth. Most have learning difficulties. According to the Warnock Report (Department of Education and Science, 1978), out of every five UK children one will experience some form of learning difficulty requiring special educational provision. The report uses the term 'learning difficulties' in a positive attempt to get away from damaging labelling such as 'educationally sub-normal'. It covers all kinds of physical and mental difficulties except those caused solely by a child having to learn in a language different from that of his or her home.

In the UK Education Act 1981, which was a sequel to the Warnock Report, a child is defined as having special educational needs if he or she has a learning difficulty which requires special education provision to be made. The important point is that the child must have significantly greater difficulty in learning than his or her peers, or have a disability that prevents or hinders use of normal resources in local schools. 'Significantly greater difficulty in learning' covers a wide spectrum. Students are sometimes still divided by degree into those with mild, moderate or severe learning difficulties. The last group usually includes students with profound and multiple learning difficulties. In addition, there are students with specific learning difficulties, such as dyslexia, who otherwise function within the normal range. 'Disability that prevents or hinders use of normal resources in local schools' is also a broad phrase. It includes physical and sensory handicaps, chronic medical disorders such as epilepsy, and emotional or behavioural problems.

The 1981 Act dealt with actual learning difficulties being experienced by individual pupils. It did not call for causes to be established, but Postlethwaite and Hackney (1988) suggest that special educational needs arise out of interaction between pupils' characteristics and the nature of their learning environment. They offer the example of a history teacher who uses a text written in complex language too difficult for a poor reader quite capable of grasping the historical concepts involved, or a teacher who lectures with his or her back to the window, thus depriving a partially-hearing child of an opportunity to lip-read. Both learners are being deprived of access to the curriculum.

Access to the curriculum and mainstreaming

Children with special needs, like Zack, who are integrated into ordinary schools for some or the whole of the school week must be helped to participate in their class's usual learning activities. In England and Wales, under the Education Reform Act 1988, 'all pupils share the same statutory right to a broad and balanced curriculum, including access to the National Curriculum' (Department of Education and Science, 1989a). Only children who have been 'statemented' may lose this right. A school may not be obliged to provide access to a broad and balanced curriculum for a child for whom a Statement of Needs (a Record of Needs in Scotland) has been prepared. For all others, it is the law.

For the average teacher, working in a mainstream classroom, providing such a curriculum for children with special educational needs is by no means easy. Daniels and Ware (1990) consider the impact of the 1988 Education Reform Act on special education in England and Wales (Scotland and Northern Ireland are affected by similar legislation). They note that the Act poses 'a severe challenge to our definitions of good practice'. By introducing the National Curriculum, it changes what can be regarded as progress by pupils with special educational needs. By introducing local management of schools, it also changes the principles on which provision is made for special education. Lastly, the Act establishes procedures for exempting individual children from the Curriculum. As Ware (1990) points out, the Act makes no mention of categories of pupils (except those in hospital schools) who should or can be exempted from the National Curriculum. In practice, children with profound and multiple learning difficulties, and those with severe learning difficulties, will have few opportunities to be taught according to it. How much may the curriculum be modified for an individual child without infringing his or her entitlement to a broad and balanced curriculum? When the child is 'statemented' his or her needs, and how they should be met, are specified (see Chapter 14). If the curriculum is to be modified or 'disapplied', this must be included.

Opinions differ on whether mainstreaming and the other changes brought about by the Education Reform Act benefit most children with special educational needs. On a positive note, Paveley (1990) argues that the National Curriculum may elicit flexible and innovative responses from the schools. Postlethwaite and Hackney (1988) take a neutral stance, looking instead for ways of helping schools and teachers to respond to the new requirements of the law. Daniels and Ware (1990) are critical, noting tensions created for teachers and hazards for children. The fact is that teachers in mainstream classrooms as well as those in special education must now grasp the significance of these changes and decide what to do about them.

What is special education?

Academically, special education is the study of the education of children and adults who have special needs because they find learning difficult. Isn't learning always difficult? No, it is not. Learning is easy for 'clever' people. Learning under favourable conditions is easier than learning under adverse ones. Learning certain kinds of knowledge and skills is easier than learning others. In other words, there are three aspects to the notion of difficulties in learning, which are very closely related: innate human abilities, the conditions under which learning occurs and the nature of the learning task. Psychologists and others helping students to overcome their learning difficulties have studied each of these three intensively. Clearly, the difficulties experienced by a learner who cannot control her limbs are not the same as those of one who can remember very little, or those of students who are disabled in more than one way.

Practically speaking, special education is a term that also covers the policies that govern practice in schools, and the practice itself. It has legal connotations, too, because children can be designated as in need of special education. The term is broader than it was before the recent Acts, covering what used to be called remedial education, but is seldom applied at post-secondary levels.

Who is special education for? Out of 100 children born in one year in the UK, about 20 are likely to receive special education at some time during their school lives, suggested Warnock (Department of Education and Science, 1978). Most will be learners with cognitive difficulties: they range from individuals with dyslexia (reading problems) or dysgraphia (writing problems) to very slow learners who are unlikely to become literate.

We think it is useful to look at Wedell's (1990) summary of principles developed in British special education during the past 20 years:

- Special educational needs are no longer seen as caused solely by factors within the child. They are recognised as the outcome of the interaction between the strengths and weaknesses of the child and the resources and deficiencies of the child's environment.

- It is therefore not meaningful or even possible to draw a clear dividing line which separates disabled children from the rest. Special educational needs occur across a continuum of degree.

- All children are entitled to education. The aims of education are the same for all children, but the means by which the aims can be attained differ, as does the extent to which they may be achieved.

- All schools have a responsibility to identify and meet children's special educational needs, and all children should be educated with their peers as long as their needs can be met, and it is practicable to do so.

The issue of assessment

How do we know what learning difficulties a child or adult has? In this field, the medical model dominates: diagnosis, followed by treatment and possibly cure. Assessment is essential for diagnosis. Without accurate diagnosis, the treatment may be wrong, and 'cure' (in this case, learning) is unlikely if the treatment is wrong. The Department of Education and Science emphasises, however, that assessment of individual school children should reveal their strengths as well as their difficulties. The assessment should touch on matters such as the child's physical health and development, emotional state, cognitive functioning, communication skills, perceptual and motor skills, adaptive skills, social skills, approach and attitudes to learning, educational attainments, self image, interests and behaviour (Postlethwaite and Hackney, 1988). Assessment should also be holistic and rank children's special needs. For example, one sight-impaired child may simply need glasses, but another with no worse impairment may need, even more than and in addition to glasses, to have his or her confidence restored after a long period of scholastic failure.

Statements of special educational needs (in Scotland, Records of Needs) must be produced for all children judged to require them, based on careful assessment by and advice from as many as possible of the significant adults in their lives, including medical and other professional advice where appropriate. Testing and observation are the usual methods. Tests are never infallible, nor are human observers. Teachers of 'statemented' children must in turn produce individual educational plans for each one, and must record what they are teaching and what each child is learning. Above all, teachers must seek individual solutions for individuals' difficulties. For example, an infant who is born deaf and blind needs help to function in many ways, but not the same help as an old person who is mentally retarded, or a young person who is orthopedically impaired. We return to assessment in Chapter 14.

US learners with difficulties

For comparison, it is interesting to note the broadly similar situation in the US, where there are about 4 million schoolchildren with learning difficulties of one kind or another. The US Department of Education uses the following categories of disabilities (Middleton, 1990):

Learning, emotional and mental impairments: learning disabled, mentally retarded (includes mildly, moderately and severely retarded learners), seriously emotionally disturbed, and other health impaired learners (e.g. autistic children).

Physical and sensory impairments: orthopedically impaired, deaf and hard of hearing, visually impaired (includes partially sighted and blind), deaf/blind, speech or language impaired, and multiply handicapped learners.

The Department is responsible for special education policy at federal level, but since much education policy-making is devolved to the states, the state office or division of special education has legal responsibility for administration and supervision of special education in schools and colleges. There is also a National Council for Exceptional Children, which operates the Center for Special Education Technology, based in Virginia just outside Washington DC.

In US schools, the picture on 'statementing' is much the same as in the UK: the law requires all children in need of special education to have an Individualised Education Plan (IEP), agreed by a team of teachers and other carers, including parents.

Benefits of using computers

Computers can ease learning difficulties. They can help learners to overcome their difficulties. They cannot work magic. They are not necessarily the best solution. Because each learner's needs are slightly different, there are few standard rules for using computers in special education. What helps Zack may not help Jack at all. On the other hand, looking at what helps Zack may well suggest ways of helping Jack.

Though some teachers may be surprised to hear it, the value of information technology (IT), including computers, in meeting special needs is now recognised officially for England and Wales (Department of Education and Science, 1989b):

> IT is especially valuable in enabling pupils to take charge of their own learning and to work at their own pace. In particular, pupils with learning difficulties find stimulation through enjoyable repetition, coupled with a gradual increase in level of challenge.

> IT has a significant impact on the quality of presentation of pupils' work. It enables all pupils, including those with difficulties of physical coordination, to produce neat and accurate work, and to concentrate on the quality of content.

> Increasingly, specially adapted IT systems offer an unprecedented degree of individual access to the curriculum for pupils with severe visual or physical impairment.

The National Curriculum Council (1990) stresses that all pupils in England and Wales have an entitlement to develop IT capability and points out that:

> Pupils who are unable to communicate conventionally, because of physical or sensory impairment, may have access to the curriculum only through information technology. Information technology offers particular opportunities for pupils with special educational needs.

> Each school's IT policy needs to provide for special needs for pupils with intellectual or emotional difficulties, pupils with communications difficulties and pupils with physical difficulties.

The Council has identified five categories of benefits of using information technology to children and young people with special educational needs. These are heightened motivation, better opportunities for work in small groups, improvements in the accuracy and appearance of work, better access to information and the development of creativity. Mansfield (1991), writing as a former head of two special schools in Richmond-upon-Thames, comments on each of these categories:

HEIGHTENED MOTIVATION

All children are motivated by success and demotivated by failure, fear of failure and disapproval from parents, peers and teachers. Computers offer access to subject areas through trial-and-error learning. Pupils can experience the satisfaction of control, while the programs operate without being judgemental.

Although some subjects are more intrinsically motivating than others, without computers they may be less accessible to less able pupils, particularly those whose concentration span is limited or who have difficulty in mastering skills requiring coordination and manipulation.

By using computers, opportunities for success and the production of high quality results heighten pupils' motivation. Children are more likely to concentrate for longer, listen more carefully and improve their mastery of language skills.

OPPORTUNITIES TO WORK IN SMALL GROUPS

Children with special educational needs have used computers in small groups to enhance their understanding of tasks through discussion and through amicable and productive social interaction. Their co-operative activities usually involve problem-solving and decision-making. They learn quicker and more thoroughly if they discover facts and concepts for themselves and discuss them with other children, rather than having these ideas presented to them. For example, the program *Developing Tray* serves as a stimulus. Together, pupils decode letters and spaces into coherent prose, with excellent spin-offs. They test hypotheses based on their spelling skills and understanding of language. Through intense debate, they enrich their powers of language. Their concentration span lengthens, while reading and spelling improve. Their teacher can control the level of difficulty when selecting text to enter into the program. In one class, the children volunteered to stay in during break to do more English!

IMPROVEMENTS IN ACCURACY AND APPEARANCE OF WORK

By using computers, children with special educational needs can achieve considerable improvements in the accuracy and appearance of their written work and graphical work. Wordprocessing can have a strong impact on their language and reading skills through use of simple programs such as *Prompt/Writer*. Pupils suddenly realise they can produce high quality work they can be proud of and want to show to their parents. Some write their own illustrated books for other children to read. Others design and produce headed notepaper for their parents. Where laser printers are available, professional-looking products result. Older pupils develop mini-enterprises that demonstrate the relevance of good presentation and increase their awareness of standards in the world of work.

BETTER ACCESS TO INFORMATION

Better access to information in the form of computerised databases motivates children with special educational needs to engage in co-operative problem-solving. They learn how information can be stored and searched. They may also learn different ways of presenting information. For example, with *Grasshopper*, pupils can collect and record data concerning cars in the staff car park. They can interrogate the data to see if petrol consumption rises with the size of engine, and so on. With the computer, they can draw line graphs, scattergrams, pie charts and bar charts or histograms. When pupils are in control of the data, they can test hypotheses and come to understand graphs without spending time on intermediate skills. They can use the printer to prepare enlarged versions for display or detailed notation.

DEVELOPMENT OF CREATIVITY

Some pupils' creative urge is stifled by their poor physical coordination skills and what they see as their failure to produce high quality work. They often become frustrated by their efforts at writing, design, art and music. Despite having a clear picture in mind of what they want to produce, frustration sets in if they fail to match that image in their drawing or writing. They even destroy their partly finished work, and sometimes refuse to make any further effort, convinced that they lack the ability. Their self-esteem suffers grievous blows.

Computers can help. For example, with a simple art and design program called *Degas Elite*, a Downs Syndrome girl, 11 years old, discovers the joys of creativity. She draws perfect rectangles, circles and lines, then fills the shapes with wonderful designs. She is so pleased by her new-found success that she does not want to leave the computer. Her work becomes more organised and she begins to produce increasingly sophisticated images. Her hand-eye control improves: she is more precise about drawing intersections of lines. Her greatest delight is to see her work coming off the laser printer, to be enlarged on the photocopier and displayed in the front entrance to the school. As part of an integration activity with a mainstream primary school, she demonstrates the computer and software to primary teachers and instructs ordinary primary children. The teachers are amazed and delighted.

We pick up many of Mansfield's points later in the book, with more detailed examples. Her Majesty's Inspectors, after reviewing classroom practice in England in the late 1980s, declared that IT was making a unique and valuable contribution to the learning of pupils with special educational needs, enriching their learning experiences and enhancing their access to a broad curriculum. Their summary was as follows (Department of Education and Science, 1990a, p. 1):

Schools for pupils with physical and sensory disabilities make extensive use of IT to increase pupils' independence in learning, although opportunities to broaden pupils' educational experience through the use of IT are insufficiently exploited. Pupils with severe learning difficulties (SLD) benefit particularly from the common practice of using the computer in small groups, often with adult help, so that social competence and linguistic abilities are developed. For pupils with profound and multiple learning difficulties (PMLD), use is often made of IT alongside other technology to enrich the curriculum.

Many schools for pupils with moderate learning difficulties (MLD) make effective use of IT with younger children in increasing their attention span, and developing the use of language and social skills. Older pupils in these schools often use software which provides practice in mathematical and written language skills; the role of IT in broadening the pupils' experience in other ways is limited.

Schools for pupils with emotional and behavioural difficulties (EBD) are generally at an early stage of development of effective use of IT; there is often an emphasis on the use of software which practises skills in literacy and numeracy, and on computer games.

Recognition is growing, but is not yet widespread, of the possibilities IT offers to pupils with special needs in mainstream primary schools and secondary schools. Much of the work supports pupils with learning difficulties and involves the practice of skills in literacy and numeracy. Limited use is made of IT to improve pupils' access to a broad curriculum. At present, subject departments in secondary schools make little use of IT to support pupils' special needs.

Mansfield (1991), now an inspector of schools in the London Borough of Sutton, suggests that information technology has in fact spearheaded moves in many LEAs to make the curriculum available to a wide range of pupils with special educational needs. Much good practice has emanated from special schools, where the problems have had to be addressed urgently, especially in some areas of the National Curriculum. We discuss examples in later chapters, and also draw on practice in mainstream classes, and for adult learners.

Computers, communication and learning

Computers have two overlapping main roles: as communication aids and as learning aids. In both, they can and should serve a 'philosophy of empowerment', as Male (1988) calls it. They should make it possible for learners with special educational needs to communicate and learn in ways previously impossible for them. Words like 'handicapped' and 'disabled' imply dependence and powerlessness: with computers, learners can be less dependent and more capable. In dramatic style, Brightman (1989) puts the case for computers aiding communication:

Consider a 15-year-old child in a wheelchair, who is paralysed from the neck down and without speech. How is that child typically regarded by his peers? Perhaps even his teachers? What's truly expected of him? And given how he's probably seen by others, how is he conditioned to see himself? Now we say to that child, 'You can raise your eyebrows up and down. You have a movement you can control that enables you to pass instructions along to a computer, so you can do wordprocessing, use a modem, and draw pictures. You can even acquire a voice. For the first time in your life, you can say here when attendance is taken. You can demonstrate what a whiz you are at baseball statistics. You can display your artistic talents. You can become known, in other words, for *who you know you are* rather than for what others have interpreted you to be.'

On first sight, a computer may not seem a useful device for learners with special needs, particularly those with physical or sensory disabilities. Means of inputting and outputting information were designed with able-bodied people in mind. Operating the standard hardware is particularly difficult for people without good control of their movements, or without good sight. Screen and keyboard are the usual basis of communication between people and computers, yet are a problem for many disabled people. Fortunately, a wide range of devices now exist to enable learners with disabilities to take advantage of computers. The QWERTY keyboard is a barrier, but keyboard emulating interfaces, such as the Adaptive Firmware Card, which enable learners to avoid having to type, are available (Luebben and Oeth, 1990). 'Smart' software such as *PAL* or *MindReader*, can increase learners' typing speed through predicting word choices after a few letters have been typed.

In the long run, learners with special needs suffer to some extent from having to master hardware and software systems adopted in education, rather than those in industry and commerce. For example, in California, PCs using the MicroSoft disk operating system (MS DOS) are favoured by companies, but Apple IIe machines dominate the schools. Screen readers that speak the text and numbers (see Chapter 5) work exceptionally well on PCs, moderately well on Apple IIe machines and on the Macintosh. Graphics remain a problem: systems for Apple IIe computers are hardware-based and expensive because a separate monitor is needed, whereas PCs and Macintosh computers can magnify text and graphics on the screen. The Macintosh is an example of a graphically-oriented computer, inaccessible to blind people through screen readers because the bit-mapped displays could not be read by existing systems for blind users and the mouse interface depended on sight of the pointer on the screen. New screen reading techniques, such as *Outspoken* (see pages 73–74), now provide access to icons and other features of graphical user interfaces (GUIs). Unfortunately, the intuitiveness of using a GUI is unlikely to be matched for blind people.

Most disabilities are not self-contained: a disability often has consequences which affect learning in several ways. For example, a physically-disabled person may be unable to spell well because he or she has missed much early education, as well as having difficulty with a keyboard. That learner needs a combination of assistance, possibly including special hardware and special software.

Computer-assisted learning incorporates systematic instruction in small increments, with immediate feedback and positive reinforcement. It provides for repetition and even to some extent for individualised instruction. On the face of it, computers could be very useful to teachers trying to cope with the special needs of learners with cognitive difficulties, particularly in 'mainstream' or 'integrated' classes. Although we found examples of computers being used well with such learners, Cartwright (1984) is right to note that software for them may need to be less complex and demanding than that which is generally available. For US teachers, Male (1988) suggests six guiding principles for selection of special education software. We think these are useful, though they are not the only ones.

1 Does the software empower the user? That is to say, does it enable the user to do something he or she wanted to but could not otherwise do?

2 Does the software address the goals of the student's Individualised Education Programme (similar to a Statement)? Put this another way for the UK: does the software give the learner access to the curriculum?

3 Is the software adaptable? If the program is truly adaptable, learners will be able to enter their own problems, and teachers will be able to suit the program to different learners. Programs should allow physically-disabled learners to use switches or games paddles, possibly at a slower than normal speed, and visually-impaired learners to use a speech synthesiser.

4 Does the software offer cues and appropriate reinforcement? Male does not favour programs that simply suggest 'try again' or do not respond at all when the learner enters the wrong answer. She wants personalised feedback for each learner.

5 Is the program easy to use? Must many commands be memorised? If a manual is essential, children and adults with learning difficulties may not get very far.

6 Is the program's text, onscreen and in print, big enough and clear enough? Male criticises programs with small print and no colour. Large, sharp-edged print onscreen can be vital to sight-impaired learners.

Even when the 'right' software is available, there is no cast-iron guarantee that computer technology will help every pupil who has learning difficulties, as Stansfield (1991) reminds us. She outlines George's case:

GEORGE'S STORY

George is an intelligent boy, aged 9, whose behaviour problems were partly caused by difficulties with handwriting and spelling. He always used to dither and prevaricate rather than write, in case he made mistakes. His teacher thought he might do better if he had access to a laptop computer, and he was lent a Tandy WP2 for wordprocessing. Initially, this strategy was successful in giving him prestige in his class. Having the machine encouraged him to get on with his writing and worry about the spelling afterwards.

Strangely, perhaps, after three months of the WP2 George began to forget how to carry out the commands. He used it less and less, and eventually it was returned. His teacher considers that he makes a greater effort now to write and organise himself, and that bringing in the machine was a good way to get him to do so, even if he no longer uses it.

For George, the computer and its wordprocessing program were not a permanent solution to his problems. For another child, they might have been. In teaching learners who have difficulties, the technological help must be suited to individual needs. Is the Mac right for Zack?

On the evidence we have, information technology can often give children and young people with special educational needs access to a broad, balanced, relevant and differentiated curriculum. Can computers help to develop a profoundly disabled student's capacity to deal with signs and symbols? Can they train perception by the eye and ear? Can computers improve psycho-motor skills? Can they increase communication between a disabled learner and other people? Can they motivate such a learner, enabling him or her to continue learning for longer than usual? Can such a learner develop creativity or hone problem-solving skills through using a computer? These are not rhetorical questions. If the answer to any of these is Yes, then all who teach learners with special needs should know how computers can help. The essential principle we work to is that the technology should be used to magnify abilities that are there, bypassing as much as possible cognitive, emotional, physical and sensory disabilities.

Summary

Zack's considerable learning difficulties might have been overcome at school had he had access to a computer there. We defined terms such as learning difficulties, mainstreaming and special education, and discussed briefly access to the curriculum for children with special educational needs, particularly those with statements. The value of computers in meeting the needs of pupils like Zack is now officially recognised. We identified broadly the benefits of using them. Computers can aid learners to communicate, but they can also aid learning itself, provided that suitable software is available. We touched on some criteria for evaluating software. We stressed that individual solutions are required for individuals' problems. Teachers should use the technology to magnify abilities and bypass disabilities.

Part 2

Learning Difficulties

2 Learners with Cognitive Difficulties

The largest group, least served

The largest group of learners with special educational needs consists of those with cognitively-based learning difficulties ranging from low general ability to specific difficulties such as autism and dyslexia. Some experts, Brown and others (1989) suggest, recommend using one or more of the following strategies in teaching such learners: a multi-sensory approach, frequent repetition, modelling of desired behaviour, brief daily review, demonstration, visualisation (by learners), checklists, a written syllabus and presentation of only the information needed. Conventional wisdom about slow learners is that they need patient teaching, through which they can learn much, step by small step. This is rather general advice, however, and does not tell us why computers may be a good medium for providing that kind of teaching.

In the UK and the US , this group also happens to be the one least served, as yet, by information technology, though we shall describe some promising developments in this and later chapters. As we pointed out in the Preface, English schools are indeed using the technology for children with special needs. That is encouraging, but three-quarters complain that they have insufficient software and equipment, and large numbers of teachers say they are not confident in using it (Department of Education and Science, 1991a). This general picture is even gloomier when the children with physical and sensory disabilities are excluded, because these are the ones for whom most provision has been made. Middleton (1990) notes that in the US the group is big enough to seem to offer a large market to commercial software developers. She reports, however, that most computers available in US schools and colleges have only limited memory, and that software developers perceive the group as containing very diversified capabilities and needs, a very fragmented market. She might have added that developers really do not know very much about how to teach such learners. No wonder she suggests that the programs which have proved most useful in the US and elsewhere are those that can be modified by teachers or parents. Among these are framework (content-free) programs, which we discuss a little later in this chapter. First, we look at work with learners who have mild or moderate difficulties.

Mild learning difficulties

Mild cognitive learning difficulties may occur due to individuals' visual, auditory or tactile-kinaesthetic processing problems of neurological origin. These problems, sometimes undetected for many years, result in children falling behind in their schooling. Teachers eventually notice a chronic but intermittent inability to read and write in an organised manner, perhaps due to poor visual processing. Fortunately, software and speech synthesisers can help. Such learners can correct their spelling and hear what they have written. Learners with auditory processing problems also seem to have an intermittent inability to deal with auditory information. A computer display assists them to receive, discriminate, retrieve, retain, sequence and/or associate it. Some learners have specific difficulties with tactile and kinaesthetic processing. Certain fine and/or gross motor tasks are hard for them, as are rhythmical movement and/or orientation in time and space. They may be unable to write legibly or place text on a ruled line, have difficulty with columns or rows of numerals, or fail to remember their place on a printed page. Computers reduce these difficulties, because wordprocessing programs control the text and offer assistance in reading columns and rows or finding one's place, as Anna found (Brown and others, 1989).

CONTROLLING MEMORY OVERLOAD: ANNA'S STORY

Anna, a Californian college graduate with multiple scelerosis, has memory problems as well as poor muscular coordination. Although technology can compensate a good deal for the latter handicap, the crucial issue for her is whether she can cope with the amount of information presented at any one time. If she becomes overloaded, she finds she does not learn. The computer helps her by enabling her to control how much is presented to her at a time: she decides when she is ready to move on.

Moderate learning difficulties

Children with moderate learning difficulties may have poor language development, short attention span, bad memory, perceptual problems and so on, as Buckland says (1991). Their early numeracy development depends on cognitive skills such as recognising object permanence and function, using tools to gain an objective and readiness to follow instructions as well as on attention, spatial location and other basic physical skills (Paveley, 1990). As consequences of their cognitive difficulties as well as other forms of disability they may have, many such children have a long history of failure and low self-esteem. Their needs must be met in integrated classes in ordinary schools, in special units, or even in special schools. They show little motivation and are easily distracted. They find it almost impossible to work collaboratively.

In Buckland's experience, computers can foster constructive work patterns among these children, motivating them to participate actively and even to take control of their own learning environment:

BUCKLAND'S *TIG*

Most children are eager to use computers and they demand programs that motivate and challenge them. The challenges must be realistic for children who experience difficulty with many aspects of learning. Teachers in special education understand their pupils' strengths and know what is likely to prove successful for them. In particular, there are now open-ended 'framework' programs that enable teachers to design the content. Most teachers see these as a valuable resource, provided they can find time to learn how they work, design individual applications and key in the information. Regrettably, they seldom have the chance to carry out research as well.

My own experience as a teacher in a school for children with learning difficulties led me to study, with help from my class, the development of a program, *TIG* (which stands for Turtling in Glevum). This is based on Logo – a programming language children like to use – and a floor turtle. It provides simple access to Logo and the turtle for children who would not be able to cope with conventional Logo. The children use non-verbal, pictorial input via a series of overlays on a Concept Keyboard, a board divided into touch-sensitive areas.

My early observation of children using *TIG* led me to think that they were lengthening their concentration on tasks in hand, while collaborating better than usual. Systematic observation of their behaviour in *TIG* sessions and other classroom activities enabled me to make precise comparisons. I studied their *TIG* work closely by devising and giving them some tests, and through analysing naturally arising outputs from *TIG* sessions. Here, in the change of behaviour patterns, was the strongest evidence of benefits to the children from using the program. They concentrated significantly better, cooperated more and were less easily distracted, compared with their behaviour in other classroom work.

I found, remarkably enough, that once children became familiar with *TIG*, they set their own tasks, with the teacher rarely instigating the problem. True, at first the teacher needs to assess the nature of the *TIG* problem and the individual child's approach to it. She must recognise when to step in, when to hold back and allow the child to experiment and make his or her own decisions. For a while, she may explore alongside the child. Where there is no right or wrong solution to the problem, several possible solutions may have to be discussed and tried. This style of teaching can be quite demanding, calling for plenty of contact with individual pupils, especially at the start. Soon, however, the children are interacting a great deal, discussing the problem, and they demand less contact with their teacher, who becomes more a facilitator as they take control of their own learning (Buckland, 1988).

Framework (content-free) software

Much early software for computers in education was directed towards specific, and often narrow, curriculum objectives. In many cases, this software had a specific content with very little flexibility to match it to individual needs. In special education this problem was often exacerbated by inappropriate language content of explanatory information and menus on computer screens.

Recently teachers have been making more use of content-free framework programs. Within the special needs curriculum, these can be matched closely to the language and intellectual abilities of learners. They provide opportunities for teachers to design their own materials, linked to other resource materials in the classroom. For example, teachers can enhance language schemes developed for a card or paper medium by using a computer with the same material. Often the Concept Keyboard, which can be overlaid with characters, words, phrases, pictures or drawings matched to an individuals' intellectual and language abilities, replaces the conventional keyboard. It enables children to create stories and other written work through an individualised interface to a computer, perhaps with *Prompt/Writer*, developed for this purpose. A simple large print wordprocessing program, *Prompt/Writer* can be used with the Concept Keyboard to provide 'on-touch typing' of difficult words. Teachers can easily prepare vocabulary sets for individual students (see Chapter 8).

Framework programs play an important part in a twelve-week induction for older students joining the Special Needs Section at Dudley College (Homer, 1990).

INDUCTION COURSE AT DUDLEY COLLEGE

The students, aged 16–19, all come from special schools and have moderate to severe learning difficulties, sometimes coupled with behavioural problems. One part of the induction involves mobility and travel skills. First, students learn to move around the college finding toilets, exits, and so on. This is then extended to include travel around Dudley.

Right from the start we decided that computers would enhance what students did on travel, complementing field trips, discussion and photographic/video sessions in which students produced their own materials. Where possible their work is displayed in the computer room and incorporated into Concept Keyboard overlays and Touch Poster sheets.

Students use the Concept Keyboard with *Touch and Learn* to develop their vocabulary. They answer questions on the screen by touching an appropriate word or picture on the overlay. The pictures include photographs taken in the college, which contribute to a College Words vocabulary, and illustrations of commodities found in shops. Teachers use a Touch Poster Board to build up a database which has a poster size overlay made up of photographs taken by the students, with added captions.

Framework programs offer an opportunity for teachers to use just a few programs for a wide range of curriculum applications and special needs. Hence, training can focus on access to the curriculum rather than the technology. Wood (1990) offers another good example of a framework program applied to learning difficulties, at Derby College.

NEIL AND *PENDOWN*

Neil came to the Multiskills Course from a special school. His main problem is his low reading ability. In fact, he is almost totally illiterate. His school report stated that 'He will do almost anything to avoid reading or writing, and becomes very emotional when put under pressure. He desperately needs to have his confidence strengthened and re-enforced, and is very afraid of failure.'

All students on the Youth Training Scheme must complete a log book each week in which all their activities and achievements are entered. Neil was unable to do this on his own, so teachers wrote down what he had done, and Neil laboriously copied it out, often not understanding a word. While this may have satisfied requirements, it certainly did nothing for Neil's confidence, nor did he learn anything from doing it.

In an attempt to overcome his problem, Neil's teacher designed an overlay for the Concept Keyboard and *Pendown*. It contained all the words Neil might need when making entries in his log book. His initial attempts at using the overlay proved slow and difficult. Neil could not recognize any of the words (including words like 'did') and it took a lot of prompting to produce just a few lines. When he saw the final printout (in jumbo lettering which made the amount written seem greater), Neil was impressed with what he had achieved. This spurred him on to make the effort needed to improve his word recognition.

As a result of this type of work, Neil's word recognition has improved considerably. He is now able, with help, to complete his log book in one session without resorting to copying. Filling in his log book has become an educational activity for Neil rather than a copying exercise, and his progress has surprised and delighted everyone. He is justly proud of his efforts and for the first time looks forward to his writing. As his word recognition and his confidence increases, it is noticeable that he spends more and more time actually typing in the words rather than using the Concept Keyboard.

The Keyboard's main disadvantages are that the number of words is limited and new words cannot be added easily. Without it probably Neil would never have got started, but because of what is for Neil a rapid and dramatic improvement, these disadvantages are becoming apparent. The next step is to enter words under a group list in *Pendown's* dictionary. This way, his teacher can easily expand the word list as Neil's abilities improve. Continuity will also be maintained: Neil will merely have to increase his familiarity with the program rather than learning to handle a new one.

Severe learning difficulties

Children and adults with severe learning difficulties, mostly cognitive in nature, cannot pay attention and seldom persevere at anything for longer than a few minutes. They may benefit from sensory stimulation. Many special schools now possess a comfortable room equipped with bubble tubes, disco lights, fibre optic fronds and sound generators for this purpose. The 'White Tower' is a commercially-available set of such equipment. Once a learner responds to one or more of these stimuli, the teacher may be able to move towards helping him or her to understand cause and effect. Electrical toys attached to a switch can be useful, because as soon as the child realises that actuating the switch operates the toy, a similar switch can be used to produce effects on a computer screen. Alternatively, a Touchscreen fitted to the computer monitor enables the learner to change an image by touching it. Suitable programs for children are *Early Fingers*, *Brimble Hill Suites*, *Switch On*, *Switch On Travel* and *Touch Games 1* and *2*. A Micro-Mike, which operates like a switch in response to noises, may be more suitable for some learners. *Blob 1*, *Blob 2* and *Going Places* are programs that can be used with a Micro-Mike: they offer a progression of stimulating pictures designed for young children. Learners' visual attention, fixation and tracking may improve through using computer programs that create bright, colourful images, possibly with sound. Those who develop attentional skills can move onto manipulating images. Non-speaking learners can learn how to use images to express choice.

As learners becomes more adept at using the computer, they may develop better hand/eye coordination and tracking on the screen. From there, they may go on to cope with matching of real objects with those on the screen, or simply matching objects on the screen. Sequencing and other pre-reading skills may follow, depending on the abilities of individual learners. Some of this work can be through the medium of computer games. Even the smallest success is rewarding, building up confidence and self-esteem.

Computers can also serve as a focus for interaction between teacher and learner. But learners may not understand images on the screen, and their teacher may have to teach pairing of real objects with their screen images. Once images are understood, it may be possible for the teacher to substitute symbols for them (see Chapter 8).

For non-reading learners, computers can create sounds as well as images. Speech synthesisers can speak instructions slowly and clearly, and if necessary repeatedly. Sound effects are often strong stimuli. With *Touching Sound* plus a synthesiser, amplifier and speakers, learners can use a Touch Screen or a keyboard to make musical sounds. They can also control the computer through making sounds, perhaps with a Micro-Mike, which encourages vocalisation (Paveley, 1990). A teacher in a Wiltshire school taught a profoundly disabled child to operate a Touch Screen, through which he could control the computer (Butterworth, 1991):

GETTING STARTED: GEOFF'S STORY

First, Geoff, in a wheelchair, needed to have his head up, facing the screen, so he could establish eye contact with it. Next, he had to reach out his arm towards the screen, then extend his hand or fingers to it. Getting Geoff to touch the screen with his fingers or fist – or even just his wrist – followed. His teacher wanted him to respond, first vocally or by some physical action, to the changes he made on the computer screen. Lastly, she wanted him to pull his hand away from the screen of his own accord. She said

'Geoff responded so well that his progress was recorded every month. At first, he touched the screen but needed physical support to direct his arm towards the screen. I helped to support his elbow throughout the session. He pushed forward with his hand and touched the screen but kept his fingers splayed out. Two months later, however, he reached out to touch the screen without help.

'I decided to pursue using the computer as a tool for increasing Geoff's independence and self-confidence. Could he use a single switch? I attached one in such a way that actuating it required a similar action to the one Geoff had developed for using the Touch Screen. I organised intensive practice for him, 10 minutes every schoolday for three weeks. During these sessions, I prompted him with words ('press the switch') and gestures, but slowly phased out the physical prompts almost entirely. I rewarded him verbally ('good boy'). In the first two sessions, he needed a full physical prompt to operate the switch. Gradually his ability improved until he could operate it reliably, with only minimal physical prompting. The next stage was for him to develop independent use of the switch or Touch Screen. Now I'm concentrating on teaching him tracking skills, and am happy that he needs only a little prompting.'

Logo: an open-ended learning environment

Children with severe and moderate learning difficulties can be taught how to control a turtle robot or a screen turtle with the Logo language. Haigh (1990) sees Logo as offering an open-ended learning environment for these children, in which they can develop thinking skills and mathematical concepts. They discover relational concepts in a meaningful way, at their own pace. Any mistakes they make are merely points for reflection and readjustment of their ideas. Through eventual success, they acquire a positive self-image, essential to further learning.

Haigh offers the children a structured approach based on Buckland's *TIG*. He considers that through it they can work towards levels 3 and 4, and perhaps 5, of AT5 in the National Curriculum in Technology. What are these?

Level 1   Be able to work with a computer.

Level 3   Be able to give a sequence of direct instructions to control move ment.

Level 4   Be able to develop a set of commands to control the movement of a screen image or robot; understand that a computer program or procedure is a set of instructions to be followed in a predetermined sequence.

Level 5   Be able to understand that a computer can control devices by a series of commands, and appreciate the need for precision in framing the commands.

In addition, these children may be able to work towards level 2 in Mathematics.

Level 1   AT10 Shape and Space: draw 2D shapes and describe them. AT11 Shape and Space: state a position such as on, inside, above, under, behind, next to, etc. Give and understand instructions for moving along a line.

Level 2   AT8 Measures: use non-standard measures in length.
AT10 Shape and Space: recognise squares, rectangles, circles, etc. and describe them, recognise right-angle corners in 2D and 3D shapes.
AT11 Shape and Space: understand the notion of angle. Give and understand instructions for turning through right angles.

This is what happens in Haigh's school, The Park Special School, Wakefield, for children with moderate and severe learning difficulties, mostly cognitive in nature:

PURPOSEFUL PLAYING IN THE PARK

Our children begin by playing with a floor turtle and become familiar with the 'control panel', usually a Concept Keyboard, or, with *Floor Robots*, switches, a joystick or Micro Mike. They develop spatial concepts such as on, off, under, over, between, inside, outside, up and down, by being asked to move the turtle under a table, over a bridge, between towers, and so on. If the child operating the control panel has to follow instructions from the others, listening and speaking skills can be improved.

Next, the children pretend to be turtles, moving around the floor by turns of 90 degrees and in slow steps or strides. Then the children, in small groups, set up mazes for the turtle and steer it through them. To do so successfully requires collaboration and a little planning and consultation. They enjoy doing this work.

Trying their hand first at *Mazes* helps some of the children. They try solving the eight graded mazes either on screen or as print-outs. On screen, they steer Sid, a cartoon character, through the maze by using cursor keys or arrows on a Concept Keyboard. In *Mazer*, for each of the six graded mazes the children must enter the whole set of moves before RETURN is pressed. If they can do this, they can move on to *M/Mazer*, with which they make and save their own mazes, as well as program Sid through them.

Drawing shapes and pictures on large sheets of paper with the turtle usually follows. By changing the pen, children use different colours. If the paper is thin newsprint, the turtle with pen down leaves a small blot each time it stops. Using these blots, the children can count how many moves the turtle made to draw a given line. Together, they estimate how many moves the turtle will need to make to reach an objective, and use it to check their estimates or guesses.

The children make number ladders, using the reverse side of vinyl wallpaper, which does not tear easily with repeated use and wears well when they walk on it. To make a ladder, they advance the turtle one move, and write the number 1 where it stops, and repeat the sequence to construct as many rungs as they want. They make ladders of different lengths, for comparison, and we practise addition and subtraction skills.

The children move on to Buckland's *TIG*, a Concept Keyboard version of the Logo-type game, *Dart*. The approach is described in Detheridge (1990). Seven graded overlays for the keyboard enable them to control the turtle even better. The first overlay helps children with problems about right and left rotations. A large red ear is attached to the right side of the turtle, a blue one on his left, on the floor and on the keyboard. Entering a command on the keyboard is in two stages: press a red ear, press the turtle (which is RETURN) and the turtle turns 90 degrees towards its red ear. Press a green arrow, press the turtle and the turtle moves forward a set distance. The two stages allow time for thinking. They can over-rule the first command as long as the second has not been given. There is a hoot command as well, which they like to include.

Using the first *TIG* overlay, they can copy shapes with the turtle, too, and this demands understanding of how the task can be broken down and sequenced. The shapes they draw include squares, rectangles, Ts and Ls. Later overlays provide more commands. For example, the turtle can be turned 30, 60 or 90 degrees (little, middle and big turns). With the seventh overlay, it can be moved forwards up to ten moves, and backwards five, and the pen can be moved down and up, to leave a track or not, as the children decide.

The children learn to write simple programs for the turtle to draw shapes, using a meaningful symbol notation as required for level 4. They learn to record their programs using a symbol notation: whenever a symbol is pressed on the keyboard overlay, another child in the group glues a similar symbol at the top of the paper, thus building up the sequence of commands. Alternatively, they draw the symbols with felt pens. They also experiment, entering sequences they choose and seeing what shapes result. Our children set up a 'library' of programs for drawing different shapes.

In further work, they use Overlay 7 of *TIG* (see Fig. 2.1) to construct more number ladders. One might be for 50, with lines for 10, 20, 30, 40 and 50 drawn at each stop the turtle made when a value of 10 was entered before RETURN is pressed. A child is asked to mark on the ladder where a number such as 37 belongs. The child's response is then tested by the group entering three 10s and a 7 and watching the turtle move along the ladder. Our children's understanding of the four rules of number, and of concepts such as 'more than', is enhanced by using the turtle and number ladders.

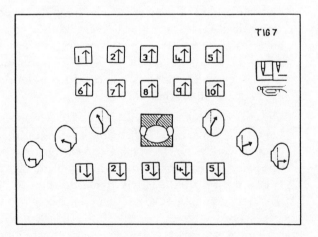

*Figure 2.1 - **Overlay 7 from TIG***

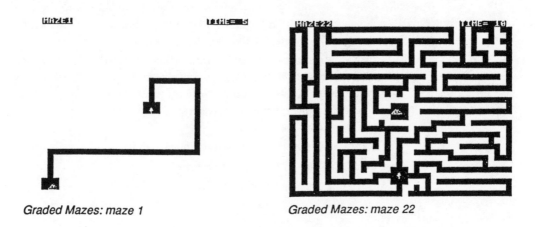

Graded Mazes: maze 1   Graded Mazes: maze 22

Figure 2.2 - **A printout from Graded Mazes**

By this time, some at least of the SLD and most of the MLD children gain from using *Graded Mazes*, a program which demands more planning and memory skills as they try to solve the more difficult ones in the set of 22, either on screen or on paper (see Fig. 2.2). Finally, SLD children making good progress and MLD children advance to *Dart*, from which *TIG* was derived. To use *Dart*, they must enter commands by typing them or through the function keys. Each command must be followed by a number, as in FORWARD 60, LEFT 100. Children who have some understanding of numbers and know left from right use this program successfully to create interesting patterns by combining simple structures with the BUILD command.

Some of the SLD and most of the MLD children also use *Contact* to turn on lights, buzzers, electric motors and models. This program requires children to enter strings of simple commands such as SWITCH ON 1, WAIT 10, SWITCHOFF 1.

Haigh (1990) believes that there are many advantages to using Logo with such children. The main ones he sees are:

- The teacher can diagnose the children's language and thinking skills, especially where the latter are far in advance of the former.
- In carrying out the work, the children engage in considerable interaction with each other and the teacher, as they ask questions, give instructions and listen to others' ideas, thus breaking down the isolation suffered by many such children.

The children, even those who are hyperactive, show sustained concentration on the work, beyond normal expectations and remember well what they learned in earlier sessions.

The children gain in confidence as they succeed in using Logo and the computer, with positive effects on their other school work, in which they begin to apply the problem-solving skills learned with Logo.

Such optimism is refreshing, and Haigh's school has produced a video showing the children gaining access to the curriculum with Logo. Is Paveley (1990) being too ambitious when she suggests that pupils with profound and multiple learning difficulties, with the help of computers, can aspire to Attainment Targets 1–3 and 9 from the Science National Curriculum?

1   Explore and experience a variety of materials.

2   Develop and extend sensory awareness.

3   Understand simple cause and effect.

4   Increase own body awareness.

5   Make choices in activities.

6   Increase own observation and concentration skills.

7   Gain an awareness, however simple, of own environment.

8   Respond with face or body movements or through vocalisations.

Autistic learners

Within the much larger grouping of learners with cognitive difficulties are autistic learners. Little is known about the causes of autism, which may have a physical, organic foundation, but result in cognitive and emotional difficulties. Autistic children usually have problems of speech, language and communciation. They may be mute much or all of the time, or say over and over again what they have heard (echolalia). They may engage repeatedly in stereotyped actions, appear to be especially interested in sameness or order, and be totally unresponsive or respond unexpectedly, sometimes in violent or otherwise socially unacceptable ways. They avoid direct eye-contact. This is a broad description, and individual children may show one or more of these traits at any one time. They may refuse to communicate at all, or in particular situations, or with certain people. They are reputed to have poor short-term memory, which makes sequential tasks difficult for them, yet they often have a great interest in objects. Until recently, most autistic children were regarded as virtually ineducable. Kanner (1943), who provided the first definitions of autism, later raised again the question of whether autism is usually accompanied by low general ability (Kanner, 1971). There is some evidence that most autistic children become autistic adults although improvement comes with maturity, the greatest improvements being made by those of greatest ability (Green, 1990).

Integration or mainstreaming of autistic children is a debatable issue. Ordinary classes seldom accept them, and they rapidly become isolated and ridiculed. Their bizarre behaviour is difficult for teachers and other children to interpret. At times, violence may be an attempt to communicate. Autistic children seem to depend less than others on non-verbal communication through gestures and facial expressions. They make little use of these means themselves and do not appear to note them in other people. Despite this, many incapable of speech may learn sign language.

Even if they cannot learn to speak very much and appear to comprehend speech poorly, autistic children may learn to read and write. They may start to type, with help from a 'facilitator', though this can be a long and difficult learning process, during which a kind of echolalia may persist, for example when they type what they have heard even though it is not appropriate in that context. Many can type only when 'supported' through the facilitator placing a hand on their shoulder or arm (see below for the Crossley approach).

On the face of it, computers should be able to help autistic learners, particularly those interested in machines and repetitive procedures. Indeed, some teachers worry about letting autistic children use a computer lest it reinforce too strongly the obsessive side of their condition. Some of these children do seem to be motivated by computers. Green (1990), working in a Unit for Non-Communicating Children in Abbey Hill School, Cleveland, describes one case typical of brighter, speaking autistic children, who often show considerable interest and aptitude, and another typical of those who do not speak:

SAM'S STORY, AND SUSAN'S

Sam is a bright boy who can speak. He came to the Unit before the age of four and left before his sixth birthday. When he was four, Sam was introduced to the computer. As a chatty individual who relates well to adults despite language problems, would he take to the computer? He started with *Keys*, a program developed at the Unit and offering practice in using a QWERTY keyboard and copying words. By the seventh session he was doing well, showing reasonably high levels of interest and concentration on computer activities.

Susan is mute, though she can use British Sign Language to a limited degree. She showed the same levels of interest and concentration on the computer as Sam had, but took much longer (almost 50 sessions) to reach criterion in using a program called *Time,* another one of the Unit's programs, which is admittedly more difficult than *Keys*. The program teaches time-telling. She was easily put off by anything new. On one occasion the introduction of a synthesised voice caused scores and interest levels to drop dramatically. The very silence of the computer appeared to be an attraction to her. Like many autistic children, Susan shows considerable resistance to change.

Green's work suggests that quite high levels of concentration can be achieved by autistic children engaged in computer activities, although negative behaviour may make computer use for some impossible or less effective. Most require little supervision, but he also notes that computer usage may not encourage active communication, vocal or signed, with other people. He concludes that the lower functioning autistic children paid attention to the screen, could control the keyboard, touchscreen and joystick for inputs and exhibited little inappropriate or obsessive behaviour. The autistic children of average ability adapted their keyboard strategy to the program they were using. They were able to use the touchscreen to select quite complex sets of positions and words, and could handle more complexities in the computer environment than they could in a physical one. They acquired new vocabulary and used correctly some simple grammatical structures. They were obviously motivated, particularly by computer simulations. The higher functioning children were able to go as far as communicating with the computer by using complex sentence structures as a logical tool.

Leading US workers in this field see computers as offering opportunities to autistic learners. Disdier (1988), noting that the autistic population has not yet been significantly influenced by computers, says that the main problem is the lack of appropriate software for low-functioning autistic individuals. Much educational software contains too may distractors and is too complex for these learners, she asserts. From another source, however, there is now controversial evidence that some autistic learners, even those classed as low-functioning, can learn to communicate using the technology. Biklen (1990) reports how two autistic Australian adolescents, using a Canon Communicator (a small electronic typing device with a dot matrix printed tape output), 'talked' to him. He was surprised at their grasp of abstract concepts, and returned to Australia to study 21 autistic individuals, aged 5 to 23, who were non-speaking or spoke only in echoes of what they had heard (see Chapter 6 for Louis' story). Biklen analyses the controversy that arose over whether the evidence of 'facilitated communication', based on the Communicator and the methods of Crossley (Crossley and McDonald, 1980), was dependable or not. Critics of the approach claimed that the words and sentence structures used were those of facilitators, not the children's. So vehement were they that the matter was the subject of a court case and, later, a public enquiry. Biklen suggests that autistic children may suffer from a neurologically-based problem of expression, but not necessarily one of cognition. Crossley and her colleagues expect their learners to communicate and facilitate their communication through adopting quite complex procedures. The Communicator was added only recently: it makes expression easier than if learners have to write by hand or use a typewriter. For comparison, Biklen mentions earlier research in the US during which autistic children tried the Edison Responsive Environment, also known as 'The Talking Typewriter'. The researchers argued that the Environment helped the children to express abilities not measured by conventional psychological tests (Goodwin and Goodwin, 1969).

Or take the case of Jamee Kleiman, an autistic American boy of 14, who had never learned sign language and whose speech was limited to a few phrases (Nolan, 1990). At Biklen's suggestion, his teachers tried Crossley's method and Jamee was soon spelling out words. His mother could not believe it, because nobody thought Jamee could read. Other autistic children in Biklen's research project use, with the help of facilitated communication, various computers as well as the Canon and Casio Communicators. Despite controversy concerning the method (not the equipment), children and adults seem to be benefitting (Swezey, 1991).

Dyslexic learners

People with dyslexia are otherwise able-bodied and of normal intelligence but have difficulty in acquiring reading, writing and spelling skills (Karnes, 1990). There is some evidence that dyslexia is accompanied by anatomical differences in the brain and may be related to the presence of antibodies in the mother during pregnancy (Masland, 1990). In the UK, since the Warnock Report this medical approach has been de-emphasised. Indeed, dyslexia has been put under the broader label of learning difficulties.

Welchman (1990) summarises the characteristics of individuals who experience these difficulties:

- [They are] of average or above average intelligence. They experience marked difficulty in learning to read and even if this is attained, spelling and writing continues as a problem. They sometimes have difficulties with arithmetic. When confronted by the written printed symbol, they reverse, invert or transpose letters in reading and writing. They confuse letters which have similar outlines.
- [They have] problems. . . in sequencing, so letters are read or written in the wrong order.
- [They produce] bizarre and unintelligible spelling. . . [with] difficulty in remembering and distinguishing like sounds and. . . persistent failure to link the sound and symbol.
- [They] frequently confuse left and right.
- [Their] minor or gross motor skills may be affected, the latter showing as clumsiness.
- [They have] difficulty in remembering and holding instructions.

In the UK, there is now a substantial body of research on teaching dyslexics. A structured multi-sensory approach to teaching language skills is usually advocated. Sight, sound and touch should all be involved, using the different senses to produce the same phonological representation, which must then be associated with, say, the right person, object or event (Miles, 1990). Simultaneously, counselling may help to reduce the learners' anxiety levels about reading, writing and spelling. There have also been trials of drugs, such as piracetam, said to improve dyslexic children's reading (Wilsher, 1990).

Adult dyslexics have somewhat different learning needs. They have developed their own coping strategies and these must be taken into account. They may well prefer to work on pieces of writing they have brought from their jobs or other classes. They may need to have the learning process made explicit to them and their misconceptions cleared up (Klein, 1990).

Since a multi-sensory approach to the teaching of phonological skills to dyslexics is widely advocated, computer technology should be useful, and in the UK several centres pursue its potential (see Singleton, 1991). Its capacity to present appropriate visual and auditory stimuli is obvious. With modifications, it can even present tactile stimuli as well, though this is not easy. The computer can also offer frequent encouragement, though it cannot readily be programmed to respond to learners' attempts to read aloud. Describing some of the early uses of microcomputers to help dyslexic learners, Kelly (1988) mentions that at a clinic operated by Southampton University's School of Education they used a program called *Crackit* (transcribed for IBM PCs), which turns messages into code. She says 'The messages became harder and harder, and teachers suffered along with the other victims, since the pupils decided that teachers were not allowed to look up the answers if they were not the creators.'

More recently at the same clinic, dyslexic learners have used *MindReader*, a predictive wordprocessing program (Kelly, 1990):

SECOND-GUESSING WORDPROCESSING PROGRAM MAY HELP DYSLEXIC LEARNERS

With *MindReader*, after the first few letters of a word are typed, a list of up to five possible words appears; typing the number of any word inserts the whole word into the text, or the list can be ignored. The lists change to reflect the words used most frequently by that particular student. Increased writing speed and discriminating reading of similar words are the usual benefits for the student. The program is of no help where there is a mistake in the first few letters of a word, or where the student is not attentive to the lists as they appear on the screen. Like any device, this one does not do the thinking for the student; it is useful partly because learning to use the aid involves thinking about language.

The clinic students are jointly compiling a computer file of the words they need for topics in each subject. Selecting important words for each topic is a useful skill in itself, and the finished lists can be sorted and printed out in several forms. They are used for reading practice, kept in exercise books for spelling reference, and form useful revision aids.

Ease of correction and revision, and production of neat finished copy, are important benefits of using *MindReader*. Neat print-out allows work done by one student to be read by others. Ease of use, an uncluttered screen display and good colours are important. Typing may be shared by teacher and student, and a student can edit a piece which was originally dictated.

Some teachers think that dyslexic learners make far more mistakes in the first few letters of words than non-dyslexic poor spellers. This could be a problem in using a predictive program: a dyslexic can become very frustrated if the program supplies none of the alternatives he or she wants. A dyslexic with really poor spelling skills will not be able to recognise the correct word from a given list. Spelling checkers that guess the correct word on a basis of the first few letters are of little value to some dyslexics.

Such problems for dyslexics, and how computers may help to solve them, are considered by Newell, Booth and Beattie (1991). They note that the burden of producing well-spelled and grammatically correct text still falls on the learner, despite the availability of predictive wordprocessors, thesaurus programs, grammer checkers, spelling error detectors and spelling correction programs. We summarise in Chapter 4 results of their work in developing and testing *PAL* (Predictive Adaptive Lexicon), a predictive text entry program originally intended for physically-disabled learners but now proving useful to dyslexics.

Write This Way is a US wordprocessing program prepared specifically for learners with difficulties, and it may be particularly helpful to dyslexics. According to Fenwick (1991), it has the usual spelling and grammar checkers, but the teacher or student can decide which features to activate, to suit individual needs. For example, the spelling checker can be instructed simply to point out errors, not provide alternative spellings. The grammar checker can search for items such as noun-verb agreement, missing words, double negatives, verb form problems and so on.

Summary

Learners with cognitive difficulties make up the largest group, least well-served, among learners with special educational needs. Computers can help, in various ways, learners with mild, moderate or severe difficulties, as we show through several examples. Some leading teachers in this field look to Logo to provide an open-ended learning environment for such learners. A few teachers of autistic learners have developed techniques for encouraging their charges to express themselves through computers. Similarly, dyslexics' problems in reading, spelling and writing may be eased through using computers with appropriate software.

3 Learners with Emotional Difficulties

Emotionally-disturbed learners

Within the much larger group of learners with special educational needs are those with emotional difficulties. Causes of their difficulties are not easy to determine precisely, but certainly include physiological as well as psychological ones. Children in this group are still sometimes labelled 'EBD', those with emotional and behavioural difficulties. Many are mainstreamed, but special schools do exist that cater for the needs of children with the greatest problems. Our examples are drawn from across the range. Adult learners with emotional difficulties come into this chapter too.

Helping any such learners with computers may seem unusually hard. Why should computers appeal to children or adults who are poorly motivated, have problems with concentrating on their work and seldom persevere long enough to complete anything? Are these learners capable of mastering concepts and memorising material taught with the help of computers? Do their emotional problems interfere with their learning with computers as much as, or even more than, in conventional contexts? Can they collaborate with others on computer-based learning tasks, rather than behaving in what are sometimes very anti-social ways? There is some evidence that in fact computers help these learners to bypass their difficulties and to achieve success.

As an advisory teacher on IT to serve special educational needs, Haigh (1991) worked half a day a week for a year with Dorothy Matthews at Knottingley High School, Wakefield, who taught a class of ten disruptive boys who had been withdrawn from the third year mainstream classes. The teachers planned an information technology course for the children, who had little experience of working on computers.

YOUNG DISRUPTIVES GAIN CONTROL

They were lively boys with anti-school values and low self-esteem. They were low achievers, with very little respect for people in authority (except Dorothy) or their peers. The uneasy peace in the classroom could sometimes flare up into a violent confrontation, without warning.

During the first term of the new information technology course, the class enjoyed developing wordprocesing and desktop publishing skills using BBC machines. The computers gave them a fresh start and they were proud of their results, which were always well displayed in the classroom. Class behaviour improved, the atmosphere in class was pleasanter and individuals co-operated better. I looked forward to my Friday morning when I worked alongside them. They enjoyed showing me some of their work done during the week.

In an effort to tackle problems the children were having with mathematics, Dorothy and I decided to get them to try Logo. During the second term I brought a Valiant turtle, which has large ears, one red, the other blue, suitable for teaching younger children. We linked it to one of the two BBC Masters available to this class, and loaded the program *TIG*. I felt they lacked proper spatial concepts, yet some of the work with a turtle with big ears seemed scarcely appropriate. I overcame this problem by asking the boys if they would like to look at computer activities I had arranged for children with severe learning difficulties. They were very enthusiastic. After talking about the handicaps of some of the SLD children at my own school, I showed them the work I had done with *TIG*. I let the boys have a go for themselves at operating the turtle from the Concept Keyboard.

Dorothy and I posed problems for the boys to solve and gradually they became at ease with the new microworld they were beginning to enter. From working with them, we were certain they were more capable than their school record showed, and the Logo environment offered them the chance to demonstrate their ability perhaps for the first time.

After the hands-on session with *TIG* the class had a good foundation for using *Dart*. We divided the boys into four groups, two to work on the computers while the other two did planning in readiness for their turn. By entering a few commands, the boys were able to observe the turtle's movements. They had problems with angular rotations but soon discovered through trial and error that 90 degrees was a square angle. They calculated and tested the angles for half a turn, a whole turn, and two complete rotations.

Dorothy and I had decided that we would give the children plenty of time to explore and develop their ideas together. We agreed to introduce new commands only when the children asked for them or if they were ready for them.

We realised some would need prompting, and we gave help in open-ended form: 'I wonder what would happen if you. . .'

The boys experimented with commands, looking at and discussing the turtle drawings that resulted. At first they drew simple shapes, but soon progressed to more complicated ones, quickly developing some understanding of the size of angles.

The next stage was to use their new knowledge to draw patterns and pictures. We encouraged them to keep records of the commands they entered, so that they could make changes later if they wanted to. Some children extended their note-taking into the planning periods, using graph paper and protractors. A good example of planning was the helicopter (see Fig. 3.1), which led to a remarkably good first attempt on-screen.

Over the next few weeks the boys learned the Build, Change, Repeat and End commands, which enabled them to experiment with more advanced pattern-making and picture-building. They used procedures they had learned earlier as building blocks for more advanced designs, and to save their work on disk. A group would set itself a problem, such as to draw a tank, and would break the problem down into small steps. For each step, the group decided on a procedure, linking the procedures to form a whole.

Finally, we introduced the boys to *Contact* and the *Cambridge Control Kit*. *Contact* uses a similar language to *Dart*, and the boys received it enthusiastically. We asked them to write procedures to operate traffic lights, buzzers and electronic counters. Both Dorothy and I were amazed at the speed with which they arrived at correct solutions. The next week, the boys, in their groups and equipped with jotters and timers, observed traffic light sequences at a Pelican crossing. On returning to school, they constructed a model, with coloured lights, a buzzer

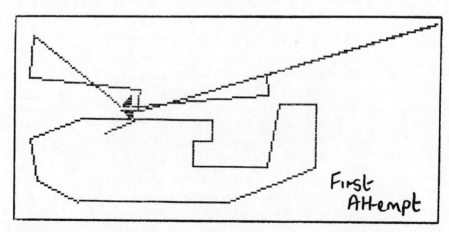

*Figure 3.1 - **First attempt at the helicopter***

and switches. They connected it to the computer, and successfully entered a program to control the model.

The boys' behaviour changed considerably that year. They found out a lot about themselves and others in their class. They learned to be more understanding of other people's problems and how to enter discussions and argue a point effectively. They ended up feeling more confident in new learning situations. They developed planning skills, learning to question, predict and reason while programming the computer. The mathematical skills they gained are a good foundation for more advanced work.

At Ackworth Moor Top School, near Pontefract, boys with emotional and behavioural difficulties successfully used computers to draw and paint. About 40 pupils attend this residential school. The teacher concerned, Les Kemp, had seven in his class, all aged 11-13. Haigh (1991) tells what happened when he arrived at the school as an advisory teacher:

PATTERN MAKERS, PORTRAIT SNATCHERS AND BADGE MANUFACTURERS

These children find it hard to co-operate with others, to enjoy school work and to concentrate for long periods. I had had experience of working with such children within a school for children with moderate learning difficulties, but had never worked with so many EBD children at the same time. Computers were new to Les and his class. He and the children learned together, and he and I supported each other. The usual way of introducing the children to computers is through wordprocessing, but after a few weeks of working in the class half a day a week I realised these children needed something more stimulating.

Image is an open-ended program that grows with the child, so to speak. With it, the child can create, enlarge, reduce, rotate, invert, cut or paste pictures and patterns, adding text of various sizes as desired. With a colour printer, the child's creations can be printed out.

These children became confident with the computer amazingly quickly. I soon realised that it was part of their sub-culture: they had probably spent many hours playing arcade games, and already knew how to use menus. *Image* was a challenge to which they responded by producing exciting and original work.

At first, the children drew shapes and simple pictures. They particularly liked the FILL command, which enabled them to experiment with colours and patterns from those stored on disk, but they were not content with the default colours and patterns and wanted to create their own. They were very concerned about being original in their thinking and design. They soon moved into the 'mixing room' to create their own patterns, saving these for later use.

The boys, working in pairs, also tried connecting a video camera to the BBC Master via a digitiser. This enabled them to snatch frames from the video camera, for modification on the computer. They specially enjoyed having their own pictures snatched, because they could then insert coloured borders and add text, to create 'Wanted' posters! Les encouraged them to discuss the quality of their work and how it could be improved.

Once they had mastered such skills, Les introduced his class to a badge-making mini-enterprise project. The aim was to design badges with slogans or pictures, for sale towards school funds. The boys asked staff, visitors and other children to describe a badge each would like, then filled the orders. There was a big demand for their 'product' and the boys worked very hard together to meet it.

Later the boys, accompanied by Les and myself, paid a visit to the Humber Bridge and the Beverley War Museum. One of the aims of the outing was to teach them some of the skills of using a video camera. The outing was very successful and once back at school we all reviewed the video, the boys joining in well and showing surprising ability to criticise the camerawork. They decided to snatch some of the pictures from the videotape and pull them into *Image*. The boys added text before printing out each in colour for display. Then they practised editing the tape, with two video recorders, and experimented at using *Image* to create titles for the video.

By the end of term, it was clear to me that here was one of the most outstanding examples of how computers can help learners with emotional difficulties.

Another outstanding example comes from Mansfield (1991), who describes the remarkable case of Maud, a girl of 14 who was excluded from her secondary school.

MAUD WINS THROUGH

There was nothing positive the school could say about her: Maud's behaviour was disruptive and she was aggressive and foul-mouthed to staff and pupils alike. Her work habits were poor and attendance minimal. She made little attempt to complete or return homework. Her handwriting was illegible and her use of language restricted.

Maud was moved to Clarendon School, Hampton, for children with moderate learning difficulties. She immediately turned out to be a serious drain on its dedicated staff. She was involved in several fights with other pupils. During one such incident, a staff member was knocked down. The headteacher visited Maud's home: her parents were very concerned, and were having problems with their other children, aged 3 to 17. The elder ones were frequently in trouble with the local police.

Although slightly-built, Maud competed for Clarendon in inter-school cross-country races. She had a natural talent for running and a competitive spirit. The staff focussed on this talent and heaped praise upon her during assembly, when she was presented formally with her certificates. Staff built on her positive feelings and raised her self-esteem by suggesting she should work with a friend to show what she could do on a computer.

Maud's teacher asked her to write a page about her family, a subject she would talk about freely. Maud produced a page of illegible script, but the fact that it was done at all was a surprise. The teacher asked her to type it into the wordprocessor: that took two days, and was full of grammatical and spelling errors, but the printed product was a revelation to Maud. Over the next two days, Maud and her more capable friend worked through several drafts, without staff help. The final product was still full of mistakes but looked good. They had debated long and hard over each word and punctuation mark, and had looked up many spellings. The original went home to show Maud's parents what she had achieved. Her teacher photocopied and enlarged it, and helped Maud to display it in the school entrance.

Maud was amazed. Never before had she had a piece of good work displayed nor had she received so much praise for her literary ability. When her work was shown in assembly, a broad grin crossed her face instead of the usual scowl. To the surprise of the staff, Maud completed at home another piece of handwritten work, not quite as illegible but still with many mistakes. Over the following months, without any specific instruction, Maud's handwriting, punctuation and spelling improved markedly as she gained confidence in her abilities. The motivation to improve and receive more praise was obvious. Everyone was so pleased with what she had achieved. Equally unexpected were the other benefits: improved personal hygiene, appearance and attendance. When she eventually left school, she found a job in a fashion shop in Hounslow.

Elsewhere we have included other British examples, such as Howard's distinctive work in Hemel Hempstead (Chapter 10).

Hyperactive children

Hyperactive children will seldom give learning tasks their sustained attention. Surprisingly, many will play video games for hours on end, to the chagrin of their parents and teachers. Margolies (1990), Director of The Motivation Center in Stratford, Connecticut, suggests that the reasons why they do so are that they receive instant gratification, including very frequent visual and auditory reinforcement. They like the short bursts of action and the extraordinary excitement. They enjoy the 'barrage of attention-grabbing stimuli'. They persist at the games, practising, improving and feeling rewarded, until they have a sense of acquired competence, rare indeed for them.

The question is, does their keenness for video games carry over to learning through computers at school? Margolies says that software which merely mimics paper and pencil tasks does not interest these children. He tells how one hyperactive lad had a habit of coming home late at night because he ignored the time he was due back. Margolies introduced him to a program, *Decision Maker*, which asks the 'player' to make decisions based on criteria rated 1 to 10 in terms of their importance. This boy was very willing to see how his decisions would be rated. Of course, for him the two decisions were to stay out or to get home on time. The criteria he chose were what mattered to him at that moment, short-term consequences with his friends and with his parents, and possible punishments. Margolies wanted to add long-term consequences, but the boy said these had no impact on his decisions. When the boy did the ratings, the game showed him that he would far rather choose to come home on time. Margolies does not report whether he always did after that!

Working with young adults

Again from the US, Scott and Viola (1990) describe a course for emotionally-disturbed youths aged 15–20 at South Richmond High School, a residential establishment on Staten Island, New York. The youths attend not out of choice but because the courts have ordered them to. The course is ostensibly one in BASIC programming, but also introduces them to reading, writing and organisational skills using the computer. It runs on Apple IIe machines.

SOCIAL REPROGRAMMING THROUGH BASIC?

The goal of the course is not to produce programmers but to improve learners' language and cognitive skills, as well as their self-image. To write successful programs, learners must use logic and proper sequencing. When successful, they discover that they possess expertise. They have control over a machine and can make it perform many operations. When this occurs, it works to bolster the confidence of learners, who, because of their past experiences often see themselves as powerless and incompetent.

Students also work at wordprocessing. For the lower functioning learners, the focus is on reading. To do this, a cloze program is used, in which students must read a sentence and supply the missing word. In any other classroom, these learners would most likely balk at such an exercise. In the context of the computer class, they are delighted because they perceive it not as reading but rather as computing.

For the higher functioning learners, wordprocessing has a unique and exciting application. Every day, the students use the computer to write in their personal journals. For some, this may mean relating the day's events from their own perspective. For others, it may be a time for looking back and expressing life's pains. Wordprocessing takes on a quasi-therapeutic air as students learn to express their feelings through writing and deal with past and present problems.

The students are given no formal instruction in keyboarding because an emphasis on it would probably lead to intense frustration and possibly to avoidance of the computer.

Some students are learning to create spreadsheets and databases. These skills are presented and applied in relation to such everyday experiences as balancing budgets. Students who have jobs create worksheets to track the number of hours they work and the amount they should be paid. Others have compiled a database of the software in the school.

Summary

Learners with emotional difficulties need, above all, to experience success and gain some self-esteem. In this chapter we gave examples of children and young adults benefitting in these ways from using computers. No teacher, US or UK, suggests that the learners' emotional problems will be solved by computers. Rather, teachers see that with the help of computers learning can occur despite the problems. With the learning comes justifiably improved self-confidence.

4   Physically-Disabled Learners

Being physically-disabled

Physically-disabled learners are unable to move normally or to exercise proper control over movement. Some children are born physically-disabled. Physical disability can arise from early disorders, possibly congenital, of the nervous, skeletal and muscular systems, such as cerebral palsy or spina bifida. Since people with this kind of disorder are likely to have been at a disadvantage since birth, their problems are often less tractable than those of people who become physically-disabled later in life. Some of the latter experience brain and spinal injury, usually in accidents or warfare. Others contract diseases such as poliomyelitis, multiple sclerosis, tuberculosis of the spine, motor neurone disease, myasthenia gravis, or brittle bone disease. Still others, not all old, have disorders such as arthritis, Parkinsonism, muscular atrophy, progressive muscular dystrophy and cerebral vascular accidents (strokes). A few experience disabilities with unfortunate physical side-effects, such as severe haemophiliacs, who are bruised by touching objects.

For all of them, life is much harder than it is for able-bodied people because they find gross or broad movements difficult, or the finer ones, or both. They may experience decreased range and strength of movement, or they may have unwanted and uncontrolled movements. For example, a child with cerebral palsy (paralysis and associated disorders of motor functions arising from damage to the brain during birth or soon afterwards) may be unable to hold her hand still enough to write clearly. An adult with muscular dystrophy (disorders of muscular function and structure that lead to increasing weakness and degeneration of the muscles) may become quickly exhausted by writing, which demands great effort. A child with Friedreich's ataxia, a hereditary progressive disease of the nervous system that causes increasing inco-ordination of movement, may find it impossible even to press the keys of a calculator. A severe haemophiliac may be unable to do so without bruising.

As learners, physically-disabled people need help above all in communicating through the written word. Many cannot write or type. Some can do so only slowly, very poorly or for short periods at a time. Their writing may be nearly illegible, even when it has cost them much exhausting effort. Not all learners are as badly off as Scott, who after four years of therapy could open his hands and now uses a modified keyboard. For a few, poor hand-eye coordination is due to visual handicap as well as lack of fine muscle control (athetosis, or uncoordinated involuntary movements associated with brain damage). Even directing their own gaze at the television screen may require vast effort. Drawing can be difficult, if not impossible. Some cannot reach very far, not even to pick up a book from the nearby table. Others have impaired speech or none at all. Physically-disabled learners with good speech are at a disadvantage, but those without speech are doubly so.

Access to the curriculum is hard for physically-disabled learners. 'Normal' study habits are impossible. Handling pieces of paper, books or index cards may be difficult. Activities such as reading, note-taking, diary-keeping, essay-writing, television watching, listening to audiocassettes and carrying out practical work of any kind may require exhausting effort, or simply be impossible. Using a 'scratch pad' or 'rough notebook' may be out of the question. On field trips they must probably rely on memory or other able-bodied learners' goodwill. Manipulating objects in a chemistry or physics laboratory may be impossible. Drawing any kind of figure in mathematics, geography or science may be too demanding. Playing a musical instrument, or composing a musical score, may be beyond their physical capabilities.

Physically-disabled learners may have little hope of exploring a library on their own or expressing their individuality through painting.

Adapting computers to help physically-disabled learners

An essential principle is that the technology should be used to magnify abilities that remain, bypassing the disabilities as much as possible. How much a computer can help an individual depends on these remaining abilities, as well the degree and type of disability. It also depends on how much the computer can be adapted to that individual.

The goal is to enable physically-disabled learners to achieve as much as they can by using the technology for the same functions, such as wordprocessing and graphics, as able-bodied people, with appropriate modifications to hardware and software. If they can manage the inputs, the technology can help them with the processing and provide the outputs. There are three strategies, for use singly or in combination. One requires modified behaviour from the learner, as in using a headstick with a standard keyboard. Another requires adaptation of the computer hardware and/or software. The third requires a specially-adapted piece of computer technology as a medium between the computer and the person with disabilities.

Mildly physically-disabled people may be able to use the keyboard and screen in normal positions. They can usually type with one hand, using accurately one or more fingers. Moderately physically-disabled people may require repositioning of the keyboard and/or screen, and can accurately access all keys using a hand-held stick, head- or mouth-stick, toes or other body extremity. The best position will depend on each individual's history and parts of the body over which he or she has some control, but keyboard height, angle and accessibility from a wheelchair must be taken into account. The height and angle of the screen need to be right, too, to avoid reflections so that the learner can see well. For somebody who is supine, a screen mounted overhead may be right. To reduce input errors and fatigue, finding the best keyboard position is important.

In addition, the keyboard may have to be adapted, or even dispensed with altogether. For example, it is possible to remove the automatic repeat, which causes a letter to be repeated if a key is held down for too long. Or the keyboard can be 'desensitised', to reduce errors due to accidental touching, through lengthening the keys' activation time and/or adding a keyguard. Cerebral palsy may be accompanied by a rhythmic tremor. People with this tremor may need slightly stiffer keys. The need to hold down two keys (e.g. control and another) at the same time for commands can be removed through a software or hardware adaptation, such as *Sticky Keys* for the Apple Macintosh. Alternatively, a keypad can be provided on which they 'set up' their input, perhaps through using a stick or headpointer to press a sequence of keys, and then enter it. This allows them to be sure it is right before actually entering the 'code'. Command selection using a mouse or some other pointer can be replaced by selection via the keyboard.

Some adaptations, such as touch tablets, bypass the keyboard entirely by providing a separate set of switches for complex multi-stroke commands. Some physically-disabled learners have small hands, often through thalidomide or brittle-bone disease. For them, standard keyboards and keypads may present difficulties. To control the cursor on screen, they and others may be able to use switch arrays, trackingballs (which can be swivelled by gross movement of the limb) and joysticks. Other people may have difficulty hitting a single switch at the right time to select an item from an array scanned by a light or cursor, but often the scanning speed can be adjusted to suit their own rhythm or speed of movement. Those who are also blind or partially-sighted may be helped to use a scanned array by means of an audible signal, such as a rising tone. Morse code may be the fastest form of text input for some learners, especially those with visual-perceptual problems who find scanning difficult. But scanning is widely used, in at least five forms: step or manual, automatic, row-column, directed and auditory. Step or manual scanning usually requires one switch to shift the scanner to the next item in the sequence; another selects the item desired. Or if the scanner stays long enough on an item, it is selected. Automatic scanning offers each item in sequence. A switch starts and stops the scan, and selects the item the scanner stops on. Scanning speed can usually be changed to suit individual needs, but many learners anticipate the scanner rather than waiting until the required item lights up, then operating the switch. In row-column scanning each row is presented, in sequence. The switch can select a row and the scanner moves along the row until the switch is operated again. Directed scanning requires 2–5 switches, which control the scanner almost like a cursor. Auditory scanning speaks each item. Though slower than visual scanning, it is excellent for learners who cannot easily anticipate the point at which to select the item desired by hitting the single switch. It is also good for learners who are unable to deal with visual information such as non-readers.

A CURRICULUM ON *HYPERCARD:* MATTHEW'S STORY

At the Center for Applied Special Technology in Peabody, Massachusetts, Matthew obtained an aid which enables him to participate in first-grade work (Meng, 1990). Matthew has cerebral palsy and cannot speak or control his limbs. He cannot use ordinary school curriculum materials. When he switches on his Apple Macintosh computer, it displays a set of buttons, highlighting them in sequence. He can select the one he wants through a chin switch, instead of a mouse. Each button leads to a different *Hypercard* stack (see Chapter 8), developed by the Center. Most of the stacks cover some aspect of the first-grade curriculum. Matthew can also play games, type, read sports stories or books, look at pictures and control equipment in his home.

Severely physically-disabled people need to attain control over the technology if they are to have access to the curriculum. Their individual needs must be carefully assessed. Most cannot access the standard keyboard and usually require an input device such as a single switch. Provided comfortable seating can be arranged, a student unable to use a keyboard directly, even with modifications, may use a scanner: when the pointer on the screen rests on the desired symbol, he or she activates a switch which sends the selected symbol to the screen or carries out a particular command. Or a touch tablet, such as the Concept Keyboard, may prove more suitable.

It is astonishing that learners with physical disabilities which prevent them from drawing a straight line with, say, a pencil can now create perfectly-drawn architectural or engineering plans of great complexity, using a computer with special input attachments. They may use different means but the output is identical to that of able-bodied learners. By looking at the drawings, nobody can tell that Mary, a woman with multiple scelerosis, operates her equipment with an eyebrow switch.

Butterworth (1991) tells how Steven, a teenager with spinal muscular atrophy, and Ruth, a girl with a strong tremor, cope in the real world of their respective Wiltshire secondary schools.

FITTING COMPUTERS TO LEARNERS: STEVEN AND RUTH'S STORIES

Steven is in the mainstream for all subjects except games periods, when he does other activities with support staff. He uses a motorised wheelchair, controlled by a joystick, to get around the school. For all work requiring fine motor skills, he needs a gantry support system for his arms, which have poor muscle tone and tire very quickly.

Although Steven can write neatly and legibly, he cannot produce by hand the amount of writing needed for his GCSE coursework. The solution for him is to have a Toshiba T1000 portable computer, provided by the Local Education Authority. Steven says he finds it easier to type using two pencils rather than his fingers. He writes:

'My name is Steven Richardson and I attend Downton Secondary School. I am in the 9th year now, so I get many projects and essays, which have to be written up at home. After a long day at school my arms are very tired, so my handwriting can become messy and unreadable.

'This however is no longer a problem, as I now do these long pieces of work on the portable Toshiba T1000. Now I can write more work, as I don't get as tired using it, but also the work I do is neat and readable. With GCSE work on the horizon, I am very glad I have the use of this great, little, machine.'

Ruth attends another Wiltshire secondary school and is now preparing for her GCSE. Her condition includes a strong tremor whenever she tries to concentrate on an activity requiring fine motor skills. She can walk around the school by herself, carrying her books, but when she sits down to draw or write her problems become obvious. She has to concentrate very hard to produce legible handwriting, and the process is very slow. She cannot focus well at the same time on the content.

The Local Education Authority provided her with a Cambridge Z88 portable computer, which is light and compact, with a virtually silent keyboard. Ruth was already quite a proficient touch typist, because she had taken lessons in order to use a Canon Typestar, predecessor to the Z88, but she decided to take a typing option to improve her skills. She has a printer at school and another at home, so she can print out her assignments and notes almost at any time. She also uses a small taperecorder in class to take notes sometimes when her slow handwriting would hold her up too much.

For learners who cannot manage as well as Steven, three main categories of single-switch devices are available: those activated by pressure, movement or puff-and-sip. Heavy pressure switches include treads, treadles, single rocking levers, thumb pads and plates. Light pressure switches include levers, pushbuttons, platforms, plate, pinchers, pillows, membranes and bite devices. Movement switches include tip, tilt, infrared, photocell and magnetic finger. Puff-and-sip switches are breath-controlled, by changes in pressure in the oral cavity. Raised keys provide visual, auditory and tactile feedback, which membrane switches do not, but the latter can more easily be relabelled and can be easily provided in various sizes. There are also specialised keyboards activated by eye gaze, light-pointing and voice. The display from which selection is made can be on the screen or on a separate monitor or panel. The Dvorak keyboard has the keys pressed most often under the strongest fingers, and is made in right-, left- and two-handed versions. An alphabetic keyboard can be best for learners using a single pointing device, as it is simpler to find the required letter.

Physically-disabled people without speech difficulties may be able to use voice-activated systems. These are expensive, and individuals wanting to use them must be trained. They are versatile, however, and can be programmed to write, check spelling, use spreadsheets and search documents and databases. Usually the student speaks a one- or two-word command into a microphone.

Speeding up writing

Electronic text is much easier for physically-disabled learners to create and handle than printed text. Through the computer, they can also reach out via networks, obtain information from distant databanks and bulletin boards, and even read some software manuals in electronic form. It is a fact, however, that their ordinary rate of response is often so slow that remedial drill and practice becomes very time-consuming for them – and for staff who help them. They fall further and further behind other learners, becoming very discouraged. Speeding up their writing by means of 'smart' programs may be possible. Smart word predictors use rules based on the English language, word frequencies and the student's previous choices. On the basis of the first two or three letters typed, the screen displays a short list of possible words, and the learner need make only one further key stroke to select the right word if it is listed. These programs also insert the right number of spaces after punctuation marks, and start each sentence with a capital letter. Commonly used phrases can be stored, along with headers and footers for documents such as letters. Acceleration strategies usually focus on reducing the keystrokes needed to type words or phrases, but for individuals with typing speeds of more than 15–20 words a minute, these may be counter-productive. Automatic spelling checkers and correction programs are available to physically-disabled learners just as they are to able-bodied ones.

For example, Stansfield (1990) describes *Speedwriter*, which works in conjunction with wordprocessing and desktop publishing programs. Built into *Speedwriter* is a dictionary which learns new words as the pupil types them, although this option can be turned off if the pupil is a poor speller! Typing the first letter of a word causes a list of nine numbered words to appear. If the pupil sees the word he or she wants in the list, typing its number will insert it in the text. If the word is not there, a second letter brings up a new list. A fullstop or question mark brings up a list of likely sentence-starting words, beginning with a capital letter.

Some predictive programs were originally written with the 'busy professional' in mind, but may now prove useful to physically-disabled learners trying to gain access to the curriculum. For example, one-handed typists and those using a headstick or headpointer can speed up their writing by using *MindReader* (see Chapters 3 and 8), sold as a 'smart' wordprocessing program. As well as predicting words on the basis of the first few letters typed in, it learns a user's vocabulary up to the limit of memory available. A spelling checker, which works either in real time or after a section of work has been completed, is included. Similarly, *Turbo Lightning* checks spelling as the text is being written. When the user makes a mistake, a tone sounds. He or she can press a key to display a window with possible correct spellings, based on phonetically-alike words, rather than orthographically-alike ones. The correct spelling will automatically replace the wrong one if the user selects it. Either the teacher or the learner can add new words to the spelling checker. It is easy to replace a word with a better one chosen from the program's thesaurus. The trouble with *MindReader* and *Turbo Lightning* is that someone with very few skills would be unlikely to be able to use the programs at all. There are other criticisms, as we found at Foothill College in California:

MIXED BLESSINGS FROM SMART PROGRAMS

Wally Manville, the Centre Supervisor, himself disabled, thought the *Mind-Reader* program only learned properly if one person used it. When four or five used it, the program did not serve their individual needs. Version 2.0 does not capitalise the initial letter of a new sentence, as did Version 1.0, and he thinks this is a pity. He believes a bad typist can be helped. A bad speller might even be helped, though the program is very slow and bad spellers often lack the grammar to write good English – *MindReader* does not correct grammar.

Turbo Lightning slows down students, even if it is replacing mispelled words automatically – it adds the correctly spelled word immediately after the mis-pelled one – very annoying. It signals, with a tone, any word it thinks has been misspelled. If you have typed on further, you have to move the cursor back to the 'wrong' word. That drives you crazy. The fact that it provides a menu of similar-sounding words assumes that writers tend to produce wrongly spelled but similar-sounding versions of the words they want, presumably because they learned their phonics badly. *Turbo Lightning* will try to match its words even to nonsense, ignoring completely the context, of course.

Wally says that Foothill College students with disabilities who tried *Turbo Lightning* turned instead to the *WordPerfect* Spelling Checker. They prefer to type a paragraph or two, then use the checker to clean up any mistakes they may have made.

A smart predictive program developed for children

The most reliable evidence to date of success in using a 'smart' program is from Newell, Booth and Beattie (1991), who describe a carefully conducted experiment in which children with varied learning difficulties tried out a predictive text entry program, *PAL* (Predictive Adaptive Lexicon) and its accompanying wordprocessing program, *PALSTAR*, both developed by researchers at the University of Dundee. We summarise their findings from the experiment:

PAL IS SMART

This study confirmed that *PAL* reduced the number of keystrokes necessary for a physically handicapped child to enter text, allowing children with severe motor problems to produce work much faster, and with much less effort.

After using *PAL* for two or three weeks, the children became aware that prediction could assist their spelling and they looked to the predictions window for assistance. Children with severe spelling difficulties (with or without physical disabilities) were very often able to produce the first letters of words although they could not spell the word correctly. They were also able to recognise words in the prediction list even when the list was composed of a number of similar looking words. By using *PAL*, these children changed their written work from being barely intelligible due to their bizarre spelling to being easy to read if not always spelled correctly. There was also some evidence that long-term use of *PAL* improves unaided spelling ability.

While using *PAL*, most of the children vocalised as they wrote, articulating clearly and breaking down the words into syllabic units. This vocalisation helped to stress the initial letter of a word that the child wanted to find in prediction.

The overall response of the teachers to *PAL* was very positive; they saw improvements in all aspects of the childrens' work with particular emphasis on the quality of their written work. Increased independence, motivation, vocabulary size and language skills were also noted. *PAL* was found particularly relevant for children with special educational needs of long standing, who had associated feelings of failure and frustration. The introduction of *PAL* often produced a happier and more relaxed atmosphere, resulting in emotional as well as academic progress being made.

It was also observed that the use of *PAL* helped to bridge the gap between home and school. Parents who previously had not shown any interest in their child's progress became involved. The program gave pleasure both to parents and to the child – who was often experiencing a measure of success for the first time.

Teachers whose pupils were part of the research study also voluntarily and successfully introduced *PAL* to other children in their schools.

Access to text

Reading books may be difficult or impossible for many physically-disabled learners. Mechanical page turners can help with physical access to a book but the process can be slow with a dictionary, encyclopedia, or other reference book where reading is non-sequential. Two potentially valuable developments in information technology are electronic publishing and compact discs. Most new publications are produced in an electronic form by a computer system capable of 'exporting' it into hypertext or browsing software giving detailed access to the text. Together with pictures and diagrams that can be scanned into a computer, complete books can be made available on a computer screen. For anyone unable to use a conventional keyboard, alternatives such as keypads and switches can be added as with other computer-based applications. By adding a wordprocessor, a disabled student can have a combined reading and writing system.

The significance of the compact disc technologies is that large quantities of information can be stored on a single disc. For example, a CD-ROM can hold about 250,000 pages of A4 text. This has led many publishers to transfer books into this medium. The complete works of Shakespeare are available on a single disc as are an increasing number of encyclopedias and dictionaries. The medium's potential is being exploited even further as moving image sequences are added to still pictures and diagrams.

AN INTERACTIVE ELECTRONIC BOOK

At Hereward College, the national college for students with physical disabilities, staff have made a leap forward in providing interactive access to books. There, the Nuffield Interactive Book System (NIBS) project is using hypertext software, *Guide*, to retrieve and display text and images from books translated into a computer readable form. Material was assembled for biology and sociology courses, with text from books being supplemented by worksheets, plus articles from newspapers and magazines. Information extracted could be structured to meet individual needs. Initial results are encouraging, though the teachers have to change the way they manage their learning resources.

Physically-disabled learners with speech impairment

Apart from speech disorders resulting from deafness (see Chapter 5) or paralysis, some learners experience other kinds, and computers may help them. Computers can be made to speak by the addition of speech synthesisers or the digitisation of human speech. In either case the speech can be recalled by entering commands from a keyboard, keypad or an alternative to a keyboard such as a switch. Compact disc technology extends the possibilities further: an hour or more of speech as individual words or phrases can be stored on a single disc. To meet mobility requirements, speech prostheses devices can be based on portable computers or customised for speech production only, without other computer facilities, which makes them even smaller. An advantage of a computer-based system is that the person can use a wordprocessor to make up (and store for recall later) phrases from the available vocabulary. The Equalizer communicator is one example, based on an IBM compatible computer.

Touch Talker and Light Talker use the symbolic language Minspeak. These devices differ in the way that the keyboards are used. Touch Talker is appropriate for someone who can use a keyboard with their fingers, stick or headpointer. Light Talker uses a light sensor to activate the keyboard. Combined with a range of selection methods including row and column scanning, it caters for non-keyboard users. The basis of Minspeak is that by selecting sequences of icons, pre-stored utterances can be retrieved and spoken (Edwards, 1991).

MARILYN GOES PORTABLE

When Marilyn first went to the Fife Assessment Centre for Communication through Technology (FACCT), she communicated by using Blissymbolics on a BBC computer. The greatest difficulty that this caused was that the computer was not portable and Marilyn, totally wheelchair bound and only able to operate a single switch, could only use the communication device in one place. This was extremely frustrating for her and the staff involved at the home and social work day centre she attended.

After assessment by FACCT, Marilyn was provided with a Light Talker which she uses with a single switch. Staff from the centre were also trained in the use of the device as several of them felt awkward communicating in this way. Marilyn is now successfully using the Light Talker and there has been a considerable improvement in her reading ability. Staff are delighted with her progress, although they say life is not quite so easy for them anymore as they have to respond to Marilyn's requests which are expressed quite clearly (FACCT, 1989).

A THEMATIC APPROACH TO MINSPEAK

A boy aged ten, with cerebral palsy and athetoid movements, started with an 8 symbol overlay for Touch Talker and soon progressed to a 32 symbol overlay, according to a Scottish Minspeak User Support Group newsletter (June 1988). All messages are in themes which correspond to a day's timetable. Examples of messages include 'I would like to listen to a story', 'I want to play', 'I want down' and 'can I have the computer' (play theme). The overall strategy has been to build one theme at a time and within each theme to open out possibilities. The teacher reports that now the lad is using Touch Talker full-time in class, it is encouraging to see how his hand function has improved. He is also communicating with and getting responses from other children who are enjoying the humorous parts of the language programmed.

Disabled learners can also speak to their computers, through speech recognition software, which now provides users with a way of speaking multi-syllabic and distinct commands. Lahm (1989) reports that disabled people's speech is more varied than that of able-bodied people, with the result that many speech recognition systems do not work as accurately. This is because the speaker has to 'train' the system to recognise his or her pronunciation.

DO WHAT I SAY: ROBBIE AND HIS COMPUTER

Robbie has physical disabilities and poor vision. He is a high school student and uses *Voice Navigator*, a speech recognition system (Meng, 1990). He trained it to respond to his voice, and through it can command the Macintosh to open a file, type a word or dial a phone number. The text is enlarged on the screen by *CloseView* and read back to him with *Talking Keys*, a public domain desk accessory that uses *Macintalk*, the Macintosh speech facility. To organise his hard disk and do his homework, Robbie can also use *Hypercard* stacks developed for him by the Center for Applied Special Technology in Peabody, Massachusetts.

One study (Coleman, 1988) showed that a simple speech recognition system could recognise 12 single-syllable, consonant-vowel utterances of speakers with cerebral palsy. Accurate recognition happened more often than chance would lead one to expect, but certainly not invariably and well below levels for able-bodied people. Rapid advances have been made in this field, however, and *Dragon Dictate* is one of the first commercially available systems with the potential to be used in a learning situation where the demands on accuracy and versatility are significant.

PHOENIX RISES FOR MICHAEL

Michael has been severely disabled from birth by spina bifida. He is very keen to write computer programs for children with learning difficulties. To help with this objective he took an Open University course, Fundamentals of Computing. With the help of the Honeywood Trust, he obtained an Aptech Phoenix workstation, as a means of undertaking the programming part of the course and of producing written assignments. This workstation uses the *Dragon Dictate* speech recognition system which is appropriate for Michael's need as an alternative to a conventional computer keyboard.

Expectations were high when Michael started the course in 1990. The computer's hard disk had been configured with the course software and integrated with the speech recognition system before he received the workstation. Progress was not as fast as everyone had hoped, however, partly due to the many simultaneous changes Michael experienced. Besides being new to distance learning and having to cope with communication and teaching methods that he had not experienced before, he had a new course, a new computer system, new software and a new input device. After initial difficulties, Michael decided to put the course aside temporarily and concentrate first on mastering the computer.

This experience highlighted the need to ensure that when enabling technology and computer applications are brought together for a user for the first time, sequential training should be provided. This should first give the user skills in the enabling technology, before the application is introduced. During acquisition of these skills, a user makes mistakes which, in many cases, cause problems with an application because the mistakes result in incorrect commands. It is encouraging that training modules are now being developed that allow simulation of keyboard actions without carrying out the commands, thus helping learners to build up skills and confidence.

Summary

Because computers might not seem, at first sight, to offer much help to physically-disabled learners, we dwelled on the special problems of physical disability before showing how computers could be adapted to help overcome them. Learners young and old in this group often want, and obtain, access to the curriculum through faster writing, as this chapter demonstrates. Electronic communicators and adapted computers can speak for these learners, whether or not they have speech impairments.

5 Sensorily-disabled Learners

Helping blind learners to read the screen

The main senses through which humans learn are vision and hearing. If either of these is impaired, or still worse both, then teachers must overcome this barrier to communication. Most people with impaired vision, particularly the old, are not truly blind but do have serious learning difficulties. Unable to see detail, they misunderstand pictures, maps and diagrams, cannot read text, and are deprived of many learning opportunities. Admittedly, among the aged the incentive to learn may not be there, but poor vision is a serious handicap for all ages. For those few who are totally blind from birth, the barrier preventing them from obtaining a normal education must seem insurmountable. Can computers help?

Before computers came on the educational scene, a few technological solutions to the problems of sight-impaired learners already existed. Among these were large print displays, often through closed circuit television. These proved cumbersome and expensive to buy and maintain. Computers can provide a range of magnifications of text and graphics, in colour or not, via cheap software compatible with commercially available software. Besides giving an ordinary-sized display when required, they can also offer a smooth, fast display of enlarged text and graphics, with automatic, adjustable scrolling, movement of the viewing window to any part of the screen and automatic return to the cursor location.

KEVIN'S STORY: ACADEMIC ACHIEVEMENT WRIT LARGE

Kevin, a Californian, lost most of his central vision at age 13 due to a congenital eye disease (Stargardt's). By 28 he had lost the rest of it. He coped reasonably well at high school without computers and started at college. He found college work unsatisfying and soon went to work instead for eight years. When he returned to college, he began to use a enlarged print system on a computer, and learned wordprocessing, which in turn improved his spelling and expanded his vocabulary. His academic work was so good that he expected to be able to transfer to a university to complete a degree. He says he appreciated tremendously the opportunity the computer gave him to express himself clearly in writing (Brown and others, 1989).

For blind learners with good hearing, the greatest advance has been the development of screen readers, which can provide a spoken (synthetic speech) equivalent to the visual screen display for computer software that functions in a text mode. Screen readers are being developed for computer software that uses a graphics mode such as *Windows* 3 on IBM compatible computers. Conversion of icons, graphics and mouse movements to a spoken output that enables blind people to use these features is far less developed than for text displays.

When speech synthesisers were first added to computers in the 1970s, the interface was often simple and crude. Typically, text would be spoken at the time that it was displayed on a computer screen. This was adequate for many applications as text was written to the screen sequentially (like a teletype terminal or printer) rather than to single screen displays where characters can appear anywhere at anytime as with most current computer applications. If large amounts of text were involved then significant delays would result as all of the text was spoken. For a sighted person the display of large amounts of text was not a problem as the eye could quickly scan the screen for information that could lead to the next action.

Development of screen readers in the 1980s significantly improved access for a blind person to computer applications. A screen reader usually works in two different modes: review, and live or application. In the review mode, the screen output from an application (wordprocessor, spreadsheet, database) is 'frozen' and the text on the screen can be interrogated with a set of functions through the computer keyboard or a separate keypad. These functions are associated with a speech cursor that can be moved anywhere on the screen and characters, words or lines of text can be spoken. There are usually additional facilities to assist with 'navigation' around the screen such as the speaking of the x and y coordinates of the speech cursor, or directional and positional tones as the cursor is moved. Information about the attributes of a character can be reported such as the colour or brightness. These review facilities provide detailed access to text or other ASCII characters on a screen but slowly because of the amount of navigation around the screen. Review mode is likely to be used by blind learners unfamiliar with a screen layout, or by programmers. For effective access to computer applications, the live mode is better.

In live mode, the screen reader is programmed to match the display of a particular application to various speech windows and event markers. Speech windows define areas of the screen which can be read using a sequence of keystrokes, or automatically. These windows are used in conjunction with an event marker which is programmed to monitor changes in pre-defined locations on a screen.

Consider a blind person working with a wordprocessor to set up a table of data. She wants to use the tab facility to ensure columns are aligned. Wordprocessors have an indicator for the tab position: either an arrow or other character shows on a ruler, or the column number is displayed. *WordPerfect* gives the number. A speech window can be defined which covers the two character positions occupied by the column number, and the screen reader is programmed to speak this window when the tab key is pressed. Similarly, the page number can be spoken by monitoring the position of the page number on the screen, and speaking out the contents of the speech window containing the number when it changes, thus giving a spoken prompt when a page change occurs.

For complex screen displays there may be numerous speech windows and event markers that combine to provide a spoken output when appropriate. Skilful programming of screen readers minimises the amount of speech and maximises the amount of information required for the next action. This action should be as obvious as when a sighted person has a screen display. The output from the application at any one time is a single line of speech compared with a screen that might have 25 rows of 80 characters to convey information.

Enhanced screen readers can also change the rate of speech and automatically mute their speech. For example, when a learner wants to check text on a wordprocessor, he or she may move through the text at a fast rate of speaking until an unexpected message, which he may need to have spoken slowly. Automatic muting is helpful too: a long message can be curtailed when any key is pressed indicating that the next action is being taken.

Speech windows, event markers, speech rates, and other features, together make up a speech environment which can be customised both for a computer application and an individual user. Good design of these environments can make all the difference between efficient and frustrating access for learners to a computer application.

Similar environments can be developed for large character displays of the same information, which is sent to a speech synthesiser but also appears in a window on the application screen (Fig. 5.1). This technique is not so widely used as speech output because the text has to be scrolled across the screen which makes it difficult to read even though it is enlarged. This type of screen reader resides in computer memory alongside an application. Less common types are hardware based such as those that have vertical and horizontal sliders, adjacent to or built into the keyboard, which move the speech cursor around the screen. Positional tones are also used, and push buttons on the sliders activate a spoken response in relation to the cursor position. Together with automatic spoken responses that are built into these screen readers, access can be provided to computer applications. These types of screen reader have an advantage for braille users as the output can be provided on a single line refreshable braille display (40 or 80 characters) that directly relates to a line on a screen display. This method is often favoured by blind programmers when using a computer as a terminal to a mainframe computer.

Graphical user interfaces for blind learners

Software for the Apple Macintosh, and more recently for IBM compatible computers, uses a graphical user interface. Conventional screen reading techniques only give access to text on screens. Hence the heralding of these interfaces as a major step forward in user friendliness can only be described as a step backwards for blind people as the techniques associated with these interfaces are so visually dependent.

Consider a typical screen from an Apple Macintosh (Fig. 5.2). It is acclaimed by many sighted users as a highly intuitive interface. Actions can be carried out by pointing at an icon (using a mouse to control the position of the pointer) and then clicking a button on the mouse to activate an application. Visual windows are designed to be resized and placed anywhere on a screen. All of these features mitigate against a blind learner successfully using this interface.

Outspoken, designed to overcome this problem for blind people, makes use of the internal speech synthesiser, *Macintalk*. The mouse is programmed to speak anything (including icons) over which the mouse pointer passes, but in fact the

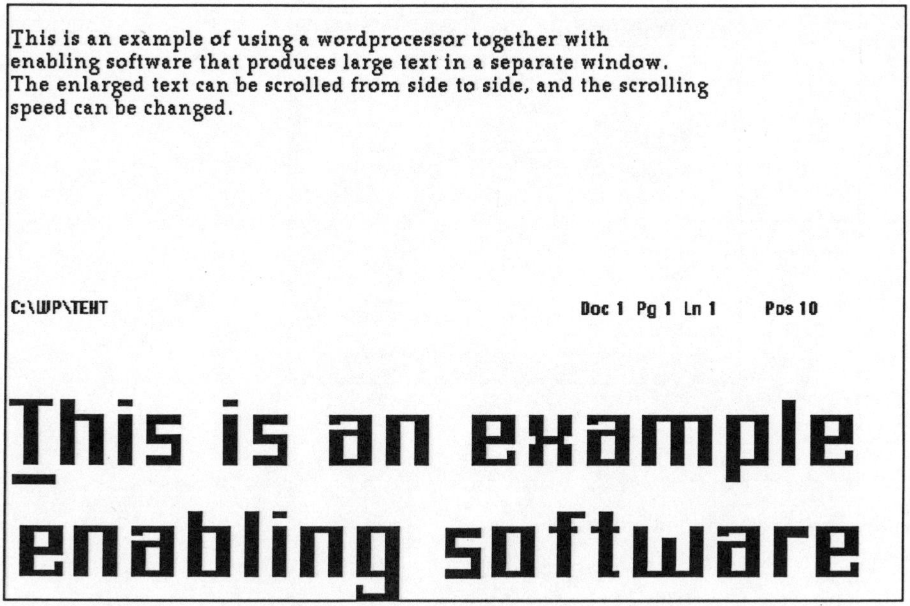

Figure 5.1 - Large characters diplayed in a separate window on screen

cursor keys provide a more realistic (but relatively slow) way of navigating around the screen. *Outspoken* has keyboard equivalents for commonly used commands, windows that can be selected from a spoken menu, and spoken outputs for the dragging and release of icons.

It is a major challenge to match screen reading facilities to intuitive features of visual displays associated with graphical user interfaces. The development of *Outspoken* for the Apple Macintosh is an important step forward in making graphical user interfaces accessible to blind learners. Case studies will show how effective it is. Adaptation of graphical user interfaces is discussed more fully by Edwards (1991), and in a special edition of the Journal of *Human-Computer* Interaction (1989).

Screen readers are not easy to learn to use. Mastering basic commands may take only an hour or so, but the full set may need weeks of learning, or even months for the most complex, but this is true for sighted users learning to use wordprocessing programs, spreadsheets, graphics packages and so on. It helps if the blind person is a competent touch typist before starting to use one. The quality of speech output is important for some users, but others are happy with the robotic voice of much cheaper synthesisers than DECtalk, the top of the range. Most blind and sight-

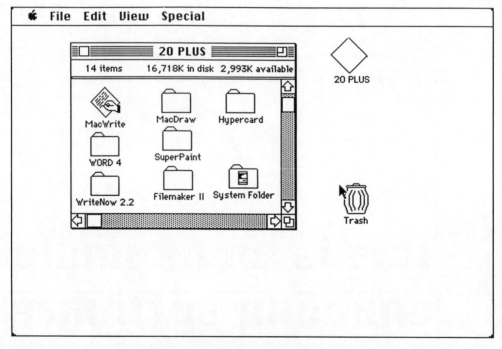

*Figure 5.2 - **A typical screen from an Apple Macintosh***

impaired people using a screen reader quickly learn to listen to and understand synthesised speech.

Braille and print

Screen readers have fostered widespread use of wordprocessors by blind learners, who can thereby produce printed text, perhaps for essays or examinations, even though handwriting is impossible or very difficult for them. For someone who prefers to retain copies in braille, computers can provide braille as well as print output.

MEETING ANDREW'S NEEDS FOR BRAILLE AND PRINT

Andrew is a student at the Open University. Both he and his wife are blind. His preferred medium of communication is braille. When he started on the Technology Foundation course he was provided with a computer, screen reader, printer and braille embosser as part of a project sponsored by IBM. The facility to switch between print and braille output from the wordprocessor that he used was crucial in meeting his needs to produce written assignments that could be passed to his tutor for marking (in print) and retained by himself for study purposes (in braille). In this way he was able to attain independence in writing and at the same time be confident that the paper sent to the tutor was as accurate and as well layed out as any sighted student. His written work was no longer associated with being produced by a blind person which is a tribute to the equalising effect of the technology.

A similar problem was addressed at Chorleywood College (Vincent and Schofield, 1986) with a pilot study into the automation of braille transcription for examinations. The Perkins Braillers conventionally used for examinations were interfaced to computers that collected all of the keystrokes and transcribed the braille to text which was printed at the end of the examination, for use by the examiners. The students did not have to make any changes to the way that they normally brailled their answers. Even if the computer technology failed, the answers in braille were still available for conventional hand transcription by sighted teachers. Comparing manual and automatic transcription was interesting. The potential for time saving was very high. Hundreds of examination papers were written each year. Hand transcription involved almost all college staff for several days. By comparison, the printing out from the automated version only required one person to oversee the rapid printing of each script.

It may seem strange that Chorleywood did not install permanently the automated process. The reasons for this lie in the ambiguities in braille and the difference a missing dot can make to a translation into braille. The latter can arise through lack of pressure on a key, a mistake in braille spelling, or by the use of a finger nail to erase an incorrect dot – a traditional and efficient method which is impossible to detect by a computer! Automatic transcription produced 97 percent accurate printed scripts but this has to be compared with the 100 percent accuracy achieved by hand transcription where ambiguities and errors could be treated in a consistent way. Although the difference is small, the Chorleywood teachers saw it as lowering the standard of scripts presented to examiners, and felt that saving time was not sufficient compensation. A similar method employed for producing essays and internal examinations proved to be very successful, however, as teachers were content to accept the 3 percent inaccuracy level within the college community where external examiners were not involved.

Since that time numerous products have appeared that achieve a similar outcome, including small portable devices, with electronic braille keyboards, that can store and translate braille for subsequent transcription, printing or embossing. The portability and silent operation of these devices makes them better-suited to activities such as notetaking for which a computer system would be too inconvenient. The ambiguities associated with the context sensitive nature of braille remain. It will need a significant level of intelligence within a computer transcription system before it can understand the difference between the word 'disabled' and 'eight Australian dollars' which have the same braille representation and would have an obvious meaning for a braille reader when used in an appropriate context!

Access to printed text for blind learners

Complementary to the needs of a learner to have a means of writing for essays, note taking and examinations, is the need to be able to access printed text such as books. Currently, the most popular way that blind people have access to books is by audiotape recordings made by sighted readers. These are commonly known as 'talking books'. A disadvantage of this method is that audiotape is a linear medium: reading reference material such as dictionaries and encyclopedias is particularly awkward, and frequent cross referencing between different parts of a book, often essential for study purposes, is impossible.

Access to printed text through computers with speech output is not well developed. Hypertext software for personal computers (see Chapters 6–8 for examples) offers new opportunities if it can be integrated with speech environments and associated learning strategies developed for blind learners. Hypertext provides mechanisms for compact storage and rapid retrieval of enormous volumes of textual, numeric and visual data. Hypertext systems contain features which, combined with speech output, offer blind learners new means of accessing, retrieving and interrogating information. Many publications are now produced electronically using wordprocessors or desktop publishing: the complete text can be transferred easily to browsing and retrieval software such as a hypertext program.

AN OPEN UNIVERSITY EXPERIMENT WITH *HYPERBOOK*

During 1991, two students at the Open University received all of their course material on floppy disk in a form that can be read with hypertext software. *Hyperbook* has been used as it is compatible with screen reading techniques. One student uses speech output; the other uses a refreshable braille display. In both cases they have detailed and non-linear access to the text, and extracts can be taken for notes or essays. Neither of these techniques was available to them in the past when they used audio recordings. This development has been extended by the use of compact disc technology (CD-ROM) so that an entire course can be provided on one disc.

General developments in compact disc technology are also proving beneficial to blind learners. Numerous CD-ROMs are being produced by publishers that take advantage of the high storage capacity of the discs. With approximately 250,000 pages of A4 text per disc, the complete works of Shakespeare go on one disc. Encyclopedias and dictionaries have been transferred to this medium. By adding a speech interface such as a screen reader, blind people can access books that were difficult or impossible to access by any other means. This is particularly true of dictionaries which have often been produced in a shortened form to overcome the problem of the large amount of space taken up by a complete braille version.

Incidentally, compact disc technology is also proving to be beneficial in managing and accessing interactively large amounts of audio recorded text. Standard audio compact discs used on home CD systems can only hold about 70 minutes of audio recording, but new compression and recording methods have already put up to 20 hours on a single disc. The compact disc interactive (CD-I) discs used for the recording can be indexed at any point within the 20 hours: direct access to selected points is almost instantaneous after entering an index number from a keypad.

As CD-ROM and CD-I players can be interfaced to a computer, blind learners can gain interactive access to electronic and audio versions of a book, a powerful combination when linked with other facilities such as wordprocessing.

Another technique that has become more widely available is based on optical character recognition (OCR). The first specialised device based on OCR was the Kurzweil Reading Machine, which can read a book to a blind person by tracking over pages when they are placed on a flat bed scanner. It reads optically the characters on a page, identifies and assembles them into words, and then converts them into synthetic speech. Tracking and page selection are controlled by the user.

A table top device, the Kurzweil is now in libraries. Not least amongst its advantages is the increased independence in reading it offers.

Quite cheap ordinary OCR systems have arrived wherever there is a need to scan printed text into a computer. Screen reading, with speech synthesis, can be added to several of these systems, thus providing some features of the Kurzweil. They also provide for immediate transfer of scanned text into other applications such as wordprocessors.

Access to diagrams for blind learners

Although braille transcription, hypertext with speech, audio recording and OCR methods have been successful in providing access to text, these have severe limitations when a document has diagrams or pictures. Tactile diagrams can be used. In the past, their production depended on skills and time being available to make masters from various materials, from which plastic sheet copies could be vacuum thermoformed. More recent developments include use of a special microcapsule paper which can be formed into a raised diagram after a black outline drawing is added. The paper has a uniform coating of hundreds of millions of thermally-formed microcapsules. Upon absorbing light energy or heat, these capsules expand to hundreds of times their original volume. It is the black areas or lines representing a diagram that absorb the energy and expand. Diagrams can be drawn or photocopied onto this paper. A Raised Diagram Toolkit has been produced by Moray House College and the CALL Centre (Odor and Buultjens, 1987) to assist with production of masters for the photoembossing process using microcapsule paper. It is an accessory for the Apple Macintosh, to accompany *Superpaint* or *MacDraw*. The Toolkit includes fill patterns, line patterns, rub down sheets (like Letraset), and point markers. It provides a wide range of distinguishable features derived from earlier work in testing patterns, lines and points for tactile diagrams. There is also a braille font. Together, these tools are an enhanced facility for creating diagrams that can be printed on microcapsule paper and embossed.

Tactile diagrams, with other methods, can provide better access to text. Use of the diagrams can be extended by adding them to touch-sensitive keyboards such as the Concept Keyboard, interfaced to a computer. Interaction with other software, and speech and braille output, can thus be achieved. This method has been used at Exhall Grange School to motivate and help blind children to read tactile images and diagrams. One of the first programs was based on a tactile representation of a musical keyboard with features to change speed, octave and volume. Tunes could be created and played back. Its function was not to teach music as such but to enjoy the experience of exploring various tactile shapes and patterns. More recently the school has introduced Nomad keyboards linked to computers. Curriculum materials are being developed for these systems by the tactile diagram research unit at the University of Loughborough. The objective is to produce geographical and scientific diagrams with speech output, giving access to many visual aspects of these two curriculum areas.

Helping deaf learners

Deafness perhaps seems a less serious problem than blindness, yet the few who have been totally deaf from birth experience great difficulty in learning and using language in all its forms. Hearing impairment varies in type and degree. Some individuals hear certain frequencies well. Some only hear loud sounds. Some hear nothing at all. Others hear but cannot decipher what they hear. Most people with impaired hearing are not wholly deaf, particularly the aged.

Deafness is a communication handicap with serious implications, particularly for learning. Understandably, the earlier the onset of deafness, the greater the communication problems. People who have been deaf since birth have not simply been deprived of hearing. If they became deaf before they acquired language (pre-lingually), they may have had very little chance to develop it. They may lack the vocabulary, grammar and syntax, and have considerable difficulty in acquiring these, particularly the last two. Even those of substantial innate ability may be unable to express themselves clearly in speech or writing. Their limited vocabularies, slow speech and difficulties in pronouncing words hinder their expression of ideas, and lack of syntax may prevent them from dealing with abstract concepts. For example, schools for the deaf have trouble teaching the concepts of physics. Acquiring spoken language is a process which depends largely on auditory feedback. Because the written word depends greatly on the spoken, acquiring written language normally comes after rather than before spoken language. People who become deaf after acquiring language (post-lingually) are in a much stronger position to pursue their education than those pre-lingually deaf.

Needs differ with degrees of deafness. Profoundly deaf people, who have no hearing at all, particularly those pre-lingually deaf, are in the greatest need. For example, profoundly-deaf students may have to depend mainly on communication systems, such as signing, that are not accessible to the majority of hearing people around them. Manual sign languages are structurally different from word languages. They are a source of controversy. Although they enable deaf people to communicate with each other by using an unimpaired function, manual dexterity, they also isolate deaf people from hearing ones. Profoundly-deaf students need to be able to communicate with everyone. The alternative, oral communication, depends on speech, lip-reading and body language, and is very hard for profoundly-deaf students to learn. It does enable them to communicate with all around them except deaf people who only use signs. Cued speech, in which the speaker uses signs near the mouth to aid lip-reading of similar phonemes such as 'b' and 'p', is an advance on solely oral communication. Total communication, using to the maximum signs and oral communication, is a solution that places a double learning burden on students and people around them, but enables them to communicate to some extent with everyone. Profoundly deaf students need to be relieved of that burden as much as possible if they are to become literate, secure in pursuing intellectual discoveries and capable of following reasoning. Their teachers and classmates need relief, too. Some schools will not let profoundly deaf children do chemistry because it may be dangerous for them and those around them.

PAUL'S PROBLEMS

Paul has been almost completely deaf since birth. Sign language is his first language, but he needs to develop English written language skills. Unfortunately, the syntax used in sign language is somewhat different and interferes with his English. His use of the wordprocessor is fast, but his written English lacks good sentence structure and is sometimes incomprehensible. Even the use of a finger spelling program, which helps by demonstrating in 'finger language' the spelling of written words to be learned, does not compensate for Paul's misunderstandings about syntax. These must be dealt with through painstaking explanation by a human teacher (Brown and others, 1989).

Partially hearing or hard-of-hearing learners, who can hear with an aid, are not in quite such dire straits. If they became partially deaf pre-lingually, despite being able to hear a little they may need better listening skills. Their acquisition of spoken and written language may be slow because they are shut off from many of the auditory experiences which are commonplace for all their hearing classmates. Some of these experiences may be essential for learners' welfare and safety. Hard-of-hearing learners may have to rote-memorise what their classmates learn simply by hearing. Function words, such as pronouns and prepositions, and word endings are difficult to hear or lip-read because they are usually spoken quietly and quickly. A problem for learners who use British Sign Language is that the word order differs from spoken English. Hearing people silently rehearse language for reasoning, writing and talking, but deaf learners trying to do the same may be using distorted grammar and syntax, or simply be at a loss for words (Griffiths and others, 1989). Such difficulties with language are almost certain to cause problems in studying other subjects. Unfortunately, language deficiences often have cumulative effects in education, so that children who are deaf find it hard to keep up at school.

How can computers help deaf learners?

Deaf or hard-of-hearing learners can use computer technology and be helped by it to build their language skills, provided that adaptations are made. Computers are interactive, like language. They respond, engaging in a kind of 'conversation' with the learner. Computers offer a visual medium, turning language into something concrete and clear on the screen, but not always. For example, auditory prompts such as beeps and tones should be replaced or supplemented by visual ones. Use of a screen reader with a carefully adjusted speech synthesiser to suit the individual's hearing may prove very beneficial for some hearing-impaired students. Computers can combine sound with text and graphics, even with movement.

The National Council for Educational Technology (1991) suggests a number of specific educational needs of hearing-impaired children that may be met with computers:

- at primary level, development of literacy skills, vocabulary and language extension, with more direct reinforcement of selected aspects than is needed by hearing peers, can be achieved through wordprocessing with the help of symbol systems and voice synthesis.
- at secondary level, development of scientific and technical language and vocabulary can take place with the help of suitable software.
- at both levels, improved expression and communication, with enhanced receptive language skills, can occur through use of age-appropriate listening and reading programs.
- at both levels, improved general cognitive and communication skills can be developed through collaborative decision-making and problem-solving programs, including simulations and adventure games.

To extend vocabulary, the Council suggests programs that use new words in context, with animation, such as *Moving In*, *Podd* and *Scenarios*, are particularly valuable. Reading, spelling or typing problems can be reduced through using a Concept Keyboard, with vocabulary development programs such as *Match*, *Complete Speller* and *Crossword Call-up*. Discussion among older deaf children of words they want to put on the Concept Keyboard can be very valuable to them.

To develop reading and writing, wordprocessing enables deaf learners to jot down their ideas with time to redraft and improve vocabulary, spelling and grammar. Spelling checkers, dictionaries and thesauri (e.g. *Wordweb*, *Viewbook* and *Pendown* dictionary) are undoubtedly helpful too. Pester (1988) tells how she used the Concept Keyboard and *Prompt/Writer* to help Nigel, 5 years old, who had been having problems, because of his poor hearing, with the initial stage of independent writing.

NIGEL TACKLES PROBLEMS CAUSED BY POOR HEARING

Typically, Nigel has quite a large sight vocabulary but is slow in acquiring phonic skills, therefore word cards and dictionaries do not help him much. His poor verbal memory makes lengthy searching for a word difficult: he forgets what he is looking for. His word and sentence structure can be very muddled, too. Crucially, he lacks confidence in his ability to tackle anything.

To introduce Nigel to the Concept Keyboard as a means of finding words, I decided to set him to work on three overlays. The first is a tightly structured reading game based on his sight vocabulary from the school's reading scheme. Nigel soon found his way around the keyboard and loved the game.

The second overlay goes further, taking him into creative writing. It provides a vocabulary related to a story ('Roger and the Pond') and words Nigel knows well, suitable for use in writing his own simple story. Vocabulary and sequence of events can both be problems for hearing-impaired pupils. I colour-coded verbs green, nouns blue, to help him locate words and in hope of thus demonstrating something of the structure of language. Nigel first watched some of his classmates use the overlay, then successfully wrote four sentences of his own story,

The third is a more flexible overlay, a larger word bank he can use for further stories. It combines words from his sight vocabulary with ones he seems to need often. Again, I colour-coded words, and placed commonly-used ones like 'and' and 'the' in prominent positions. I also introduced the alphabet and a word line. Pupils are encouraged to use the initial letter of a word, plus the word line, if they know the initial letter, rather than stumbling over the word.

This third overlay was an instant success. Nigel's first piece of writing was completed quickly and easily. He is learning the layout. I hope he will soon be writing independently, on the computer and in his book.

Electronic mail, telephones that display text, simulations, adventure games, teletext and TV subtitles all motivate hearing-impaired children to read for meaning, and provide them with examples of correct language usage to emulate. Electronic mail also links them with mainstream children.

DEAF LEARNERS COMMUNICATE THROUGH AN AUSTRALIAN NETWORK

A remarkable network to help deaf students was set up in Sydney, Australia, in 1989. The telephone company for the area agreed with the University of New South Wales to provide 100 people with microcomputers and modems. Of the 100 people, over half were deaf learners of various ages, many of them congenitally deaf. The rest were either hearing students, retired people or others willing to learn to use the equipment. Since the price of calls in the Sydney area is A$0.21 per call, no matter how long, users are able to meet the cost of using the network from time to time for longish periods. Although no formal evaluation has yet been conducted, early reports (James and Eyland, 1991) indicate that many deaf students very much like to 'talk' to their hearing and non-hearing friends through the system. Students who have been deaf from birth benefit from seeing correct syntax and spelling in messages sent by hearing people in the network. They try hard to emulate the written continuous prose, whereas in oral conversation students deaf from birth resort to speaking mainly in nouns, in a kind of shorthand, in an effort to make themselves understood in the fewest possible utterances. They cannot emulate the spoken language they cannot hear.

This example should be balanced against experience at Doncaster College for the Deaf (Boyce and Turfus, 1990), where 1987 and 1988 surveys of newly inducted students showed that few knew about computer-related technology such as viewdata and telephones with keyboards and visual displays. The College installed six terminals on the campus, but these deaf students needed keyboard and wordprocessing training. After lessons and practice, they started well, but were stuck for words! They were not used to instantaneous communication.

To develop syntax, hearing-impaired children must perceive and learn to use correctly words such as pronouns and prepositions that they do not easily hear because these words are usually short and unstressed. They must also perceive and learn to use correctly syntactical endings of verbs and nouns. Without such understanding, they continue to make mistakes in syntax. Computers can help by providing plenty of experience of meaningful language. Hearing-impaired children can benefit from using text handling software such as *Tray*. Language on screen is easier for them to try than the fleeting spoken word, partially heard. They can emulate word order and sentence structure from correct usage. Colour and position of words on screen or on a Concept Keyboard may help.

To develop listening and speaking, hearing-impaired children may find it useful to have a visual 'peg' on screen, on which to hang what they are hearing and their own spoken ideas. These children often depend on non-verbal clues in decoding a speaker's meaning. *HyperCard* enables teachers to integrate text, graphics, animation, speech and sound. Children rapidly pick up the techniques to exploit *HyperCard* in their own work (again, see Chapters 6–8 for examples).

Teaching a science topic to hearing-impaired learners

Hearing-impaired learners may have a more limited vocabulary than their peers, especially specific vocabulary relating to a science topic, as Pester (1991) explains. Their hearing peers may well have absorbed incidentally some of the terminology used (such as potential or kinetic energy), whilst hearing-impaired learners have to understand a host of new words in the science class. The text books to which the teacher has access, although educationally appropriate, use vocabulary which is new and probably meaningless to the students. Teachers want the children to understand the scientific concepts (which were quite complex). They don't want them to get bogged down by the vocabulary used, although the children must learn to use terms consistently and accurately. Where text books offer a variety of terminology, the most meaningful label must be adopted. Spring energy, for example, is referred to as elastic energy. Some of the correct scientific terms can be introduced along with a brief explanation. Kinetic energy is described as 'energy in use'. Pester tells of one attempt to overcome scientific terminology and conceptualisation problems for hearing-impaired learners through use of a computer.

GETTING TO GRIPS WITH SCIENTIFIC TERMS AND CONCEPTS AT ELMFIELD

At Elmfield School for the Deaf in Bristol, a mixed ability group of 14–15 year old severely and profoundly deaf youngsters were about to study energy. As is often the case in special schools, the topic was being introduced by a teacher who was not a science specialist but who wanted to provide the group with an appropriate science curriculum. In fact, the group was working towards Attainment Target 13, Level 6 in the Science National Curriculum. They had to be 'able to recognise different types of energy sources and follow some processes of energy transfer in terms of the principle of conservation of energy'.

To help the children, a set of useful terms were suggested and approved by science teachers in the local comprehensive, Henbury School, who agreed it was more important to understand the scientific concepts than to learn the correct scientific terminology.

Starting from these concepts and terms, I developed some teaching materials in conjunction with the teacher, Gaynor Robinson, for use in practicals and discussion sessions. They included reinforcement activities aimed at helping this group of youngsters to clarify for themselves new terms and concepts to which they were being introduced, to absorb the words and to use them to record some of their hypotheses and findings. We only started them on the computer, with Concept Keyboard attached, after the children had been introduced to some of the concepts involved and had experienced some simple classroom-based science activities (such as dropping a pencil, winding up a clockwork toy).

The EnergyPic overlay, for use with *Touch Explorer Plus* was intended to illustrate two important principles: Everything contains energy (all our energy comes ultimately from the sun), and energy is not created or destroyed, it simply changes its form. This first overlay was developed to introduce more complex ideas relating to energy and to allow the pupils to generalise their understanding beyond the classroom and the fairly limited activities they had experienced in it. The overlay is therefore relatively unstructured, designed for free exploration leading pupils to a wider understanding of the topic. We also hoped it would develop their ability to apply their ideas to more varied situations.

When pupils used the program, they first pressed the 'Help' squares on the overlay. These gave them a brief description of different forms of energy. The 'Pupil Task' square (see overlay) then asked them to explore the picture to find further examples of each type. They were asked to record their findings in the 'Notepad' (a wordprocessor within the program which pupils could use by pressing 'N' on the overlay). Level 1 described potential energy examples, Level 2 kinetic energy and Level 3 energy changes; the levels cannot be changed from the Concept Keyboard and initially pupils were limited to one level of exploration at a time.

When they pressed some areas of the overlay, the relevant energy being used in the scenario depicted was described on screen. For example, when the boy reaching for fruit was pressed, the screen read 'This little boy could fall. There is stored gravitational energy in his body.' Others gave a clue and allowed the pupils to suggest their own hypothesis: 'Perhaps the cupboard is not fastened to the wall properly. . .' Not all the examples of energy had been identified (they didn't all contain a message). We explained to the pupils that we had not included a message for every scenario on the overlay, but that they should feel free to identify examples for themselves and write a hypothesis in the Notepad. Some pupils found this difficult because they were used to the computer as an infallible object containing preset and correct information which could not be altered.

The computer was situated just outside the science lab and the pupils had the opportunity to use it for their work during the part of the lesson set aside for individual work. Thus, exploration of the overlay took place over several weeks and complemented the practical activities they were experiencing in the lab.

This activity and other *Touch Explorer Plus* activity served to extend the group's understanding of the nature of computers and incidentally to acquire new information technology capabilities. Information Technology Capability Attainment Target 5, Level 4, says that pupils should demonstrate that they are able to:

- Use IT to retrieve, develop and organise their work
- Amend and add to information in an existing database
- Understand the need to question the accuracy of displayed information and that results produced by a computer may be affected by incorrect data entry.

The *Prompt/Writer* overlay was developed to allow pupils to record their class activities and experiments. It used the same terminology as introduced in the EnergyPic *Touch Explorer Plus* overlay described above and enabled pupils to use the correct terminology without problems of spelling or having to remember the vocabulary. It also enabled them to record their work much more quickly and neatly than would otherwise have been the case.

The EnergyPhoto overlay (not reproduced here) was created using photos of the children taken during an initial practical session when the topic was first introduced. When the photos were taken they were starting on the concept of potential energy. By the time they had created the file they were near the end of the topic and we used it to recall and record their thoughts and hypotheses at the time and to apply what they now knew about energy. This generated a great deal of discussion around the computer relating to the nature of scientific exploration. They realised that their hypotheses were valued and valuable. The hypotheses, although they may ultimately have been proved incorrect, had been helpful in directing the children's thoughts and explorations. This kind of discussion might have been more difficult for some of these pupils without the concrete focus of the computer file around which to work. Similarly, they were pleased with their progress in understanding as they recalled with amusement some of their initial thoughts and ideas.

The students worked within the same framework as the previous *Touch Explorer Plus* file (that is, level 1 referred to potential energy and so on) and I set it up for

Figure 5.3 - Touch Explorer Plus Energy-Pic overlay

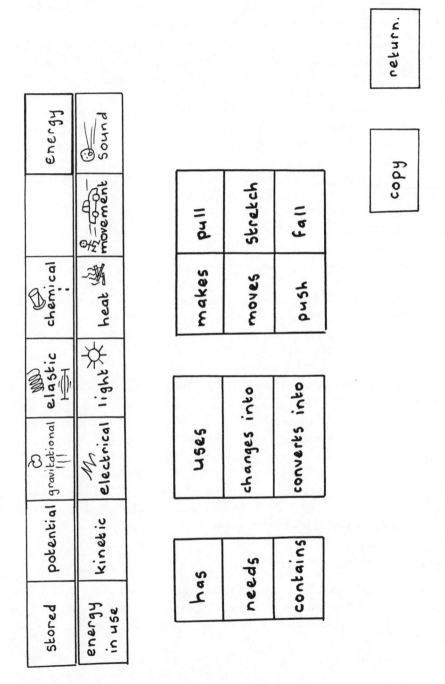

*Figure 5.4 - **Prompt/Writer overlay***

them. They thus had the freedom and confidence to concentrate on the content in a situation where the format was familiar to them.

In Level 1, the students described the examples in the photos and recalled their thoughts at the time. For example, 'Zoe held a stick in the air. She looked like she might drop it.' In Level 2, types of potential energy were identified and described. For example, 'The match has chemical energy in the piece on the end of it. Naveed thought Zoe uses gravitational energy to strike it - do you think he's right?' In Level 3, types of kinetic energy were similarly defined. For example, 'If Zoe eats the biscuits then she can use the energy for movement (for walking, running, etc)'. Using Level 4, the students attempted to describe the energy changes they believed to be happening in each of the situations. For example, 'We use chemical energy from the food we eat to give our bodies heat. We use energy for movement too'.

The support of the computer proved invaluable. It provided access to a bank of terminology and concepts which otherwise the pupils were having to absorb during sessions which were primarily activity-based. The problem of doing something at the same time as watching and listening can be significant for hearing impaired pupils. All three files enabled them to record their findings more efficiently than might otherwise have been the case. The computer presented language in a more permanent and complete form than the more fleeting, possibly distorted, auditory message. Textbooks give explanations only once, but in our *Touch Explorer Plus* file the definition of the term remains on screen throughout each level, to reinforce the unfamiliar language.

This chapter cannot end without mentioning the imaginative use of computers and interactive videodiscs by deaf children at Macalpine Primary School, Dundee, as described by Megarry (1989). She points out that these children are at a constant disadvantage since for them English is at best a second language to signing, not to mention Urdu. They sign constantly and unconsciously, thinking with their hands. Video with words and signs, as in the *Interactive Video Dictionary* (Jones, 1989), is important to them as a bridge between languages. Memorable visuals provide a common reference point for teacher and child.

Summary

In this chapter we reviewed much of the computer technology available to help sensorily-disabled learners. We provided a few examples of it in use for the benefit of blind and deaf learners; other examples appear in later chapters.

Part 3

Achieving Access with Computers

6 Speaking and Listening

Access to language skills in the curriculum

This chapter and the next two deal with language development. In a sense, it is ridiculous to separate speaking and listening from reading and writing. We are conscious that the examples of good practice here often overlap into other chapters. Language skills must be developed in parallel, and in integrated fashion, as much as possible. What's more, they must be developed through use across the curriculum, as our examples in the whole of Part 3 show. Teachers know, however, that to gain access to the curriculum many learners with special educational needs require more assistance with some aspects of language than with others. For instance, and perhaps most obviously, non-speaking children need help in finding ways to express themselves in language, while vision-impaired children need help of another kind.

Most teachers in England and Wales want pupils with learning difficulties, including those with statements of special educational needs, to participate in the National Curriculum in English. That was a finding of the National Curriculum Council (1989c) after the consultations on the Working Party Report, and is probably true in respect of the National Curriculum's equivalents in Scotland and Northern Ireland. When the Department of Education and Science (1989c and d, 1990b) published details of Key Stages 1–4, these contained frequent mention of use of technology by pupils with special needs, so that these children would have the opportunity to experience as far as possible the full range of the curriculum in English. Her Majesty's Inspectors also noted (Department of Education and Science, 1990a) that oral and written language were widely and successfully supported by IT.

The National Curriculum defines attainment targets to which the majority of children with learning difficulties should have access. Paveley (1990) suggests that the Level 1 Attainment Targets are based on assumptions about learning during the first five years of normal life. Teachers of children with severe learning difficulties may have to look at these targets in terms of the prerequisite skills needed, but their pupils can be seen as working towards the same attainments as their more able peers. Access to the language curriculum is equally important for older children and adults, whether or not their teachers are working within a legally enforceable framework such as the National Curriculum. Our examples of good practice include learners across the age range.

Speaking and listening with computers

In English, Attainment Target 1 of the National Curriculum is entitled 'speaking and listening', and calls for 'the development of pupils' understanding of the spoken word and the capacity to express themselves effectively in a variety of speaking and listening activities, matching style and response to audience and purpose'. This sounds quite ambitious, but of course children normally acquire communication skills in the first years of life. Expressive abilities include speaking, gesture and facial expression, all of which can be limited by motor impairment. Interactive abilities include eye contact and turn taking in conversations. Receptive abilities include listening and seeing, and can be limited by sensory impairment. Where there is 'severe cognitive deficit' individuals cannot use the sensory data they receive, nor find ways to express themselves effectively.

Computer technology can stimulate development of sensory awareness, and can provide substitute ways of expression to non-speaking students (Paveley, 1990). As Stansfield (1989) suggests, for instance, synthesised speech can be very motivating for children with learning difficulties. *Stylus*, an easy wordprocessing program that can be used with either a Concept Keyboard or a standard one, speaks the children's text through a speech synthesiser. Its 'robot voice' amuses the children and they feel they can do better.

Although computers can help learners to speak via a synthesised voice, the machines can also help them to 'speak' via text. In Chapter 3 we discussed the problems autistic children and adults have in expressing their thinking, because many are non-speaking. From his Australian experience, Biklen (1990) reports how Rosemary Crossley used her methods during a first meeting, at which he was present, with Louis, an Australian student.

I'M NOT RETARDED: LOUIS' STORY

Louis is twenty-four years old, with reddish-brown hair and gold metal-rimmed, rectangular-shaped glasses with thick lenses. He was wearing a black and white sweater, black jeans and white tennis shoes when we met him. Louis had very little facial expression. He does not speak, except for a few phrases that seem involuntarily uttered and are out of context. As he entered the room where Crossley was to conduct the assessment, he said: 'Excuse me. Get mommy on the bus. Excuse me,' which didn't make sense to me. Attempts at answering his statements by saying, for example, 'There is no need to be excused, you are fine,' did not quiet him. He repeated the phrase.

Crossley introduced herself and me to Louis, who sat between us. She described her work to him as helping people who don't speak to find other ways to communicate. She apologised in advance for her assessment approach: 'Louis, I ask people a lot of really silly questions.' She commenced the session by asking him to press down on various pictures on a talking computer, a children's toy with a voice output that requests the person using it to press various pictures or letters and which announces the user's choice, for example: 'Right, that's the apple.'

As Crossley asked questions, tears began to roll down Louis's face. He was crying silently. She reassured him, telling him that she would do it with him.

Crossley took Louis through a series of graded exercises, with her hand on top of his right arm. The last few consisted of word and letter recognition. He completed all of them successfully. Next, she showed him the Canon Communicator, a small laptop computer with text display and speech synthesis.

Crossley went through the alphabet and numbers with him. 'For starters,' she asked, 'can you type your name?' At this point her hand was stretched out flat, on top of, but not actually touching, his. He typed 'LOUIS'. As he finished, she asked it there was anything else he wanted to say. Louis started typing again. First he typed an 'O', then 'PC'. Crossley pulled his hand back from the keys, saying, 'I'm not sure I follow. Let's start over.' This time he typed 'Pocco'. She was confused. Then we realised what he was typing. *Pocco* is his last name. He was still responding to Crossley's first request, to type his name.

Crossley asked again if there was anything else Louis wanted to say. He typed, 'IM NOT RETARDED,' to which she remarked, 'No, I don't think you are. Keep going.' Louis continued, 'MY MOTHER FEELS IM STUPID BECAUSE IH [he back-spaced this and crossed out the *h*] CANT USE MY VOICE PROPERLY.' A tear rolled down his left cheeck as he typed. And Crossley said to me and to Louis, 'A lot of people believe that what people say is what they're capable of.'

Louis was not done. He typed, 'HOW MUCH IS A CANON?'

'They're dear,' Crossley answered.

'I SAVE A BIT BUT NOT ENOUGH' Louis typed.

Crossley explained that she would continue to work with Louis and that she would try to get him a Canon. Then she congratulated him on his work in the session and said to me, for Louis to hear, 'Anybody who starts off typing, 'I'm not retarded' isn't retarded. First rule!'

Working with younger children

Not all teachers are able or willing to practise Crossley's methods of facilitation. Taylor (1990) provides general guidelines to those working with students who must use a communication aid. She stresses the need to wait and listen. She says that adults often fail to recognise the communicative signals of young children with severe physical handicaps. Gestures and signs often come before use of communication boards and computers.

Once younger children with special needs have been introduced to the technology, many programs designed originally for young children without disabilities can be brought into service. For example, Tanenhaus (1990) suggests that for developing language skills, *McGee*, could be useful. Children use mouse clicks to send McGee to explore a house. They can make McGee do various actions, such as brushing his teeth, as well go into the different rooms, all in excellent graphics and animation. He speaks and giggles, the animals make their own noises, the doors squeak and you can hear the water running. The program runs with the Adaptive Firmware Card, so a scanning system with single switches (see Chapter 4) is available for students unable to manage the mouse. Alternatively, they can use a Unicorn board (US equivalent of the Concept Keyboard). Such programs spark animated conversations among children.

Watchman (1990) shows how listening skills can be developed and what a positive influence they can have on disabled children's writing skills. A support teacher at Ridge County Primary School, Avon, she used *Stylus* (see above), with synthesised speech – the TALK facility. She writes about working with mainstreamed children, that is, those with special needs who are in mainstream classes:

LISTENING TO THE LITTLE ROBOTIC VOICE!

Initially, as adults, we had to suspend our disbelief as this monotonous little robotic voice read dispassionately and phonetically, with the inevitable pauses and mispronunciations. We agreed, however, that when the children were able to hear their own efforts being read out to them by 'the computer', positive educational results followed. Children who had been highly unmotivated and who had made minimal contributions to any class discussion were inspired to write considerable quantities of high quality work. One lovely image left with us was of a hushed class listening intently to a story by a child who had never been able to present a completed piece of work that was comprehensible even to his teacher.

The Concept Keyboard, with appropriate teacher-made overlays, and this magical TALK facility, motivated the targeted children to produce more and better work in every area that we explored.

Perhaps the only disadvantage is that the greater the child's learning problems the harder he or she finds it to follow the computerised voice. One 11 year old boy, of average intelligence and good hearing, but with severe specific learning difficulties, finds it almost impossible to decipher simultaneously even simple print on the screen at the time he hears it read out to him. This is the most extreme example we encountered: what motivates one child can frustrate another.

In the US, Meyers (1986) developed *Exploratory Play* and *Representational Play*, which help children with communication difficulties. First, the teacher puts a real toy, one of a set specially provided, in front of the child. When the child touches a picture that matches the toy on a Muppet Learning Keys (similar to the Concept Keyboard) overlay, the same picture appears on the screen and the computer speaks the word or words written below it. Using this output, a child can make up and describe play scenes, which stimulate meaningful conversation with other children or adults. For children between developmental ages of 18 months and 8 years, the system offers synthesised speech output under their own control. They regard the speech signal as an added voice as they converse. The speech output also provides toddlers with an acoustic signal which they can activate as often as they wish, enabling them to learn English sound patterns.

At The Park Special School, Haigh (1991) has found that children with severe learning difficulties can benefit from talking and writing about digitised pictures. He links a videocamera or videorecorder to the Watford digitiser, linked to a BBC-B microcomputer into which he loads *Image*. Or he uses a Lingenuity digitiser with the school's A3000. With *Image* the children can capture the video frames, transfer them onto a blank page on-screen and then with the help of the teacher easily change the colours, shape or size (see Chapter 9 for another example of these methods). An important aspect of his work is the feeling the children have of 'owning' the images because they helped to create them.

CAPTURING IMAGES TO TALK AND WRITE ABOUT

The children look forward to digitising sessions. They enjoy setting up the camera, 'snapping' the subject and discussing the images on-screen. They get very excited at seeing pictures of themselves, in colour or black and white, slowly emerging from the printer.

Sometimes the children make badges from the pictures. First, *Image* can reduce a child's picture. Second, the picture is printed. Third, the child cuts it to shape. Fourth, it goes into the badge-making machine, which crimps it onto a metal backing, with a plastic cover. The children are usually very impressed with their badges and discuss them endlessly. This stimulating setting certainly promotes language development. Sometimes we extend the work into a mini-enterprise:

the children invite their friends to pose for pictures, which then become badges they are expected to buy!

One class has been studying 'My Body'. The children made life-size cardboard cutouts of themselves. After lessons on the internal organs, they drew pictures of some of these and stuck them onto the cutouts, together with cardboard bones such as the ribs. These models suddenly took on new meaning when each child glued his or her own digitised face onto the head. The cutouts were displayed in the entrance hall, where many other children recognised them. Again, there was plenty of discussion.

One other way in which we are trying to use the digitiser is in recording students' achievements. From videos we make of children in various school situations, we can capture particular shots to print out. These are a valuable supplement to ordinary photographs, and with the A3000 we can get high quality images. The prints go home to parents or on display in school. In addition, we can make stimulating on-screen jigsaws with them, or use them for personalising pre-reading and pre-number software with which we are trying to develop children's matching and sequencing skills and finding the odd one out. With *Phases* 2 on the A3000 we can put the pictures on a blank page and the children or teachers can add writing about them, using the keyboard or a Concept Keyboard. If they tire of pictures of themselves or their friends, we can quickly digitise a few favourite TV personalities to provide new stimulation!

Working with older children

Bell (1991) tells the story of a hypermedia-based project at Fleming Fulton School, a special school for physically-disabled children in Belfast. She was working with a group of childen aged 15-17 who were low achievers with reading ages of 9 or 10. Her aims were broad: she wanted her pupils to develop their ability to communicate in speech and writing, but she also wanted to help them to understand what they heard, read and experienced through various media, and to respond imaginatively and sensitively to it. She believed the project could also improve their self-realisation and confidence, while encouraging interaction and cooperation.

Through introducing *HyperCard*, Bell set out to encourage the children's use of language in creating written work, in deciding how to present it and in interacting as a group. *HyperCard* would give their work a professional appearance, on screen and in print, and the children would gain a sense of audience for it. Overall, she thought that the project would encourage the children to speak and listen, by emphasising the value of what they were doing.

THE BIRTH OF HARRY AND SUPER SPOT

I suggested to my pupils that they might like to write stories for young children in the Junior school, an idea which excited them. They discussed whether it would be better to write individually, in pairs or as a group. They decided to work as a group, writing a story for the Nursery Class, which I deliberately suggested because I felt that they would approach very young children with more confidence than older ones.

My pupils began to share experiences of young children's interests: we brainstormed ideas for the 'book'. Initial suggestions were that it should be about fairies or witches, that it should have a cover and chapters. Nobody could say what a chapter was for, though one said it was something to do with the structure of the book. He couldn't explain what he meant by structure, so we spent some time investigating the meaning of the word. A considerable difference of opinion then arose about what would interest the children, and I suggested visiting the class to get to know them. Some of my pupils were very timid about this, but two agreed to go round to the Nursery teacher and propose to her that the group would write a story for the children, and that they should visit her class first. She readily agreed.

We discussed how to organise the visit. Pupils were worried about what to say to the little children, but one came up with the idea of taking something to show them. Soon the group had a small collection of picture books and one girl was commissioned to buy Dolly Mixtures.

Although some of my pupils were rather nervous on the day, most had a very successful visit. Two boys couldn't overcome their shyness: they just looked at books in the Nursery Class and talked to the teacher about the characteristics of a good book for that age. Two other boys and three of the girls were particularly good at talking to the young ones.

After this visit, the group had to revise radically its ideas about what should go into the book. They came back convinced that the story should be very simple, about something in the children's everyday experience, colourful with pictures, with a minimum of print, and with nothing scary. They felt that some of the books they had taken along were clearly unsuitable. They had had to talk to the children about the pictures in a very simple way, rather than read aloud the story as they had planned.

I introduced them to *HyperCard*, and they could see its possibilities. We spent a long time discussing how they could use it to the full while producing a book for the little ones to keep. Eventually they decided they would have to take the computer round to the Nursery and show the children the screen version as well as leaving a copy of the more limited print version for the class. They would have to mount the pages on cardboard and cover them with sticky-backed plastic. One boy suggested putting the children's names on the cover – others quickly added that authors' names should be there too. Colour was essential, they said, and they discussed how it could be provided.

To garner further ideas, two pupils visited the Junior school's library. They brought back books they thought suitable, others that were not, and explained their reasons to the group. They discussed size and quantity of print, size and colour of pictures, and the subject matter.

The story they began work on was about a toddler named Harry and a toy called Super Spot, in a Christmas setting. They agreed that each would write an outline of the story, then pool the best ideas. They decided it would help if they showed what would go on each card.

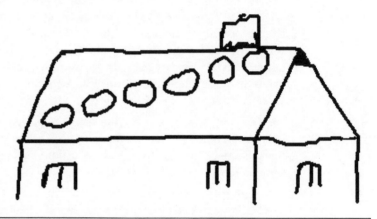

Next morning Harry saw Santa's foot prints on the roof.

Figure 6.1 - Next morning Harry saw Santa's footprints on the roof

When the group was ready, they read out their outlines and agreed a final version, which they put into storyboard form, listing the artwork and sounds needed. The best artist went off to the art room to draw. The rest were keen to start on the two computers, but before keying in could begin, they still had decisions to make about page content, size of font and positioning of text on the page. We broke up the text into small units and discussed each in detail, experimenting on the computer with fields and fonts. Questions of sequencing and isolated sentences came up. They wrote a sheet of simple instructions for everyone to use when keying in: it isn't exactly a model handbook, but they had worked it out for themselves and all could follow it:

1. Edit – new card

2. New field

3. Field info – rectangle

   – font

   Helvetica – bold – OK

4. Change tool to Hand

One advantage of *HyperCard* is that we could tackle the work piecemeal, not in a particular order. Some keyed in the story, one scanned in the artist's artwork, others did artwork onscreen. The whole could be assembled later. My pupils rapidly discovered better ways of dealing with text, graphics and sound. For example, they did the first animation by moving Harry to different positions on a series of cards. Later the artist suggested short-circuiting it by drawing a master copy with all the positions on one sheet: it was then a simple matter to delete all but one position of Harry on each card, giving greater control over the animation and its effect. Here is the master-copy of Santa in the snow with Super Spot and Harry searching for him. They animated this one in the same way, making five cards from it, each one moving Harry to a new position in his flight to save Santa.

I was particularly excited to observe that my pupils were using language so much to communicate and comprehend. The subject matter for discussion and decision-making was very specific. They were intensely motivated by using graphics and sound. They spoke about the project with greater fluency and variety of language. As they became more expert at operating the computer,

They found Santa in the snow. The conditions were hazardous and they could not rescue Santa for at least two days.

*Figure 6.2 - **Santa in the snow with Super Spot***

97

their confidence increased. They talked more and were more relaxed about it. They expressed their own ideas, feelings and points of view, even if some earned the final veto of, 'Those wee children wouldn't be interested in *that*...' They tested everything by whether they thought it would appeal to the toddlers or not. Two boys wanted to include the phrase 'The conditions were hazardous' (see Fig. 6.2), which they seemed to me to be particularly proud of. The rest thought the words were much too long for 'those wee children'. After a heated discussion, the phrase was allowed to stand, because the group felt the children would grasp the gist of what was being said even if they did not understand the words.

My group had plenty of opportunities to reason and solve problems, particularly when the computers would not do what they wanted. For example, one boy wanted to draw a parcel, with animation of it opening to reveal Super Spot. He had great difficulty drawing the outline until he discovered the 'line' tool. Then he wanted to cover the parcel with a pattern, making the ribbon solid black. He tried the 'spray' tool and of course covered the ribbon as well. With the 'bucket' tool, the pattern spilled over. In sheer exasperation, he changed his plan and prepared a card showing a half open parcel before Super Spot was revealed. This was only half successful. By now the entire group had got involved and tempers were fraying. Thankfully, somebody had the bright idea of making it more realistic by adding the sound of crumpling paper instead.

Above all, says Bell, this project provided an excellent context for speaking and listening. It gave all members of the group the chance to talk to several different audiences, adults and children. When they were working in twos and threes, they had to give and take very specific instructions. She noticed that because the children were involved in what they saw as an 'adult' task, nobody felt upset if they made mistakes, nor did they object to peers doing the correcting. This would not have happened if they had been working with pencil and paper. What is more, they never lost sight of the end-product, the book, or of its audience, those toddlers.

Summary

These few examples, mainly from schools, give a substantial but incomplete picture of how computers can help to give learners with difficulties better access to that part of the language curriculum dealing with speaking and listening. Apart from Louis' story, we have not found other examples of good practice with adults. Possibly teachers of adults see speaking and listening as less important parts of language development for older learners with special needs. More likely, these teachers have yet to bring computers into that aspect of their work.

7 Reading

Access to reading

The National Curriculum's attainment targets for reading skills might not seem too ambitious for children without special needs, but teachers of pupils with learning difficulties know that even Attainment Target 2 may be beyond their charges. This target expects them to 'recognise that print is used to carry meaning, in books and in other forms in the everyday world' and to 'begin to recognise individual words or letters in familiar contexts'. We deal with signs and symbol systems in Chapter 8.

Although the teaching of reading is a controversial subject, many schools teach whole word recognition first, introducing phonics a little later. As Slater (1991) points out, for pupils with severe learning difficulties phonic analysis of words is beyond them. They do not have good enough auditory perception to distinguish digraphs such as 'bl' and 'pl'. Their tracking is poor: that is, they cannot control well their left-to-right eye movements across the page. At best, they may learn to recognise a limited number of whole words, through such means as each word's pattern, length, starting or ending letter, or simply through contextual or situational cues. Slater says that computers can be valuable tools in helping these pupils to master a 'social sight' vocabulary ranging over, say, street and shop signs (see Chapter 13). Working with content-free framework programs such as *Collage* and *Picture Play*, she suggests preparing scenarios to which the words are added by the pupils with the help of a Concept Keyboard. Straightforward labelling can be supplemented by simple games, such as unscrambling pictures and words with programs like *Move It*.

At Ridge Primary School, Avon, Dean (1990) uses *Match*, a program which places words randomly on the screen and children have to match them with appropriate pictures or words on the Concept Keyboard. The teacher selects and enters the words to be read. Dean begins with word-to-word matching, but this does not require any understanding of the words. He moves to picture-to-word matching, which requires children to identify the correct picture to match the word displayed. He finds that the children then like to prepare their own overlays, choosing the pictures for themselves and programming the overlays (see Fig. 7.1). This develops their reading vocabulary. In his class, a mainstreamed child with reading and linguistic difficulties participates well in this work.

Another way to teach reading skills to children with special educational needs is to use a literacy and language development program such as *From Pictures to Words*, which is designed to support Attainment Targets 2–5 in English in the National Curriculum. The teacher can draw pictures on-screen or choose from nearly 300 pictures in the program, then add words. The children can practise initial letter matching, matching initial letter to picture, matching word from sight or memory, finding a word in jumbled letters, spelling from a picture prompt, using picture prompts for adding missing words in sentences or in a story, and free writing in words and pictures. All of these involve reading.

Young children with cognitive difficulties often have trouble when starting to learn to read. Teachers can help them by bringing a computer into their work, as Taylor's (1991) example demonstrates:

THOMAS' STORY

Thomas is six and lives in St Helens. He goes to Robins Lane Primary School, a large school where high standards of work, behaviour and appearance are expected. The school has two special units housed in temporary classrooms

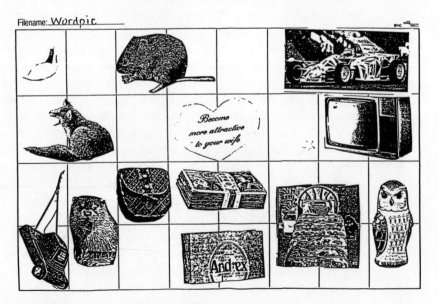

Figure 7.1 - An overlay produced by the children

beside the main Victorian building. One is for children with expressive language difficulties, and the other for children with both receptive and expressive difficulties. Both groups receive intensive speech therapy. Teachers expect most children to spend up to two years in the unit, with increasing amounts of time in mainstream classes.

Thomas, in his school uniform of grey shorts, navy jersey and school tie is indistinguishable from other infants at Robins Lane. But Thomas has difficulty in concentrating and picking out the most important thing to attend to. He misses what is said to him and can seem classically 'disobedient'. He can't find the right word when he needs it, and has already developed good compensatory strategies such as 'can I have the thingy?', pointing to what he wants. This behaviour seems ordinary until one looks at the frequency. He has been in the Language Unit for 18 months and his understanding of language has improved to the point where it is adequate for an ordinary infant classroom, so long as the teacher has his attention. To fit into a regular infant class, Thomas needs good reading and number skills. He needs to build up his vocabulary through practice in real situations where clarity is essential. He needs lots of practice at focussing on the activity in hand.

Thomas now uses the computer to help his reading. His teacher makes original and exciting overlays for *Touch Explorer Plus*, to reinforce reading and writing related to the reading scheme. For example, for The Village with Three Corners she made an overlay in 3 dimensions so that Thomas and the other children can explore, build up the scene with more houses and figures and, at a later stage, read and answer written questions. Another overlay reinforces work from the Oxford Reading Tree Series. She has hidden animals under flaps behind trees, boxes and so on. They are then 'discovered' by the children during the exploration. A third overlay features the boys in the class at a fair: she made this using photographs of the children, including Thomas, on a variety of fairground rides. The text reinforces the basic spatial vocabulary in the unit's curriculum: up/down, backwards/forwards, round and so on. Thomas and the others like seeing their own photographs on the overlay, which holds their attention and interest over a longer period than usual as they use it to improve their reading.

Reading with *HyperCard*

In the last few years, as we saw in Chapter 6, teachers in special education have started to experiment with *HyperCard*. In the US and the UK, they prepare hypermedia 'stacks' (large sets of computer-linked cards) aimed at promoting reading through text, graphics and sound. Using *HyperCard*, the Center for Applied Special Technology in Peabody, Massachusetts, has plans to help children like Nicole:

WILL NICOLE READ BETTER WITH A MACINTOSH?

Nicole is a sociable child of 11 who loves animals. She is bright and sensitive, but has a severe reading disability. She has problems with decoding and visual scanning. She cannot sound out words she does not recognise and often loses her place. These difficulties have left her with an impoverished vocabulary and limited general knowledge. Even though she thinks creatively and grasps concepts quickly, she feels she is a failure at school. Each schoolday, she spends the afternoon in a resource room because she is reading three years below grade level and cannot work by herself with printed materials.

At her request, the Macintosh will read the word aloud to her, as a whole and in sound segments. She will be able to ask it to search for other occurrences of the word, so that she can see it in context. She will be able to ask for a picture or animated sequence to help her to understand the word, or simply a dictionary definition with an example of the word in context, in text or read aloud. All this is technically feasible. Will she learn to read better?

In the UK, Davidson and others (1991) carried out a small-scale trial using *Hyper-Card* to provide a computer-spoken version of pages from story-books. On placing the cursor on a word, a child could hear it spoken by the computer, in a child's voice which sounded natural because it was digitised. Children reading the pages with the 'computer voice' did better in standardised reading tests than those reading the pages alone. The former's success may not have been caused entirely by the voice, but the researchers were encouraged by the results to propose further work along similar lines.

When computers were first introduced into schools, Skeffington (1991), a special needs teacher in St Peter's Primary School, on trouble-torn Falls Road in Belfast, saw them as a novelty likely to arouse curiosity in most children. She now sees computers as integral teaching tools that make learning exciting for children who had begun to lose all hope of ever feeling proud of their schoolwork. One group of five Primary Fives (about 9 years old) came to her for special help with reading problems for 45 minutes every day. Their reading ages were mostly more than two years below their chronological ages. Through a Language Development Project based on the University of Ulster, Skeffington was able to create a *HyperCard* stack about her school, and she used it to get the group interested.

READING TO DISCOVER

I began showing them the new computer, giving them the names of the parts. Then I went straight to the 'School' stack and showed them my map of the local area without saying where it was. They immediately recognised the Falls Road (who wouldn't!), the Royal, Ross Road and St Peter's. I was asked, 'How does the computer know about us and where our school is?' I explained that I had told the computer, by giving it instructions on how to draw the map. Would they like to see what a map of the school looked like? They were fascinated that here was a computer with which they could communicate – sure, didn't it even know where the school was, and the Falls, and all that? I had simply labelled the rooms Primary 1, Primary 2 and so on, but the children instantly identified each class. 'There's Mrs Searle's and Mrs Nixon's, there's our class. Mrs Skeffington, there's your room, the one we're in now!'

I was very pleased by the enthusiastic response, and, to hold this totally captivated audience, I whispered, 'Would you like to go in?' I clicked the button I had put on Mrs Skeff's (the rest of my name wouldn't fit on the plan). The children recognised the room at once and were delighted with the plan of the room they were actually sitting in – the washbasin in the corner, the teacher's desk, the 'wee' soft red stools, their own desks. They exclaimed, 'Miss, there's us!'

My original plan had been to take them on the *MacTour*, supplied with the machine, to show them such skills as dragging with the mouse, but I was glad I had used the stack. It was much more personal and the children felt that this 'Mac fella' was an acquaintance rather than a machine. The next step was to show them the tools, first for drawing. They were so wrapped up in mastering these that I had to switch off the machine to clear the room for the next group. Over the next few weeks, the children took turns switching on the computer and soon became confident about working with the 'School' stack, reading all the while.

In the belief that reading is one part of an integrated approach to language development, Skeffington was keen to start them on writing a group story. They wrote one about themselves (see Chapter 8). This proved so successful that when she received the *StoryMaker* software from the University of Ulster, the group was ready to write a second story, which turned out to be on Japan (see Chapter 8). Skeffington says:

WRITING TO READ: USING *STORYMAKER*

At this point there was a long delay. Emma, who was emerging as the organiser of the group, remarked that they could not write about a holiday in Japan until they knew something about the country. They used the school and local libraries to get the information they needed. For this purposeful reading activity they realised the importance of choosing books according to their reading level. After many days spent on pooling information about shared topics, they decided on a list of headings they wanted to cover. Each chose a heading, read up about it, made rough notes and often passed on pieces of information to the others. They were free to go to the computer to look for possibly suitable graphics and could print them out. I set a deadline and finally all were ready for the next stage, which involved speaking and listening. The children took turns to tell the rest about what they had read, sometimes referring to their notes and showing graphics for comment. The others asked questions and even offered advice about other sources, sometimes to the annoyance of the speaker!

At the start, I had felt pressurised to get 'all the group's other work' done – reading, phonics, comprehension and so on. As the Japanese story progressed, however, I was convinced that *HyperCard* was providing a near-perfect environment for practising listening and speaking, reading and writing, in a most interesting and meaningful way. To discover what Japan was like, the children were using library skills. The discussions required careful and meaningful listening and talking. As regards comprehension, I realised it had been taken care of the day the Project Coordinator came and asked how we were progressing. The children provided her with much newly acquired information on life, work, transport, food, clothes and homes in Japan. This was certainly a more relevant exercise in comprehension than an isolated passage from a textbook.

Even in wordprocessing, a time-consuming activity, the work typed in by two of the children at a time was scrutinised by the whole group, so that errors of spelling, punctuation and sentence construction could be corrected. I was impressed by the way in which this correction was received. The two 'typists' were grateful for the help given by the rest. This redrafting by the group turned out to be a much more acceptable approach to corrections than the usual reproachful red pen of the teacher. It made me wonder if this was why these same children in the past had written only a few lines of a story. They had now proved to me that it was not because they had nothing to say. Was it because they did not see the point in writing much when the page would be transformed into an 'illuminated manuscript' by my over-zealous attempts to help them?

Developing the reading skills of visually impaired learners

Most visually impaired people have some residual vision including many of those who are registered blind. Learners with poor central vision but a full peripheral field, have difficulty in distinguishing fine detail such as the individual letters of printed materials. Those with good central vision and a restricted peripheral field (tunnel vision) have little difficulty with individual letters but have problems such as maintaining a place on a line, and find it even harder to move from one line to another.

With poor central vision, some form of magnification is often appropriate. Depending on the visual impairment, this may be either a microscope or telescope aid. Microscope aids with their short working distance and wide field of view can help with reading. For those with tunnel vision, magnification does not help with reading. Indeed it can make the situation worse. As their major problem is getting oriented within text, they need aids which assist in maintaining or changing position.

John has poor central vision. He has developed his reading skills by using closed circuit television (CCTV), as Marsh (1990) relates, but was disappointed to find that the sensitivity in his fingers is too low to enable him to read braille. He felt very uncertain when he undertook a computing module within the foundation course at the Royal National College. He knew that he would have to read both books and information on the computer screen. After assessment, John was provided with a Frank Audiodata. With this he could access text onscreen through a movable window in which the text on a selected part of the screen appears in enlarged characters. It also has speech output that can be used as an alternative to the large character display.

JOHN'S OWN STORY ABOUT 'FRANK'

The Frank that I use has white characters on a black background which are magnified by 20 times. I need this magnification with my sight difficulties which are 1 over 60 in my left eye and 2 over 60 in my right eye. It is a central vision problem so I still have a good field of vision. I have a slow CCTV reading speed of 20 words per minute which applies to the Frank as well. When using the computer, the enlarged window follows the cursor which makes it easier when I am typing. Sometimes I spot the spelling mistakes, back space and correct them. I think that I have developed a very good memory while on the course which I need. Remembering things that I have typed enables me to go back and correct easily. I use the computer's operating system to quickly find things in programs that I need, using the search facilities which are invaluable.

I use speech output a lot, more for blocks of text. If I need to read the whole computer screen, my reading speed of 20 words per minute is too slow and then I use the speech output. Without such equipment as the Frank, I would be unable to work and I find it brilliant. Also to help me work, I use a CCTV which is kept by the computer on a trolley. I can use this to look up familiar material – not to read extensively but to just look up specifications.

One facility that John found essential to complement CCTV was a personal reader. His personal reader (human!) read material on to an audio cassette which included handouts as well as books. During a six week placement at the South-Western Electricity Board (SWEB), the reading skills that he had developed both with a computer and with CCTV were equally important in a work situation. Subsequently he gained employment with the SWEB.

In Chapter 5 we discussed blind learners' problems with orientation and moving around within text, and suggested providing students with access to course material through the use of hypertext on CD-ROM. Students at Exhall Grange School experience the benefits of this approach:

COMPACT DISCS HELP WITH READING

Because many visually impaired learners can only read books slowly and because of their difficulties in managing either large quantities of enlarged print or braille, publications like dictionaries and encyclopedias are often produced for them in a precis format. To provide access to full versions of such reference books, staff at Exhall Grange School have evaluated the potential of a CD-ROM workstation which has both large character display and speech output facilities. The computer has a high resolution colour monitor to make it easier for partially sighted children to use the standard screen display.

One CD-ROM that has already proved popular for teaching across much of the curriculum is the *Times* and *Sunday Times* disc, containing thousands of articles from the 1990 editions. It is an invaluable source of information which would normally be inaccessible, for most children at the school, in a newspaper format. A feature that has proved to be very important is the facility to search and narrow down the amount of text that has to be read. Effective search methods go some way to matching what a sighted person would do in scanning pages of text quickly before finding a section of interest to be read.

Developing the reading skills of hearing-impaired children

We touched on the language development problems of hearing-impaired children in Chapter 5. Computers can help these children to gain access to the reading curriculum. For example, Pester (1991) developed a *Touch Explorer Plus* file for a group of hearing-impaired youngsters aged five to seven in a partially-hearing unit at Henbury Court Infants School, Bristol. The children were familiar with the Concept Keyboard and *Prompt/Writer* for recording their work and for creative writing. She exploited *Touch Explorer Plus* for them within the curriculum, with five specific aims in mind:

- To reinforce a reading or spoken vocabulary (whichever is appropriate).
- To encourage reading for meaning.
- To encourage conversation and discussion.
- To encourage and motivate the children and give them the confidence to work on their own.
- To introduce and lead to activities away from the computer.

Pester said she wanted to develop an activity for children on the computer which would reinforce and support work by her whole group, which contained some older, less able pupils. She was keen for all the children to be able to use the file from a purely practical point of view; if she invested a lot of time in preparing it, she wanted it to be useful across a range of abilities. She thought it would be possible for a pupil to work at the appropriate level, out of the six she provided, but all would use the same resource without really being aware that they were working at different levels.

READING ABOUT THE HOUSE

I created a bright, colourful overlay from an Activity Book which fitted exactly on the A3 keyboard. It was already plasticised, therefore robust. The book included plastic shapes to stick on and was very tactile in its appeal – just right for the Concept Keyboard. The children were itching to use it and enjoyed it off the Keyboard as well!

Level 1 introduced the children to the format of pressing a question square (marked at this level by a finger for those who couldn't read 'press'!) and then exploring the picture for a response. At this level simple vocabulary relating to the house was reinforced. For example, 'Find the door'. Each level included an activity. Here the children were asked to draw their own house, away from the computer. In fact, they were so taken with the activity book format that they were keen to make their own models. The 'print' facility on the program allowed them to print their own labels in large print (their own idea).

Level 2 extended the reading activity by introducing further vocabulary with which the children were already familiar in other contexts. So, for instance, they were now asked to 'Find the big window'. For some children, the reading and concentration demands at this level meant that they needed an older child or adult to work with them. For these children the activity was very much a focus for developing spoken language skills, whilst the 'reading' element tended to be a process of word matching to find the correct picture.

Some of the children used only these two levels on the computer but thoroughly enjoyed playing with the activity book away from it!

Level 3 asked the children to 'open the house' at last! It then introduced them to the names of various rooms – vocabulary which they would need to complete the other levels. They were asked to 'Find the bathroom' and so on. Once they had located the room they could stick some relevant furniture into it. Again, the children enjoyed printing out the vocabulary to stick on their own house pictures. The vocabulary used at this level was that which was being used in other classroom activities related to the house topic. I wanted to reinforce a spoken vocabulary and introduce the written pattern so important to hearing-impaired pupils.

Level 4 was a game to check the vocabulary from Level 3. The children were asked to tidy the loft which had various items of furniture stuck in it. They pressed each item in turn and were asked to 'Put me in the kitchen' and so on. The purpose of this level was very much one of reinforcement and several of the group needed to do it a few times. The beauty of this level was that the items of furniture were interchangeable (sometimes they would put a bed in the bedroom, at others a wardrobe) so that each time they came back to the game they had different things to tidy up! The children were encouraged to use contextual clues in that the pictures and the decoration of the rooms obviously helped a great deal. As they became more competent with the reading, we set up 'nonsense' items so that they were asked to put a cooker in the garage, or a bed in the bathroom.

Level 5 introduced the children to the vocabulary for a few items of furniture. They worked, in fact, the other way around and pressed the room for instructions – 'Put a bed in here' – and then 'found' the item in the loft.

Level 6 gave the children a series of clues as to what should be in each room. For example, 'I am singing in a cage', 'You sleep in me'. The children enjoyed this game and it led to a great deal of riddle work away from the computer. This ability to have fun with language is a skill which requires a certain level of facility and confidence with language itself and it is one which hearing-impaired children may be slow to acquire or may simply not be given the opportunity to explore. By using the computer to introduce the riddle format, I could illustrate a use of language it would have been difficult to get across in another context.

*Figure 7.2 - **Overlay of outside view of house***

Work on this file was just part of related classroom activities and other computer work going on simultaneously within the topic. The children enjoyed coming back to this, doing a little bit more each time, and they used it throughout the term's work.

*Figure 7.3 - **Overlay of inside view of house***

Summary

In all reading classes, for young and old, the teacher's intervention is vital, for diagnosis of errors and remediation. No computer can do that work as well as the teacher. In this chapter, however, we gave a few examples of how teachers use computers to improve access to the reading curriculum for children and adults with learning difficulties. For many such learners, computers hold their attention, provide practice and integrate reading with other language skills.

8 Writing and spelling

Using symbol systems

Signs, symbols and ordinary writing are essential in a language curriculum for many students with learning difficulties. Teachers of students with severe learning difficulties often turn to symbols as a first stage in teaching communication skills. Rebus and Sigsymbols are examples of pictorial symbol systems, which cannot easily carry abstract concepts, functional words and grammar. Blissymbolics make up a more versatile system, with more abstract symbols. *Beeb-Bliss* and *Blissapple* enable teachers to introduce computers for Blissymbolics, and there are games available, such as *Bliss Snap*, *Bliss News* and *Bliss Synrel*. There is no difficulty in computerising symbol systems, as Beste (1990) shows in this Rebus example:

VIA SYMBOLS TO SPEECH: THERESA'S STORY

Theresa is 14, cannot speak and is profoundly disabled, physically and mentally. She understands speech, but communicates at school through explosive yelps. Words she can neither read nor write. Sign language is beyond her abilities, because she can control only her mouth, eyes, head and, when splinted, her arms: even these are all subject to spasms.

Because Theresa cannot control her physical movements, she cannot select items on a communication board and has to depend on a helper interpreting her eye movements as she tries to select an item. The helper says the Rebus symbol she thinks it is, and asks Theresa to say Yes or No. This process is slow and laborious.

With *Using Rebus II*, Theresa can now select her own items, without human help. She can hit the platform single switch when the scanner is on the right item. The symbol she has selected appears at the foot of the screen and is spoken in synthesised speech. Her selections are memorised by the computer: she can repeat them or ask to have them printed. In 1989, she was learning how to put two or three symbols together to make simple sentences. She was beginning to make requests, express choices and tell her experiences. She may be able to learn to print and delete. The computer and a suitably adapted program have given Theresa a degree of independent expression simply not possible a decade or so ago.

Using Rebus II is the most commonly used program, sometimes combined in the classroom with British Sign Language. Beste (1990) offers further examples of this and other programs helping learners with special needs.

SIGNS, SYMBOLS AND WORDS

At Blanche Nevile School in Haringey, British Sign Language is used extensively. There, a teacher made three Concept Keyboard overlays to go with the *Compact Suite*, which is a set of early childhood development programs covering topics such as shape, size and so on. One activity involves deciding whether to place a stick figure on, in or beside a box. Once the choice is made, the figure is animated to illustrate the concept. The first overlay the teacher made reproduced the drawings from the screen for each position. The second showed drawings of the British Signs for these three concepts, and the third was of the words themselves. Students can thus move easily from one system to the other.

At The Vale School in Haringey, a teacher adapted the program *Podd*. The original animates a creature of that name when the right verb – run, jump – is typed in. The adapted version asks children to pick the right symbol from the Concept Keyboard. Twydall Infants School in Kent has similarly adapted *Picture Play*, which contains simple pictures to be used for identification and matching. Each picture is presented in full colour, thick outline and thin outline, that is, in increasingly abstract form. The adaptation adds a Rebus symbol to each set of three.

Teachers at Amwell View School in Hertfordshire use total communication, including British Sign Language and Sigsymbols. They noted that there is very little published for children to read in symbolics, and used three computer programs to prepare several short books. *Folio* was available to wordprocess the text, and *Using Rebus II* and *Using Pictures* for inserting the symbols and illustrations. The school would like to provide a bridge, starting from symbols, moving through pictures to words, but a reading scheme incorporating such a bridge would require more symbols than the 300 in *Using Rebus II*.

Beste (1990) also discusses *From Pictures to Words*, which 'combines pictures and words in a series of structured language and literacy activities – such as initial letter matching, word recognition and word building – but also has a free-writing option which can be used to write with pictures and words, displayed in a variety of sizes'. In the program's picture library are many Rebus symbols, and teachers can use the picture editor to make their own if necessary. Beste says teachers need a large library to save time if they are to create readers with symbols. Given such a library

111

in the program, students may even create their own books, as Beste's example suggests:

NOT ENOUGH SYMBOLS FOR PETER

Peter, a five-year-old with cerebral palsy and without speech, had already learned to operate a computer with switches. Soon he found *Using Rebus*'s grid of 16 symbols inadequate for his communication needs. *Using Rebus II* enabled him to turn to additional 'pages' of 16 symbols, but before long even these were not enough. He wanted a program that combined symbols and ordinary characters, because he was learning to read.

Writing with wordprocessors at school

There is plenty of evidence that the writing of children with no special educational needs can benefit from using wordprocessors, but what about children with writing difficulties? Morocco and Neuman (1986), working with children in this group, found that wordprocessing was motivating to their pupils when they were engaged in creative writing, but not when it was used for the isolated practice of basic writing skills. They noted that wordprocessing gave the teacher access to the pupil's writing process, and that the teacher could collaborate with pupils, monitoring and praising the editing process. Children with a history of weakness in writing were less anxious writing with the wordprocessor because changes could be made simply and cleanly, and poor handwriting was irrelevant. Similar findings have been reported elsewhere. For example, Jarvis (1988) describes how John improved his writing skills by using wordprocessing. John is one of six in his year who use computers under guidance from the special needs teacher.

JOHN CATCHES UP

John, a second year pupil in a comprehensive school, has a reading age of 7.9, a spelling age of 6.3 and difficulties in writing. His major problem is the slow speed at which he can operate. He leaves the class to receive help from the special needs teacher, who introduced him to wordprocessing.

Recently the class was studying the Herring Gull and Baboons. After watching videos, all the children began completing worksheets with reference books to hand. John understood the videos and could remember the key points when questioned about them, but he could not read the booklets or write his answers on the worksheets. He produced little work even when the classroom teacher gave him extra time.

His special needs teacher taught him to read keywords, using *Prompt3* (now *Prompt/Writer*), and a Concept Keyboard. He quickly learned then to type his answers on the computer keyboard, building on the keywords he knew. The next stage was to repeat these keywords in a cloze exercise with *Prompt3*. John felt fairly confident in using the keywords in this way.

All John's 'recognised' words went onto the computer, into his own special dictionary within *Easy Type*, a wordprocessing program. At the end of term, John's file of work compared favourably with his classmates'. His teacher said he had understood the concepts, and had good recall of the facts. He himself felt he had succeeded.

Many learners with special needs can benefit from using the Concept Keyboard with a wordprocessing program such as *Folio*, *PenDown* or *Prompt/Writer*. For example, if the necessary vocabulary for a piece of writing is on the overlay, correctly spelled, a pupil can concentrate on the content. Or, if the overlay contains complete sentences, the pupil can simply focus on arranging them in the right order. Speech synthesis (available, for example, with *Prompt/Writer* and *Stylus*) may help the poorest readers with their writing. As we described in Chapter 7, *Touch Explorer Plus*, the most successful program published by the National Council for Educational Technology, enables the teacher to present information via the Concept Keyboard suited to needs and abilities of learners at various levels. Learners can start with a blank overlay and explore the text beneath, prepared by the teacher. Each area of the keyboard can have up to six levels, or layers, of information attached, each one capable of containing quite long text messages. Here is a brief example of good practice with this program:

USING *TOUCH EXPLORER PLUS*

At Corsham School, we developed a four-level file on extinct animals. On the overlay are pictures of animals which have become extinct in the last 100 years. A child working at level 1 will get only the name of the animal coming up on the computer screen, but one working at level 2 will get some basic information as well. At level 3, there are questions as well as information, to direct the pupil's thinking. Level 4 contains a glossary of terms used at other levels. Available to all pupils is a wordprocessor into which they can type notes and answers to questions, for editing and printing as needed.

We found that in this way the text could be made appropriate to the user's reading ability, unlike the difficult text of many books about extinct animals. The children were very interested in using this approach, and for those who were poor writers the system offered many advantages.

The National Special Needs Software Unit, based in Doncaster, has now produced *Touch Explorer Plus Prompt/Writer*, building on the proven success of the original content-free programs, which teachers could easily fit into their own classwork.

Scenario Designer, first in a new Designer series, includes a page creator, with a title generator, vocabulary editor and graphics editor.

Beeson (1988) reports on work done by Gee, a teacher at Kensington Junior School in inner city Liverpool. Gee introduced her children to *Facemaker* with which, in pairs, they designed a portrait for a 'Wanted' poster. As they worked, the children discussed differences and likenesses, identical and non-identical twins and mirror images. When the portraits were done, they used *Prompt 3* to write captions. Even those with little reading ability could manage this. The posters were printed and displayed. She was well pleased by her children's improved writing and social skills.

Subsequently, Gee worked with fourth year children and *Folio*, another word-processing program. For writing stories, she gave them a starter sentence about a magic umbrella. She found that the children were motivated well by using the computer. She had them working in groups, with one child as typist. They listened to each other's ideas, then agreed what to type. They gathered the stories together as a 'book', which was read to some of the infants, who in turn drew some illustrations. After this project, the children wrote more, with wider vocabulary, she said, whether they were wordprocessing or using handwriting.

In Cleveland, secondary school pupils with special educational needs used *Folio* and other programs to produce books specifically for infants, as Stansfield (1991) describes:

OLDER CHILDREN WRITE STORIES FOR INFANTS

Two years ago we organised a 'course' to develop the production of books for infants by secondary pupils with special needs. Norton School already ran a book-making project, without computers, but the special needs pupils were always at a disadvantage in the project because they felt they were incapable of making books that 'looked good enough'.

For the course, we paired a teacher from a secondary school with one from a primary feeder school and two secondary special needs pupils. There were eight such groups from all areas of the county. The secondary pupils went to the infant class and researched the infants' story preferences by talking to them and reading their existing books. Afterwards, the groups spent two separate days at the Cleveland Educational Computing Centre preparing and printing out their books.

The results were excellent. The special needs children's self-confidence and self-esteem improved because they had produced desirable products, at least as good if not better than those ordinarily produced by the project. Their motivation to write increased. They even experienced a little parenting. The infants were delighted to have more 'grown-ups, especially 'men' in their school, and were motivated to read more. Collaboration between the schools was enhanced. Some of the special needs pupils' books have now been introduced into in-service training of teachers from other schools, to encourage them to repeat the experiment. The programs used were *Folio*, *Fairy Tales/Christmas Tales*, *Fantasy Island* and *Picture Play*.

Wordprocessing within projects and themes

Commonly, however, teachers bring in computers to support writing and other activities within a project or theme approach. James (1988) tells how she used an adaptation of *Mallory Manor*. This crime detection game offers opportunities for discussion, note-taking, logical thinking, deduction and decision-making. The Manor has been burgled. Police search it and take statements from its occupants about where they were and what has been stolen. Eventually the crime is solved.

WHO BURGLED GEORGE WARD SCHOOL?

My third year special needs group at the George Ward School, Melksham, included mostly Statemented children of very low ability. Many were behaviour problems: they were difficult to motivate and unimaginative. Yet the group was enthusiastic about this project and learned a good deal during the six weeks of English lessons that it lasted.

In Lesson 1, they played the original game of *Mallory Manor*, in groups of four or five, with one member noting down which rooms they had been in, how rooms link together, where people said they were at the time of the crime, and so on. They all enjoyed this, some reading, others reasoning.

In Lesson 2, I explained to the whole group that we could make up our own program, using the *Mallory Manor* framework. The group decided to call the new game School, basing it in their own school, which they knew well. The time was to be afternoon, 'as things get stolen at lunchtime'. Each pupil chose an object which might be stolen, 15 in all, including interesting ones like 'Mark Wood's bus pass' and 'Mr. White's spectacles'. The group agreed to have 20 rooms, but it was not easy to decide which ones because each room's name had to start with a different set of three letters, not capitals. All the pupils joined in the discussion and finally chose 20.

During Lesson 3, each pupil chose a 'character'. Some decided to be themselves, others used nicknames (whose use in normal circumstances would rapidly lead to blows), and still others chose friends' names or their teachers'. Each pupil also had to choose two remarks he or she would make as that character. They had some difficulty in choosing because they had to avoid saying where they were at the time of the crime–the computer decides that. Finally, the group had to decide who would be the detectives, and chose the teachers since the crime was to take place in school.

Pairs of pupils took it in turns to enter all the data, continuing sometimes during lunchtime and after school. I edited the entries, but there were not many errors.

Next lesson, the computers were ready, loaded with the *School* game. Although the children had spent so much time working on it, they were still surprised and excited to find a very efficient and professional program working with their data and even their names in it. The program ran very well, although there were some unforeseen incidents created by the computers, like Miss Wilde, the historian, saying 'I was going to check my history money. I was in the boys' toilet with Matthew Booth'. Fortunately Matthew is not easily upset. The rest thought it was hilarious. Overall, they found it slightly easier to solve the crime than in *Mallory Manor*, because they knew the people and could more easily remember who was where and with whom.

The group's self-esteem reached new heights in the following lesson, when some other third-year pupils were invited in to play School. The group showed them the game and explained how to play it.

When the time came to evaluate the program, pupils were able to suggest how it could be improved. For example, it is boring to go into rooms with nobody in them, but this is inevitable if there are 20 rooms and, say, only 13 characters. It would be better to have fewer rooms. Matthew Booth suggested it might avoid some embarrassment if toilets were not used.

Computers played a major role in this project, but the work extended far beyond. Apart from developing the School program, James says the pupils gained from interesting discussions on questions such as, Is it right to steal? Should finders be keepers? How should a thief be punished? Groups of pupils used *Front Page Extra* to produce newspaper stories. Some of the more able pupils wrote lengthy crime stories. There were 'drama' sessions in which 'police' interviewed 'suspects': the crime was planned with the 'police' outside the room, but when questioned all the suspects had to speak the truth expect the guilty person. The police had to find the criminal.

Wood (1990), in using witches as a theme in his special needs class of 9–10 year-olds in Bryncethin Junior School, Bridgend, found ways of teaching design/technology, mathematics, religious and moral issues, science and drama, but he says the linguistic and literary area was perhaps the one most developed during the theme! The starting points were a book, 'The Worst Witch', by J. Murphy and its accompanying software developed by M. Anderson and D. Baxter. With the wordprocessor, the children wrote about 'Ghostly witches', 'Flying over the school on a broomstick' and 'Mixing assorted potions and spells'. They also did some empathetic writing, as main characters from the story.

```
My name is Mildred Hubble

I was in Miss Cackle's Academy for Young Witches.I had to find two
parts of the broomstick and glue and sticky tape.I had to find a
satchel to put the tabby cat into. I went to the magic gates.I
tapped the broomstick.I flew up and up.I flew forward and into the
forest.I landed in the forest and I saw the witches.I turned the
evil witches into snails.I flew back to the Academy.Miss Cackle
said "you have saved the day from that ugly sister of mine."

by Wizard Paul Rainbow
```

*Figure 8.1 - **Paul Rainbow's empathetic writing***

They made word pattern amulets and wrote leisure items for 'Holiday Witch!' magazine. With *Front Page Extra* they produced several newspaper stories.

Wood stresses that he takes a holistic view of the curriculum. His children show unexpected abilities when challenged with an imaginative theme and given appropriate tools, including the computer.

An example of an autistic pupil being helped to write and program by using a computer is reported from Cleveland by Stansfield (1991):

ANN'S STORY

Ann, aged 8, has Asberger's Syndrome, a form of autism, and goes to her neighbourhood primary school. When a Statement was prepared for her about a year ago, she could read well and could write, but her handwriting was illegible to all but herself. She had shown little interest in computers until the day she sat down and wrote unaided a three-page story using *Folio*. Her teachers were so delighted that they asked for the loan of a BBC, but it soon became clear that a Typestar 90 electronic typewriter would be more portable: she would be able to take it home as well as use it at school.

The only problem at this stage was that she began to perseverate, writing the same long stories about the greatly exaggerated misdeeds of her younger brother. To enable her to break out of her biographical loop, her teachers taught her to work with the BBC and a Concept Keyboard, with overlays of words and phrases.

It turned out that her parents had an Amstrad at home. Ann somehow found in it the listing of a program. She reproduced the listing from memory, with

SCHOOL NEWS £1
Wednesday 2nd May

Witch pulls off aeroplane wing

Yesterday, a witch pulled a side wing off a Concorde aeroplane travelling from Cardiff Airport to Spain. It crashed by the beach in Costa Blanca Spain near to the Olympic Hotel. Mr. Albert Thompson who was a survivor from the crash said " A witch wearing a black hat and cloak with a green face with boils and warts cast a spell to rip off the wing."
32 were killed in the accident but 20 survived. Spanish police have ordered a search for the witch. Our reporter asked what they were doing about the incident and they said that they waiting in case she came back.

New broomsticks from Wizard Supply

Item 11 Two 'Front Page' news stories

NEWS OF THE WITCHES 67p
Sunday May 25th 1989

DANGER! WITCHES!

by Richard Joyner

Witches have been seen jumping from cliffs near Ogmore-by-Sea.

Witches have for the last few days been using spells in the area. Two people have been turned into frogs!

One was Mr. Jim Toy, a 25 year old milkman. The other was Mr. Tom Broke a postman who later said "Ribbit. Ribbit."

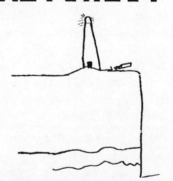

WitchyCola...The wizard drink.

Figure 8.2 - Witch news

enough errors to prevent it from running, and said she wanted to learn how to write programs. Her teachers were concerned about encouraging her to do something that might make her more introverted, but introduced her to Logo instead. They felt that Logo would offer Ann opportunities for problem-solving together with other children. She is being encourged to become the school's *Pendown* expert.

Writing with hypermedia at school

As we strongly hinted in Chapters 6 and 7, teachers in the UK and the US with computers in their classrooms are showing much interest in hypermedia, which are proving particularly valuable in promoting writing. Hypermedia are based on programs such as *HyperCard*. This enables teachers and children to prepare stacks of 'index cards' that can be linked together in various ways. Each card can carry on-screen text illustrated by graphics, including pictures scanned into the computer, plus sound recordings. 'Authors' see for themselves how the content fits together as they create it. Hypermedia also provide teachers with a record of learners' writing and the way their language develops. McMahon and O'Neill (1989) look to hypermedia to aid language development, particularly through writing. Working closely with children and teachers, they have produced tools such as *StoryMaker* which offer the young writer increasing control over his or her own 'voice' in writing.

At St Peter's Primary School in Belfast, Skeffington (1991) introduced a group of five children with special educational needs to *HyperCard* (see Chapter 7). She wanted them to start a group story because she knew from experience that their individual pieces of writing were usually uninteresting, whereas they enjoyed bouncing around ideas with her acting as scribe. She also knew that a disadvantage of group writing is that a few tend to dominate and take over the storyline while the best 'artist' usually does the illustrations. Sometimes a child contributes nothing in the face of such competition. This time was different.

FIVE TAKE OVER AT ST PETER'S

Each child was keen to start drawing and writing. Not surprisingly, they were keen to write about themselves and do a self-portrait, and I was easily persuaded as I felt that this individual effort was necessary to give them practice with the drawing and wordprocessing tools. For them, it was a guarantee that each had a go on the computer.

Using my classroom plan (see Chapter 7), I had placed each child in it with a simple face drawing, and it was while two of the girls were playing about with this map that Natasha saw the possibility of using a button. She remarked that when the button for our classroom was pressed on the diagram of the school building, then the card with the classroom plan came up on the screen. 'Can we put a button on each face so that our writing and drawings will come up?' she asked. I was surprised she so quickly picked up the button idea, seeing how it could be applied in another situation. Emma seemed to anticipate my reaction and very diplomatically suggested I show them how to do buttons for two separate cards, so that each child could do her or his own drawing and writing, linking them to the right face (see Fig. 8.3). I did exactly as they had requested, repeating the procedure several times. Emma was the first to try out the technique: the others prompted her each time she hesitated, before I could offer help. They were all determined to help each other so that they could claim this new development as their own. I became increasingly aware of this joint determination as we progressed together through *HyperCard*.

As a matter of fact, I was only one step ahead of the children, approaching anything new with caution and much repetition. I was inclined to suppose that these 'slow learners' would need a lot of help. I soon discovered that the children were filled with a desire to succeed and they rapidly gained the confidence to take charge of their own learning. They even created their own aids to learning. While I was working one day with two of the children, the other three quickly put a button on the face and linked it up with the right card. They wrote out their own simple directions for carrying out what many adults would consider a complicated task: Tools>Button>Objects>New Button>Objects>Button

My name is Natasha and I am nine years old. I have blue eyes and brown hair. I love going swimming, disco-dancing and playing on my bike. My uncle Tommy has a karate club. He brings me down to it. His sister kathy can lift heavy things. She has very big muscles. When I saw her down in the club I laughed my head off but I did not let her see.

*Figure 8.3 - **My name is Natasha***

info>Name icon>Link to>Hand. This was the start of a system of learning strategies which they created to serve their own special needs. It resulted from their ever-increasing desire for independence and competence. For example, once they had discovered the procedure for changing the text style, they insisted on creating a booklet with samples of writing in different styles to help them decide in advance which style to use. This was part of a continuous effort to improve their own performance by attention to even minor detail.

Skeffington received *StoryMaker* from the University of Ulster early in 1990. One of the children described it as simply, 'a program we use on the Apple Mac. It is a storybook and we put the words and pictures into it.' She saw the program as having great potential but its Resources file seemed too limited. In her experience, children of about nine bring a wide variety of people into their stories. The program needed a large repertoire of men, women and children, wild and tame animals, buildings, backgrounds, parks, countryside, street scenes and seasonal props. The Resources file tended to dictate what was in the story rather than enhance it. Despite these limitations, her children produced a story about two girls and their encounter with a lion, illustrated from the Resources and through their own artistic efforts.

The children were critical of the graphics in Resources, but were delighted to discover they could choose their own graphics from elsewhere and 'paste' them into the Scrapbook file as their own personal resources. Before long, the children were ready for something more ambitious with *HyperCard*:

FIVE OFF TO JAPAN

While Louise was looking through the ClipArt file of readymade graphics, she suggested we write a story about China. 'There's beautiful Chinese pictures we could use,' she said. Everyone agreed and our Chinese story was begun.

Much lively discussion and deep thinking went on as we invented a reason for us to have an opportunity to go to China. We agreed none of us could afford it, so we would have to win a holiday there. The group's oral language flourished, but with me as scribe they were under no pressure to put their ideas into print. We changed our desitination to Japan when we found that the ClipArt pictures were Japanese, not Chinese.

We constructed the pages singly, two on a good day. The group decided that wordprocessing was 'a waste of valuable time'. All the typing was therefore done by the children taking turns at lunchtime. I was amazed that in such a short time they had become confident enough to switch on, open *StoryMaker* and move to the right page. They decided to vary the print on different pages and their Print Sample Book proved worthwhile. Each child became efficient at changing the text style. Soon several pages had been created. For convenience, I suggested we put their self-portraits from the 'School' stack into the

Scrapbook, then they could cut-and-paste these into the story when required. They thought this was a good idea at the time, although now they look back on these first drawings with a more critical eye. Paul especially cringes at the sight of his big ears!

On the second page, the children really entered the world of storymaking, recalling personal experiences in an attempt to convey to the reader how it felt to be kept in suspense waiting for important news. One lunchtime, I allowed three of them to work on the computer, inserting illustrations for the first two pages. They went on to write another page. I read the last line over and over to myself: 'The teacher looked so proud of us.' I thought this must indeed be a rare feeling for most children with special educational needs, yet one it is natural for them to want.

By the time the Japanese story was completed, the children had broken away from their old stilted style of writing, which had resulted from sticking to words they could spell. They had begun to use their spoken language in their writing. Difficult words appeared, seldom spelled correctly but used in the knowledge that the group would be at hand to help correct errors.

The story included pictures. For example, the graphics were hand-drawn using different size brushes and tools.

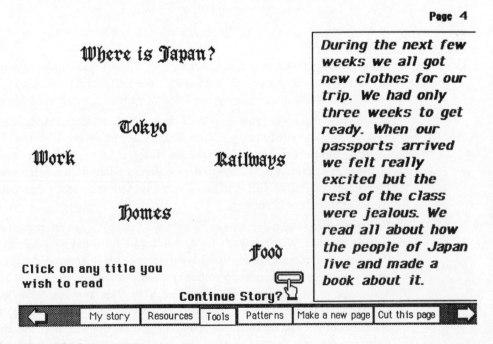

Figure 8.4 - The Japan menu page

When one girl was putting a pattern on the bedclothes, using the 'fill' tool, she became increasingly frustrated as the pattern kept leaking out and spilling onto the floor. She painstakingly went round checking for 'leaks', to no avail. The rest of the group became aware of her problem and stood round her watching in silent thought. At last one solved the mystery by suggesting changing the brush to a fairly thick one, choosing the required pattern and simply painting on the pattern. Changing the brush again to reach narrower areas was simple. This sort of perseverance and ultimate success was a new experience for these children, who were inclined to give up early, expecting failure.

One day Emma was looking through the story on her own and came up with an idea. She and Natasha had been the first to appreciate the use of buttons. She suggested it was awkward to have to flick through all the pages of information on Japan before continuing to read or write the story itself. She wanted to put an extra button on the Japan menu page (see Fig. 8.4), to enable her to jump to the story. Logical thinking indeed!

By this stage they were all well-practised in the skills of cutting and pasting pictures from page to page and from scrapbook to page. I had taught them how to animate pictures by using, say, a picture of an archer shooting with his bow and arrow. In the Japanese story, they made the minibus travel to the airport, and the plane take off.

In the second year of the project, the group learned how to record sound with the MacRecorder, saving it and placing it on a card of the story. For example, the Principal called out the names of the winners of the competition to go to Japan, and the children added clapping.

Then they recorded me announcing flight departures, improving the effect with an echo. Background noise from the class next door listening to television made the recording even more realistic. The noise of the (animated) jet taking off was created from Sound Edit noise, modified. Paul complained that the noise ended before the plane had disappeared, and was determined to change the recording, using Sound Edit, to match the pictures. Another problem had presented itself to the children, who by now had set their own standards, higher than those I had expected of them. Writing a group story had indeed become a vehicle for learning about language and much besides.

In reflecting on her teaching of these children with *HyperCard*, Skeffington noted that some people might ask what was the point of the extra work involved in introducing such novel aspects. For her, the interest and enthusiasm of all the children justified the effort. These were not normally attentive pupils. The previous year, before the project started, they had never displayed such imagination or creativity. Through the writing and associated work, they gained confidence in

Emma

Louise

Paul

Naomi

Natasha

Then Mr. Green called out the names, _ Natasha, Paul, Naomi, Louise and Emma. We were brought up to the front of the room and all our class clapped and cheered. The teacher looked so proud of us!

| My story | Resources | Tools | Patterns | Make a new page | Cut this page |

Figure 8.5 - 'The teacher looked so proud of us'

themselves. They took pleasure in producing work they themselves were pleased with afterwards, to say nothing of their peers, parents and teachers.

In Bell's (1991) story of a similar *HyperCard* project at Fleming Fulton School, in Belfast (see Chapter 6), it is clear that she wanted her pupils to develop their ability to communicate in writing as well as speech. She says that working in groups of three they made lists of ideas for the subject matter, with a scribe in each group. Then they wrote initial drafts of the story they wished to tell. They also prepared a letter to the Nursery school teacher halfway through the project, telling her of their progress. But their main use of the computers for writing was when they keyed in the story onto *HyperCard*.

WRITING WITH *HYPERCARD* AT FLEMING FULTON

The children were so keen to present their work with 'professional' accuracy that the most common request was 'Miss, do you see any mistakes?' I always let them find their mistakes for themselves, although several times I had to stop them from putting a new error into work which they corrected.

One of the positive aspects of *HyperCard* was that so few words appeared on the screen at a time. Several of these children share a weakness: they tend to scan print quickly and inaccurately. In this format they were encouraged to look specifically at each word and sometimes each letter.

A child with muscular dystrophy, with very little strength in his hands, found it easier to use a pencil to press the keys. When that exhausted him, he adopted an advisory role and was the best at giving instructions for creating fields, moving graphics and so on, despite never having done it himself! He was so keen to gain hands-on experience that he and another pupil, unaided, found a way he could do it. She held up the keyboard so that he could press the keys. They got this cooperative skill down to a fine art and both took great pleasure from it. She found it as creative as he did.

Bell (1991) tells further of working with a group of six physically-disabled children, all about 9 years old, with reading ages of about seven. The prospect of 'writing a story with the computer' stimulated their oral language. Three of them had a long discussion with her about their ideas for a story. Here is the start of it:

DISCUSSING THE SHERLOCK HOLMES MYSTERY

Gary	I'm Sherlock Holmes.
Matt	Can I do all the talking this time Gary?
Teacher	And what does Sherlock Holmes do?
Gary	A tactive.
Others	A detective.
Matt	And he always carries a magnifying glass.
Gary	He solves mysteries and all.
Matt	We're going to have this here thing about a haunted house. Right, he goes to. . . I'm doing the wee boy who goes to the haunted house?
Teacher	Right. What happens to you?
Gary	He gets caught.
Matt	I get caught.
Gary	And a witch caught him. . . a witch. . . And had him shut. His mother phones me. His mother comes round to my house. Right?
Teacher	Right.
Gary	Then I go to the haunted house with her mother and I saw footprints and there's ghosts round the haunted house. And. . . defences to Dr Watson.

Teacher	And who are you David?
David	Dr Watson.

Bell says that the children never depersonalised the story. They assumed from the start that every child was a character in it, and kept referring back to their roles throughout the project, even saying such things as 'But I don't want to do that'. Despite this strong identification, they wrote the story collaboratively, with the teacher acting merely as recorder.

Next, they keyed the story into *MicroSoft Works*, copying the teacher's record very inaccurately. In its uncorrected form, they copied this script over to *HyperCard*. To do so, they had to discuss where the natural breaks should be and what should go onto each card. Bell thought it would be better for them to edit the text when it was in short units on the cards, where they would more easily spot mistakes.

THE SHERLOCK HOLMES MYSTERY

We added graphics and sound as we went through and gradually the structure became more complex. Robert suggested that they all cheer when the screen said 'Watson was freed'. Gary wanted to add a werewolf howling. To add footsteps took several tries before they were satisfied.

The children enjoyed hearing their own voices. We spent a whole session trying out the special effects, playing their voices backwards, with echo or reverberation. They insisted on using the echo effect whenever they could. They were very excited at seeing their own drawings scanned onto the screen, even though, because the drawings were only in pencil, the results were not very clear. They all wanted to label their own drawings with their names.

Robert asked would it be possible for the scanned pictures to appear automatically one after the other. I showed him and Gary how to find the numbers of the cards. It took them most of a morning to record the numbers and key them into the script of the buttons. The following week they were very pleased when they found they could add another card to the sequence, unaided.

This led to discussion of setting up two routes through the story, one with pictures only and the other with only text. They built in other routes and loops. That they did not have to go chronologically through the story turned out to be a distinct advantage of *HyperCard* over traditional storytelling. We began to add offshoots describing each character, others giving information on Victorian dress and houses, and so on. They never lost track of the structure of the stack and were quick to suggest when a button was needed to move backwards or forwards.

With only two or three sentences on the screen at a time, the children were encouraged to look critically at each word, even each letter. For example, they became much more alert to capital letters for names. They decided together what the exact words were that Holmes and Watson spoke, and it was very simple to isolate the punctuation rules and insert them one at a time (first speech marks, then commas, then capitals for the opening words of each speech, then new lines for each person). It was a valuable introduction for them to punctuation of direct speech, which they had not studied before.

For these children, whose hand functions are poor, using a mouse was not easy, even with a mat. We experimented with two mice: one child drew the mouse across the mat, while the other clicked on the second mouse at the right point. Instead of using the mouse and pulldown menus, one or two learned the command codes because it was physically easier for them to hit the keys.

These problems were minor, however, and the children easily mastered the technicalities of the Macintosh and *HyperCard*. Bell thought it was very good for them to discover they could cope with complicated processes which few teachers had mastered! They did not approach the task with preconceived ideas that it would be difficult and very quickly they felt at home in the new medium. The secret seemed to be that they did not try to understand how *HyperCard* works: they simply accepted that it did, and turned it to the ends they had in mind.

McMahon and O'Neill (1989) have also provided *HyperCard*-based dialogue tools, such as *Bubble Dialogue*, which enable learners and teachers to depict social situations and use language appropriately within them to express themselves in thought and speech. Margin tools enable learners to make notes in the margin of on-screen text, especially valuable when they are carrying out collaborative writing exercises. McMahon and O'Neill's *WordSwopper* is a pre-spellchecker designed to help children to get their spelling right. They enter text without worrying about some words being spelled wrongly, but double clicking with the Macintosh mouse on a suspect word copies it into the margin. Its correct spelling can be discussed then with others, including perhaps the teacher, or looked up in a dictionary. The correct spelling is typed in, then another double click on the original suspect word will replace it with the correct one. Message tools enable teachers and children to exchange notes within the system.

Computer aids to writing by adults

At the post-secondary level, acquisition of written language skills is of great value to disabled students. Some of the most dramatic advances academically are made by students who have not been able to write well, but who are enabled to do so by the technology, say Brown and others (1989), offering three US examples.

GARY, ERIC AND MELANIE: THREE ADULT STUDENTS

Gary has spelling problems. Except when he is copying, he becomes very anxious when writing. He discovered that he could write on a computer without serious spelling errors by using an on-line spelling checker and thesaurus. He is now able to focus on content and structure instead.

Eric, a sight-impaired adult student, had never written any assignments and had been obliged to take examinations orally or not at all, despite the fact that he types well, because he could not read what he wrote on the typewriter. His spelling was phonetic, and inaccurate. He was introduced to a computer with large print display, spelling checker and thesaurus, though he was not used to looking at words or punctuation. He had never developed his expressive writing, despite his years of listening to books on tape.

Melanie has had mild written language problems since she received a traumatic head injury as an older child. She tends to omit verb inflections and plural forms of nouns. By using a screen reader, she can hear what she has written, and more easily identifies her errors, which she is able to correct.

At California State University, Northridge (CSUN), near Los Angeles, more than 1000 students, out of about 30,000, have special needs. All who can manage it are encouraged to use a typing tutorial program, *Typing Tutor IV*, to develop keyboard skills, and some become proficient touch typists, able to type notes on a laptop computer during lectures. Scott (1990) discusses how a well-known wordprocessing package, *WordPerfect*, was made more accessible to these learners. *WordPerfect* was chosen because it is a well-designed and supported product, widely used at CSUN and elsewhere. It is more comprehensive than students initially need, however, and during tutorials they are taught how to use the Help system, plus a small number of commands, so that they can teach themselves thereafter. They do not need to memorise commands, because for IBM-PC machines they have a mouse interface, *Mouse Perfect*, which enables them to select commands from menus on the screen, as on a Macintosh. Another add-on program, *Keyworks*, cuts down the number of keystrokes required, through redefining some keys. Thus a student may type an abbreviation, but the screen shows the whole word. If a commonly misspelled word is entered as an abbreviation, the correct word can be shown on screen, though this procedure sounds doubtfully pedagogically, as it possibly reinforces the error! Similarly, the abbreviation in English can sometimes produce a Spanish version on screen, for a very limited vocabulary, valuable to Hispanics.

CSUN has word-prediction programs which Scott claims are valuable time savers for physically-disabled students. Most of these programs display a list of likely words as soon as the student has typed a few characters. Each time, they derive the list from statistical analysis of the student's previous usage, plus a dictionary held in memory. Some display homonyms or homophones, words that sound similar to the one partly spelled. *Handiword* is an add-on word predictor for *WordPerfect*, which also has its own spelling checker and thesaurus.

CSUN students with learning difficulties report mixed experience of grammar checkers, such as *Grammatik III*, which offers advice not easily followed by such students. It marks the erroneous text and suggests corrections. It picks out missing punctuation, vague word usage, cumbersome phrases, sexist terminology, run-on sentences, missing capitals and so on. People with strong writing skills find these checkers too rigid and judgemental. Students who have poor writing skills cannot easily understand the fine points being made and seldom think the advice helpful. Outlining programs are more useful. They encourage students to give the writing task a title and to break down the work into sub-tasks, under sub-headings and sub-sub-headings. They also enable students to focus on any specific sub-task, hiding the rest of the work for the time being. As the assignment develops, students can move sections around easily if need be. Scott says that many students with learning difficulties have problems expressing their thoughts in an organised way, but with an outlining program they can jot down all their ideas and sort them out afterwards.

Students' notetaking in lectures can benefit from outlining too. Disabled students who use a laptop computer usually take down the 'headlines' during the lecture. With the help of a tape-recording, perhaps, or from memory aided by the headlines, some can now produce very good notes. Sometimes, if the topic of the lecture is known in advance, students can even set up the main headlines before going into class. In any event, outlining usually results in lecture notes that are better for revision purposes than those taken by hand.

CSUN's disabled students can also learn desktop publishing. The programs, such as *Ventura Publisher*, are usually more difficult to learn than those for word-processing, but the results can be of much higher quality.

CSUN students who cannot write because of physical disabilities may be able to use speech input systems which recognise what they are saying and reproduce it on the screen or as synthesised speech. The commonest type depends on voice prints of whole words and is limited to a vocabulary of a few hundred words. The student 'trains' the computer to recognise his or her pronunciation of each particular word, then, provided the word is pronounced in exactly the same way by the same person, the computer will recognise it again. Recognition is through matching of the two voice prints. Students who cannot control their voices well enough to replicate the original voice print cannot use this type of system satisfactorily. The second type has fewer limitations and is much more expensive. *Dragon Dictate* (see Chapter 4) is an example. It depends on phonetic models of each word in the Random House Dictionary, stored on disk. These models are in a statistical form which is updated each time the system succeeds in recognising a word, thereby adjusting the system to the user. Scott (1990) reports that at CSUN a student with cerebral palsy tried *Dragon Dictate* and within ten minutes was able to type out and 'say' a sentence that would have been unintelligible to an ordinary person.

The last word on wordprocessing for adult learners should go to Jay, a student mentioned by Brown and others (1989):

LET THE WORDS OUT OF MY FINGERS!

Jay regarded himself as a non-writer in a writing world. His handwriting was misshapen, his verbal expression confused, and the task of writing appalled him. At about age 35, he turned to a computer and wordprocessing. He could scarcely believe that the keyboard would 'let the words out of my fingers', check and change the spelling, reversing the reversals and making him unafraid to write.

Summary

We have been able to provide no more than an overview, with examples, of a rapidly-developing field in which children and adults with learning difficulties are achieving considerable success in accessing the curriculum. First we discussed using signs, symbols and computers to help learners with severe difficulties. Next, we gave varied examples of wordprocessing software in use at school by learners with special needs. We moved on to discuss the imaginative introduction of *Hypercard* into creative writing by children with learning difficulties, with examples of good practice. Finally, we looked at wordprocessing, including predictive and other ancillary programs, for adults with special needs.

9 Drawing, Design and Making

Starting with Logo

Transfer of skills developed with Logo to other activities is a matter of some controversy, as we discuss briefly in Chapter 12. Haigh (1991) suggests that computer-based drawing and design can help pupils with severe learning difficulties to develop certain 'thinking skills'. He prefers them to use programs written in the computer language Logo, because it puts them in command of events as they send commands to the computer. They can set their own pace, avoiding the failures that previously damaged their self-image, because any mistakes are treated merely as stopping to think before trying once more. The Logo environment is safe for them, with known boundaries. At The Park Special School, Wakefield, some pupils only learn to write Logo programs to draw shapes while others progress further. Haigh describes how they use the computer's function keys to enter Logo commands that include numbers and angles:

USING LOGO TO DEVELOP THINKING SKILLS

The children find out, through guided discovery, that, for example, a square angle is 90 degrees (moving the turtle on a square tiled floor helps). Once they have some understanding of measurement and degrees of rotation, these concepts can be consolidated and extended by exercises such as the creation of a turtle dance using several turtles.

After studying the body movements in a waltz, the children in small groups experiment with Forward, Backward, Left and Right commands, with the aim of making the turtles waltz to The Blue Danube. Fine tuning of the movements involves the children in developing their number and spatial concepts in a meaningful context. They also engage in much discussion and co-operation.

Next, the children use a floor turtle fitted with a pen to draw shapes such as a child's initial or a circle. Some shapes require many repeated instructions to the computer, therefore the children learn the Repeat and Build commands at this stage.

After success with the floor turtle, the children can move towards developing more abstract thinking by using the screen turtle for drawing and design. Once they have made this transition, the children are ready to advance into the exciting microworld of Logo.

Bringing computers into children's drawing and design

Children with special needs often enjoy using computers in their drawing and design. Computers may also enable them to draw and design better than they could otherwise. For example, Jones and Morgan (1990) report they used *Collage* to compile a work disk of graphics for use by children at Crownbridge Special School, Gwent.

INCREASING PERSEVERATION WITH GRAPHICS

Children with severe learning difficulties enjoyed watching the 'snippets' characters moving around the screen, some suggesting where they should move to, even offering an imaginative storyline. Snippets are pieces of graphics that can be lifted and moved around, as in cutting-and-pasting. A few wanted to use the mouse themselves. Two tried using *Paintpot* as well and with great enthusiasm kept at the task for 45 minutes at a time, well beyond their usual attention span.

In another class, children aged 16–18 worked on another teacher-created collage, showing a seascape with six snippets (anchor, seaweed, crab, shark and shoal of fish). These children had mastered the mouse and were confident about putting snippets in strange places, such as the shark on the ship's mast. They talked a good deal about what they were doing. When they discovered they could overlay snippets they played a simple memory game: which was hidden first, second, last? They were attentive for 15 minutes at a time.

Computer programs can bring art, even at examination level, within the reach of physically-disabled pupils. Stansfield (1988) tells how Fred, a boy with cerebral palsy, succeeded in obtaining a Grade 1 CSE in a special school in the North of England.

FRED PASSES HIS ART EXAM WITH FLYING COLOURS – AND A COMPUTER

Fred's cerebral palsy causes him some difficulty when walking. His slight hand tremor makes handwriting difficult and prevents him from doing fine line work with a pencil. He had always been at a special school because he depended on a typewriter and had poor mobility.

At the age of 12, Fred asked if he could go with some of his classmates to art lessons in the adjoining comprehensive school. He wanted to find out what it was like in the mainstream and had no idea of his own artistic ability. In the art class, he discovered his skill in using pastels and water colour washes to create impressionistic pictures. He got such pleasure from this, worked so hard and made such progress that he convinced the art department to let him take art for CSE.

Fred's painting progressed well, but his art teacher told him he could not possibly get a high grade in the CSE unless he could produce work from all parts of the syllabus, including fine line work. His art work had to stand on its own merits, as the examination board would make no allowance for his tremor. Fortunately, his special school acquired *Superart*, which runs with a mouse. His computer teacher, no artist, was able to get Fred started on the computer.

A church was Fred's first effort. He experimented with the angles of the walls and made attempts to get the perspective right by trial and error. The weather-cock was assembled pixel by pixel, using the zoom facility. He took three lessons to complete this stage and printed the picture out at the end of each session. He took all the pictures to his art teacher, who had not been very interested in computer art but realised that here was a means by which Fred could bypass his disability. He suggested that Fred add a landscape to his church to complete the work.

The art class was drawing a skyscraper skyline as an exercise, and Fred did his with *Superart*. He lost his first morning's work because he forgot to open the file before he started, but he never made that mistake again.

It was valuable, from Fred's point of view, that by printing it out he could keep a permanent record of each stage of his drawings. He showed two stages of his picture of the colliery winding gear in his village. In drawing a corner of his special school, he experimented with texture and perspective, and printed out several versions as he built them up.

During his two-year CSE art course, Fred produced a great range of work. His teacher convinced the examination board that his computer art should be accepted, resulting in his Grade 1 pass, and at the comprehensive school he won a trophy for creative talent. After he left, he went to Hereward College, Coventry, where he continued to develop his skills in preparing computer graphics.

Morgan (1990, 1991) describes how she used *Quest Paint* at Ysgol Cefn Glas, Bridgend, a residential and day school for 160 children aged 7–19 with learning difficulties, to design the school Christmas card for 1989 with computer images. This activity was an introduction to famous painters of the Nativity, within Critical Historical Studies.

COMPUTER HELPS IN CHRISTMAS CARD DESIGN

We wanted to involve children across the school's age range. While the older ones looked for paintings in books, deciding which ones they liked and why, the younger children 'acted out' the paintings. In the end, the children chose 'The Nativity' by Tintoretto. We did a video 'snatch' of the painting using our video camera and the Watford digitiser. Because *Quest Paint* allows only four colours, and mixtures of them, we chose red, yellow, black and white.

Next, we dressed up the two children chosen to be Mary and Joseph and they took their seats in similar poses to the figures in the painting. Baby Jesus was a doll! Again using the video camera and digitiser, we scanned this tableau into the computer. With 'airbrush' and 'pencil' options, we altered the modern-day background to resemble the stable in Tintoretto's painting.

The final stage was to print out on our Integrex colour printer both the digitised images. We stuck them onto folded card, one labelled 'The Nativity – Tintoretto' and the other 'The Nativity – Ysgol Cefn Glas (1989)'. We prepared the captions and text inside the cards using the 'Text' option in the program. The children had their Christmas cards!

I hasten to add that at our school neither teachers nor children have abandoned traditional art media in our enthusiasm for computer-aided art and design.

Morgan (1991) carried out two other computer-based projects of great interest. In the first, each child designed a logo based on his or her own name or initials, using *Pro Artisan*, for silkscreen printing onto a T-shirt.

Figure 9.1 - Equipment used to capture pictures

DESIGNING T-SHIRT LOGOS WITH COMPUTER HELP

The children drew their design onscreen using the 'pencil' option of *Pro Artisan* and coloured the design with the 'fill' option. They changed the colours until they were satisfied with their personal combination. Up to six colours were available onscreen, as long as these could be reproduced by using a maximum of three silkscreens (for example, green could be obtained by overprinting blue and yellow).

Once a child had decided on his or her basic logo, such as a simple set of two initials, the next step was to choose between using it as it was or in a more complex form using the program's 'cut and paste' facility.

The children used *Pro Artisan*'s 'edge detector', which draws a thin black line between any changes of colour onscreen, before printing out their designs on the colour printer. If they wanted to, they could enlarge or reduce the designs on our photocopier, to provide the outlines for the silkscreen stencils. At this point, the children moved away from the computers.

Our school has no sophisticated printing equipment, only wooden frames with fine nylon gauze ('silkscreen') stretched over them, plus squeegees. Polyprint inks mix well and are water-based. We avoided using light-sensitive emulsions to block out the silkscreen, instead cutting our stencils from sticky-back plastic normally used for jobs like covering books. This meant that cleaning screens was easy and by laying down the plastic with the paper backing uppermost, the children could cut the letters the right way up. Many of these children find reading difficult enough without having to recognise letters back to front!

We cut the plastic longer than the frame so that we could fold it round the edges, then placed it on a flat table with the paper backing uppermost. The children sellotaped their photocopies onto it and cut the shapes with a sharp knife. They had to decide which areas were to be printed during a 'print run' using a particular colour.

Once the areas to be printed were cut out, the children had to cooperate to remove very carefully the paper backing. Someone had to hold down two corners of the plastic while the backing was pulled off by another child. Somebody else had to hold down the other two corners while the frame was dropped precisely onto the sticky plastic and the silkscreen pressed firmly onto it. With care, a child could use the screen for up to eight prints before the ink began to seep between the plastic and the screen. To clean the screen, all that was necessary was to peel off the plastic, wash the screen under the tape and dry it quickly with a hairdryer. Screenprinting was a team effort, with all jobs given equal importance and all children involved, after the individual work of computer-aided design.

At the end of the project we held a 'fashion show' to which the whole school was invited. Several staff, intrigued by the activity, had ordered T-shirts designed by the children for them. They joined the children to model their new shirts in the show, which was videorecorded.

The third project at Ysgol Cefn Glas reported by Morgan (1991) used *Image*. This program has commands easily recognised by many children with learning difficulties, and in the video mode, linked up to a camera and digitiser, only a few simple commands appear onscreen, always in the same position (eg, EXIT is always bottom left, SNAP bottom centre). Morgan's children used it to work on portraits, following up with *Pro Artisan*.

'PORTRAIT-PAINTING' WITH *IMAGE* AND *PRO ARTISAN*

As in all the other work we do with computers in the art room, this project calls for cooperation between the children, usually in groups of three: one behind the camera, one as the model and one on the computer keyboard.

When each pupil has taken a turn and the three portrait images are stored in the 'sketchbook' – a separate disk – the group discusses how to present the final portraits. The computer offers options of printing each one as it is, or they can change the colours by pressing the key (the RETURN button) on the arrow which appears at the top of the colour palette. Doing so will alter all of the eight colours onscreen, by moving the colours up. What is white becomes yellow, what is yellow becomes pale turquoise, and so on. At the darkest end what is black becomes white, white replacing the gap left as all the colours move up.

The children find changing the colours is great fun. They can also fill areas with other colours, individual colours can be changed or areas can be filled with patterns taken from the 'store room' or new patterns made up in the 'mixing room'. Variations without end are possible. When printing out with the colour printer, children can elongate or shorten the screen, or they can use 'cut and paste' to add features.

We relate all of this activity with *Image* to the portraits painted by great artists such as Modigliani or Picasso. We encourage our pupils to paint with a much wider range of colours than they would have had the confidence to use before.

Next, with *Pro Artisan* and the A3000, plus camera and digitiser, children in each group 'snatch' 16-shade grey images of each other. We have tried three ways of using the images, with differing results. Greys can be 'filled' with colour from the program's 256-colour pallette. Children can draw on the image using the 'pencil' option. They can change the shades of grey with the 'colour change' option.

We had great fun recently when the children invited staff to 'sit' for portraits. After capturing the images in greys, pupils added unusual features in bright colours – curly hair, beards, glasses and, because Red Nose Comic Relief Day was approaching, red noses. They printed out these 'improved' faces and displayed them in the foyer for all to see and to identify who was who!

In all three of Morgan's projects she stressed group work, into which she integrated the computer. In the last project, the class looked at artists' work from across several centuries and learned about equipment and media used then, compared with what is now available. She says that she and her children even tried to imagine how these artists might have worked had they had modern equipment. What would have Leonardo da Vinci done with his Mona Lisa, Renoir with Nini Lopez, Raphael with Elisabetta Gonzaga, Picasso with Gertrude Stein or Villon with his self-portrait?

Meeting National Curriculum Attainment Targets in textile technology

At Ysgol Cefn Glas, Bridgend, the same school where Morgan teaches the art and design work discussed earlier in this chapter, Dando (1991) introduces computers into her teaching of Food and Textile Technology. She believes that her children can thus be helped towards achieving National Curriculum Attainment Targets. In one project, Water was the current cross-curricular theme for her Year 8 class, aged 12–13. Here is her account of what happened, a further example of good practice:

USING CAD AND CAM IN MAKING GREETINGS CARDS

The design brief I gave the children was to produce blank greetings cards with a printed design on the front, based on the theme of Water. They would use computer-assisted design (CAD) and computer-assisted manufacture (CAM). The design would be printed on acetate fabric, which would be padded and quilted prior to being mounted on blank greetings cards. I saw this brief as providing for Technology Attainment Target 1, identifying needs and opportunities.

Each child was asked to prepare a very simple design, based on a water 'landscape', using little or no detail, just blocks of colour. For this purpose, I gave them a small piece of paper, 20 cm square. In doing so, the children were meeting AT2, generating a design, to the best of their ability.

The next stage involved using *Image* on the computer. The children recreated their designs, first onscreen, then as a colour printout and finally on the acetate (AT3, planning and making, and AT5, using information technology). We tried other fabrics too, but acetate gave a 'watered' effect we liked (AT4, evaluating). Drawing the designs with *Image* proved very time-consuming because the children needed one-to-one guidance. I provided this while the rest of the class worked their designs on plastic canvas, using a tapestry stitch.

When the designs were all printed on fabric, the children stitched the fabric onto terylene wadding. They had their chance then to use the New Home Memory-craft 7000 computerised sewing machine to carry out the quilting. Finally, the children mounted the finished plastic canvas designs and the quilted landscapes on the cards. They were very pleased with their efforts.

There is no doubt that the children, especially those with motor difficulties, find the Memorycraft 7000 very helpful, compared with conventional models. It holds the fabric with an automatic pressure-controlled foot. It has a locking stitch to secure thread ends instead of these having to be tied and cut. Children can select the stitch they want simply by pressing a picture of it. Stitch length and width are computer-controlled instead of being adjusted manually. Bobbin loading and threading is easy, and there is an automatic needle threader.

Personally, I found this whole exercise far more time-consuming than I had expected, but judged it well worthwhile in terms of experiences it offered the children and the skills they acquired.

For another of Dando's projects, this time with Year 7 middle school children at Ysgol Cefn Glas, the cross-curricular theme was 'Shape'. Again she gave the children a design brief, to produce a simple piece of collage work suitable for a child's bedroom wall, using five basic shapes – triangles, squares, rectangles, circles and hexagons (Technology AT1).

DESIGNING IN TEXTILE TECHNOLOGY WITH THE HELP OF *IMAGE*

To start the basic designs, I gave the children attribute blocks (five basic plastic shapes in three colours, two thicknesses and two sizes), which they were accustomed to using in number lessons. They transferred onto paper, with the help of adhesive coloured shapes, the designs they made with the blocks (AT2). The computer came into the final stage, when they used *Image* (AT5) to put their designs onscreen and printed them out in colour.

Each child took his or her printout and cut out the design to use as a paper pattern, pinning it to felt fabric. Then they had to cut out the fabric. Most of the children had more trouble with these two processes than any other. They went on to pin and tack the fabric shapes onto hessian backing fabric before using the sewing machine to applique the shapes into place (AT3). Finally, they enhanced their work with machine embroidery. The children have to wear 'L' plates until they become competent machinists and can 'pass their test' on the sewing machine: they think this is wonderful!

When all the children had finished, we created a large display of their work, and they tried a little evaluation (AT4). In the end, everyone decided that their work was perfect! And why not!

Perhaps the most ambitious project at Ysgol Cefn Glas in Dando's classes was to design and make the Giant Welsh Collages. The Memorycraft 7000 computerised sewing machine was central to this work. The collages were the Home Economics Department's celebration of the school's Silver Anniversary. Dando (1991) writes:

DESIGNING AND MAKING THE GIANT WELSH COLLAGES

We picked four areas of Cymric Interest: Wales, Morgannwg (Glamorgan), The Cultural Heritage of Wales and Ysgol Cefn Glas. For each of these, the children produced design ideas on paper. On this occasion, we did not go to the computer to use CAD, but synthesised the children's drawings and transferred the final design to hessian fabric.

Each child also made a replica in Fimo clay of his or her face, to be placed in a choir appearing along a harp in the Culture of Wales collage. A few teachers got in too!

For three terms, senior pupils were very busy, using a multitude of hand and machine techniques. They knitted, crocheted, couched, embroidered, made pom-poms and so on, by hand. On the Memorycraft 7000, they did free machining, quilting, embroidery, couching and applique work. This was excellent experience in CAM, and they learned a great deal.

The collages, each one about 2 metres by 1 metre, now hang in the school hall for all to see. Each is very colourful and exciting.

Besides projects like these, Dando also brings the technology into lessons in other ways, to give her children better access to the curriculum. For example, she encourages children to use *Stylus* to prepare neat written work. If they have to produce pie charts or bar charts, she introduces them to programs such as *Datashow*. They can produce and print out their work in colour if that is needed for extra clarity.

Art and design in Further Education

Fowler (1988) describes how computer art programs can help students with special needs in further education. He cites the example of one student who seeks attention, displays an aggressive nature and cannot accept criticism:

SUSAN CHANGES HER IMAGE

Susan's art work and sense of composition have been developed significantly by using *Image*. She has done a lot of work in this area, producing cards, posters, tickets for discos, and so on. She is motivated and will take time and care to produce an end result. This is a great improvement from her earlier rather slapdash approach. Because the computer helps her to produce a piece of work of a reasonable standard of presentation, Susan wants to try again and is able to discuss her work and look at ways of improving it, accepting criticisms – amazingly – without immediately feeling threatened and becoming defensive. This has shown itself in other areas and she is far less likely to respond aggressively to criticism than she was at the beginning of the year. Her teacher is convinced that this is due to her computer work in Art and Design.

Summary

These examples of good practice suffice to give an impression of the range of work that can be done in drawing, design and making by learners with special needs, with the help of computers. They can access the curriculum, without doubt, and be very creative. They enjoy doing so, and the technology is far from being a barrier. For some, the success they achieve has a positive impact on their work in general.

10 Number and Mathematical Reasoning

Gaining access to the mathematics curriculum

Although computers have been commonly associated with mathematics (and with mathematics departments in secondary schools), we did not find a large range of good practice in using them to give children and adults with learning difficulties access to the curriculum. Our examples are mainly of Logo and turtle graphics with *Dart*, though we conclude with instances of children gaining from using framework and wordprocessing programs.

Lewis (1990) gives an account of how pupils with moderate and severe learning difficulties at Greenfield Special School, Mid-Glamorgan, use a Concept Keyboard, a floor turtle and Logo to achieve attainment targets in the Mathematics National Curriculum for England and Wales. Directionality, counting, ordering, estimation, angles, figure/ground perception and mathematical language and awareness can be covered, he says, as well as giving and receiving oral and written instructions (part of the National Curriculum in English).

REACHING TOWARDS ATTAINMENT TARGETS WITH THE TURTLE

The turtle has made many friends. Our pupils, especially those whose movement and coordination is severely restricted, enjoy this mysterious being, with its bright red eyes, lumbering across the floor, turning right and left. The trail the turtle is able to draw for the class when a pen is attached has provided a bonus for pupils visually tracking the path of the robot as it weaves an interesting pattern.

The junior classes manoeuvred the turtle by using Concept Keyboard overlays. Sending the 'creature' forward, backward, right and left helped their direction and spatial awareness skills as well as prompting their language and developing their use of prepositions. Pupils gave directions by using hand signals and also copying the movement of the turtle. They engaged in role playing and socialisation as well as pure enjoyment and movement. They devised games. In one the turtle chased a foam ball, in another it knocked down skittles, and in a third the children were seated in a circle and gave directions to the turtle to visit one another, with one child standing and acting as controller.

Older children have been able to attain full control over this equipment, using the Concept Keyboard. Even shopping trips were planned, with a large street map on an acetate screen overlay. The children instructed the turtle to move to the right shop in response to questions such as 'Where would the turtle go to buy a piece of beef?'

Howard (1991a), working with older pupils at Boxmoor House, a school for children with emotional and behavioural problems, introduced Logo screen turtle graphics to encourage them to investigate regular polygons, shapes associated with them and patterns made by rotating them. His aim was to complement and extend mathematical work and conventional geometrical drawing exercises. He designed the project to serve the needs of these pupils.

INVESTIGATING POLYGONS WITH TURTLE GRAPHICS

Using *Dart*, the pupils constructed regular polygons. To find a general principle for the construction of polygons, they had to establish a relationship between 360 degrees, the number of sides and the angle the turtle turned at each corner. They first investigated equilateral triangles, squares, pentagons, hexagons and octagons. Later they went on to rhombi and five-pointed stars.

Before putting them to work on the computer, I had most of the children measuring angles. They also constructed an equilateral triangle or square on cardboard, cut it out and used it as template to make a rotated pattern using previously drawn guidelines. A few pupils already understood these concepts and skipped this stage.

The pupils had used *Dart* before and knew the basic commands, but I gave them detailed instructions for writing the procedures for building basic polygons. Once the children had mastered these, they learned further procedures for repeating and rotating the shapes around a point. In this way they looked into the relationship between 360 degrees, the number of times the polygon is repeated and the angle turned between each repeat.

Compared with conventional geometric drawing techniques, *Dart* offers far greater speed. It also offers pupils greater scope for investigations because they don't have to draw the shapes themselves and can concentrate on the mathematical relationships. In fact, the structure of the *Dart* procedures is based on these relationships and reinforces them. For example, I found that the children developed their ability to visualise geometric shapes in different orientations.

They became more aware of mathematical properties of shapes and patterns. Their individual creativity emerged as they produced their own geometric designs, based on their new understanding. Their self-esteem increased as they turned out well-presented results (see figure below).

```
HEX

REPEAT 6
 FORWARD 40
 RIGHT 60
END



ROHEX

REPEAT 12
 HEX
 RIGHT 30
END
```

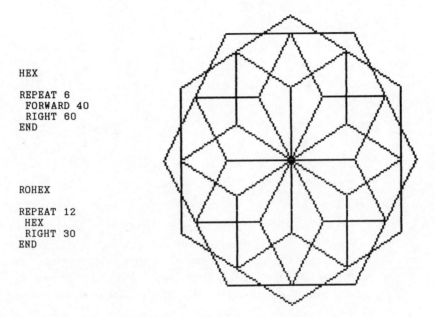

*Figure 10.1 - **Well presented results increase pupil's self esteem***

Some of Howard's more able pupils carried out another interesting investigation using *Dart*. He wanted them to develop mathematical skills by making observations, comparisons and deductions based on the multiplication tables. He believed they would gain deeper mathematical understanding by studying relationships between the sets of numbers in the tables.

THE TIMES TABLE INVESTIGATION

The idea of 'drawing' the times tables intrigued the children. I told them that by expressing the tables as shapes and patterns on the computer screen they would understand better the similarities, differences and relationships between the sets of numbers. Without turtle graphics, of course, much of the value of the investigation would be lost because the pupils would be utterly daunted by the time-consuming task of plotting the patterns by hand. The computer encouraged them to observe, enquire and investigate further.

Each table can be reduced by adding the digits together to produce single digit numbers which form a repeating pattern, as in this example:

Table	Reduction		Pattern
$1 \times 4 = 4$	$4 + 0 = 4$		4
$2 \times 4 = 8$	$8 + 0 = 8$		8
$3 \times 4 = 12$	$1 + 2 = 3$		3
$4 \times 4 = 16$	$1 + 6 = 7$		7
$5 \times 4 = 20$	$2 + 0 = 2$		2
$6 \times 4 = 24$	$2 + 4 = 6$		6
$7 \times 4 = 28$	$2 + 8 = 10$	$= 1 + 0 = 1$	1
$8 \times 4 = 32$	$3 + 2 = 5$		5
$9 \times 4 = 36$	$3 + 6 = 9$		9
$10 \times 4 = 40$	$4 + 0 = 4$		4
$11 \times 4 = 44$	$4 + 4 = 8$		8
$12 \times 4 = 48$	$4 + 8 = 12$	$= 1 + 2 = 3$	3

The children discovered that when the repeating number patterns are plotted as lengths, with a right angled turn between each length, then a line pattern emerges (see Fig. 10.2). To make the pattern clearly visible onscreen, they multiplied all lengths by 10. Then they found that after four repeats the line returns to its point of origin, producing a distinctive pattern (again, see Fig. 10.2).

Mark, a Year 10 boy, approached the investigation particularly enthusiastically. When I explained to him the times table reduction procedure, he asked if he could use the wordprocessor to lay it out. Considering the complexity of the task, he coped extremely well. He took great pride in the product:

1x	2x	3x	4x	5x	6x	7x	8x	9x
1	2	3	4	5	6	7	8	9
2	4	6	8	1	3	5	7	
3	6	9	3	6	9	3	6	
4	8		7	2		1	5	
5	1		2	7		8	4	
6	3		6	3		6	3	
7	5		1	8		4	2	
8	7		5	4		2	1	
9	9		9	9		9	9	

Observations

The number patterns: (a) have an odd number of digits,

(b) all end with a 9,

(c) with the end 9 covered up
show matching
pairs in which one set of numbers is
reversed, i.e.,

   8x is 1x reversed
   7x is 2x reversed
   6x is 3x reversed
   5x is 4x reversed

(d) with the end 9 included
show the sets of
numbers in the matching pairs as
cycles of numbers, one in one direction and
the other in the opposite direction.

The *Dart* patterns show the matching pairs of numbers as pairs of
mirror image patterns.

Mark went on to work independently using *Dart*, which he already knew, to produce the line patterns. He printed them out and stuck them in his work folder and, so that the patterns could be observed together, on card. When he had produced the patterns derived from the complete set of times tables, Mark wanted to extend his investigation. He produced the number pattern and plotted the line pattern for the diagonal sets of numbers in the 1 to 9 times tables

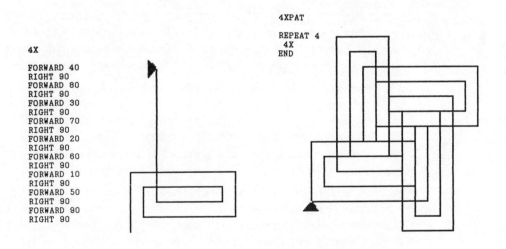

4XPAT

REPEAT 4
    4X
END

4X

FORWARD 40
RIGHT 90
FORWARD 80
RIGHT 90
FORWARD 30
RIGHT 90
FORWARD 70
RIGHT 90
FORWARD 20
RIGHT 90
FORWARD 60
RIGHT 90
FORWARD 10
RIGHT 90
FORWARD 50
RIGHT 90
FORWARD 90
RIGHT 90

Figure 10.2 'Drawing' the times table intrigued the children

chart! Next, he discovered for himself that the times tables beyond 9 also reduce to the same repeating patterns.

I am certain that Mark's mathematical understanding increased. He enjoyed doing the work. The results enhanced his self-esteem and gave him prestige. For pupils like Mark, such opportunities are of tremendous value.

That was not the last of Howard's stories about his pupils using turtle graphics, however, because they went even further, with the remarkable Roman Mosaic investigation. He wanted to lead them to understand mathematical concepts such as reflection, displacement and repetition, as well as offering a thought-provoking link with the mathematics of Roman times. The pupils involved were normally hard to motivate, with little confidence in their own abilities.

THE ROMAN MOSAIC INVESTIGATION

Boxmoor House School was built on the site of a Roman villa. During excavations in 1852 Sir John Evans discovered the substantial remains of a mosaic pavement. The mosaic, dating from around the 2nd century, is an arrangement of five panels surrounded by a continuous swastika-meander merging into an all-over lozenge pattern. This combination is considered unorthodox and perhaps unique. A diagram of the mosaic, drawn by Sir John (see Fig. 10.3), provided the inspiration for this turtle graphics project.

The aim was to investigate the pattern, attempting to reproduce its basic form with *Dart*. We identified first the basic line pattern (see Fig. 10.4).

The pupils noticed that when it was repeated four times it made a continuous loop. The swastika-meander could be made by linking the first loop with an identical loop which had been displaced. The result, in turtle graphics, was a closed self-contained pattern very similar to that in the mosaic pavement.

The swastika part of the pattern consisted of right angle turns. The inner part of the four outer panels of the design formed an octagon, indicating that turns of 45 degrees were used to produce the lozenge part of the pattern. Therefore the angles used were either 45, 90 or 135 degrees. The pupils carefully measured the line pattern, finding that the lengths of the sides were related by a 2 : 3 : 4 ratio. The FORWARD steps in *Dart* could then be 20, 30 and 40.

We built up the line pattern in three stages, using three procedures. The first repeated the basic line pattern to form the continuous closed loop. The second incorporated a small lozenge into the basic line pattern. The third included the displacement of the pattern so that two interlinked closed loops completed the design.

This was not the full design in the mosaic, which consisted of the basic line pattern arranged in different orientations to produce four patterns linked

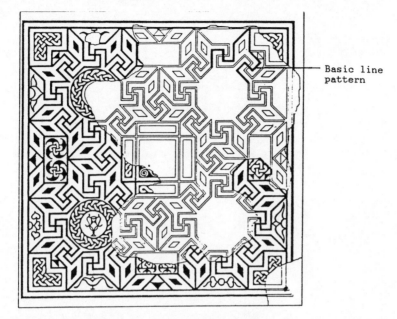

*Figure 10.3 - **The Second Century Roman mosaic pavement***

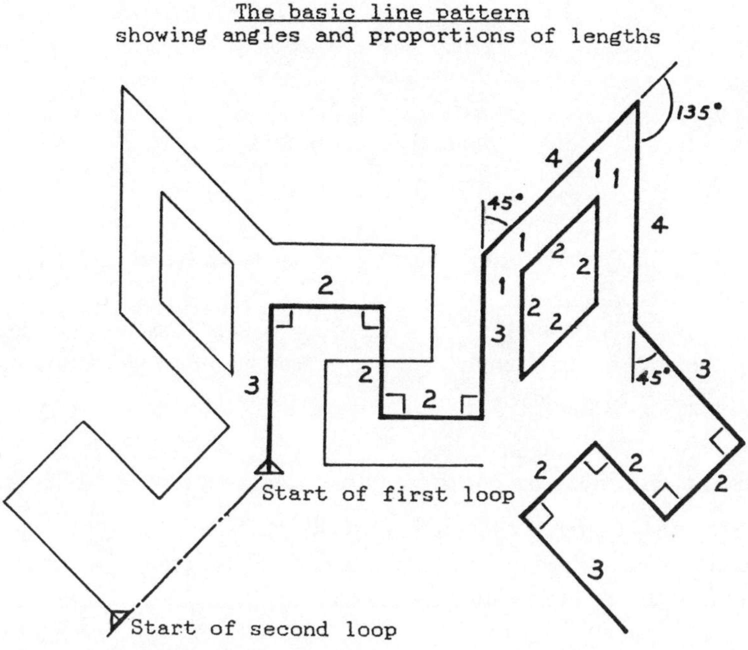

The basic line pattern
showing angles and proportions of lengths

*Figure 10.4 - **The basic line pattern for the mosaic***

A design combining a lozenge
pattern with a continuous
meandering swastika, produced
using the program 'Dart'
The design is based on the
Roman mosaic pavement found
in the grounds of Boxmoor
House by Sir John Evans in
1852.

*Figure 10.5 - **The design produced in turtle graphics by Howard's pupils***

around five panels. Despite the deep interest this project engendered, we thought that the complete mosaic pattern might prove too complex a task for our turtle graphics!

Mathematics and computers for children with moderate learning difficulties

Pratt and Richards (1990), teaching at Glevum School for children with moderate learning difficulties, describe how they developed a maths workbook based on a funfair theme and including time and money concepts.

EXTENDING MATHEMATICS TOPIC WORK

The children use *Touch Explorer Plus*, with five levels on the file, each designed to provide as much flexibility as possible for the individual child.

1 Names of funfair rides available, to enable the child to become familiar with the vocabulary and activities available, before any mathematical demands are made of him/her.

2 Price for a single ride. Questions at this level vary from 'You may have one go on everything. How much will it cost you?' to 'You have 10p to spend. What will you go on? Will you have any money left?'

3 Price per ride and the time taken. For example: 'Helter Skelter. 4p a go. It takes 2 minutes.' Questions relate to either time or money, but the pupil must extract the relevant information from each message in order to answer the specific question. For example, 'You are going to the fair at 6 o'clock. If you go on all the rides, what time will you leave?' requires the pupil to ignore the references to money in the messages and extract the information relating to time.

4 More complex instructions. For example, 'You may go on 4 rides. How much will it cost? How long will it take you?'

5 More complex instructions still! For example, 'You have been dropped at the fair at 7.00 and you will be picked up at 8.30. You have £3.00 to spend. What do you do in this time?'

Levels 4 and 5 contain a series of events which take place during his/her visit to the fair. For example, 'It cost 18p for 3 darts. You get one stuck in your finger and have to go to the First Aid tent. It takes 20 minutes to bandage you up.' The pupil builds up his or her own story of the evening's events:

You may go on 4 rides.

How much will it cost?

How long will it take you?

Dodgem Cars: 12p a go. It takes 8 minutes.

Ghost Train: 20p a go. You have to wait for a train, so it takes 12 minutes.

Big Wheel: 15p a go. It takes 5 minutes.

Swings: 15p a go. It takes 6 minutes.

It will cost me 62p and it will take 31 minutes.

This work with *Touch Explorer Plus* and the overlays was combined with worksheet and other activities, off the computer. Some of the children had difficulties with problems in the program – to some extent the program is

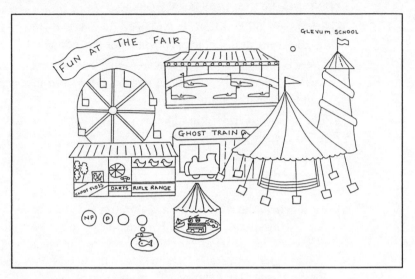

*Figure 10.6 - **Fun at the Fair overlay***

diagnostic – but most worked satisfactorily towards the Mathematics Attainment Targets 1 (levels 1–3), 6 (levels 2 and 3) and 8 (level 2b).

At a slightly lower level, *Count With Blob* provides number activities for young children who can only use switches or a Concept Keyboard or Touch Screen. They may learn to count up to nine. The program displays pictures of different kinds of transport or animals, with the relevant numbers or on their own. It leads on to sorting and counting activities. Finally, it presents a shopping scenario: the child buys items listed, by sight or from memory, and these are moved from the 'shelf' to a 'basket' at the foot of the screen. The child has to count those bought before sending the basket to the checkout.

Number skills and daily experience for Further Education students

For Further Education students with learning difficulties, linking number skills to daily experience is essential, as Fowler (1988) concludes from a project in Further Education. He suggests that they need for a clear purpose, which should be linked to daily experience. This approach is illustrated by Holliday (1987), who integrated the computer into assignments about money:

SPECIAL COINS

Once we began to use the *Coins* program, the lecturers were generally surprised to find that many of our students appear to have little true understanding of money and poor ideas of financial management. They had assumed that the more independent students who regularly travelled and shopped alone were aware of the transactions taking place but it soon became apparent that many were relying upon being given the correct money and the total honesty of shopkeepers.

We decided that one group of students should undertake some shopping assignments. Daily visits to shops started, with an emphasis on students checking their change and ensuring that they understood what change they had received and why. Students visited a local cafe where they paid for their meals. For some of the more able students, we created bank accounts using *Bank*. This was an important activity because it was the local council's policy to pay YTS students through a bank account, and other students received social security payments in the same way.

Summary

These few examples show how children with learning difficulties can be helped by computers to learn mathematics. The pupils clearly find turtles very useful, on the floor or the screen. Howard's work is an outstanding instance of students developing their work to a high standard. The Concept Keyboard and *Touch Explorer Plus* again came into their own at Glevum. Lastly, older students in Further Education got to grips with money with the help of two programs.

11 Musical Appreciation and Skills

Gaining access to the music curriculum

How can computers help students with learning difficulties to gain access to the music curriculum, to develop musical appreciation and skills? The latest music technology, linked to computers, makes possible much that was impossible for them before. There is certainly evidence that even profoundly and multiply-handicapped children can benefit from using computers and related equipment to explore, experiment with and create sounds and music. At this basic level, the children are not being 'taught music' in any conventional sense, but they learn much that is valuable to them. Haigh (1991) describes his work with two such children at The Park Special School, Wakefield.

MUSIC REACHES SIMON AND NAHEED

We offered Simon and Naheed opportunities to explore a microworld created by the program *Soundspace*. We ran the program in a computer fitted with a Touch Screen and linked to a Hybrid synthesiser.

The children soon discovered cause-and-effect relationships in producing and modifying sounds: touching the screen produces a sound through the synthesiser. Moving a finger, fingers or even the whole hand over the touchscreen modifies the pitch. Different parts of the screen can be programmed to produce different sounds for the children to investigate. These can be changed easily by the teacher from musical sounds such as organ notes or bells to eerie whistling winds or space rocket noises. The children can also create their own sounds with the system. By touching the four coloured areas at the bottom of the screen, sounds can be changed. New sounds can be stored.

Simon and Naheed both found the sounds very satisfying, to judge from the unusually long time they concentrated on the task in hand. Simon kept at it for more than half an hour at a time. This represented something of a breakthrough in overcoming his passive approach to his surroundings. Naheed wants to share the microworld with Simon: after she has had a turn at creating sounds, she waits for him to try, beckoning him to touch the screen. It is hard to find other experiences that stimulate social interaction between them as effectively.

Children with moderate learning difficulties can move quite quickly towards use of computers for learning something about music. Haigh (1991) also reports that children at The Priory Special School in Crofton, Wakefield, wrote music with *Compose* for a hymn to be sung in school assembly. The Special Needs version of the program contains a simple music-maker. Each picture displayed on the screen represents a short sequence of notes, therefore children do not need to learn musical notation in order to make music.

ALLELUIA! MORNING HYMN AT THE PRIORY

The children worked closely together to prepare the tune and lyrics. Here are the words of the hymn, Alleluia:

> *Sing out, sing this morning,*
> *Praise the Lord,*
> *Alleluia, Alleluia,*
> *Alleluia, Alleluia,*
> *God is love,*
> *God is love.*
>
> *Sing out, sing this morning,*
> *Praise the Lord,*
> *Alleluia, Alleluia,*
> *Alleluia, Alleluia,*
> *God is love,*
> *God is love,*
> *Sing his praise,*
> *Amen.*

Compose contains 'tune files' consisting of short musical phrases that can be linked into tunes. Each short phrase is represented by a picture or symbol on the screen. The children listened to the phrases, selected the ones they wanted, to match the words, and inserted them in a grid on the screen to form the tune for the hymn. Just as if they were using a simple wordprocessor, they could alter the sequence and/or insert different phrases. They could also change the speed for playback.

The children were thrilled to be asked to demonstrate their composition to a group of 40 teachers, and in doing so showed they had developed technical skills and powers of concentration. They had soon learned how to load the program, moving quickly through the on-screen menus to call up and modify the piece. They co-operated well, and their success improved their self-image.

Haigh does not claim that *Compose* is the best way to teach music, but he does see such experiences as being invaluable for the children concerned. The program introduces them to the idea of composing music, despite their limited knowledge and skills, and they can hear their own composition. From such beginnings, these children are keen to move from computer music to proper instruments, as their teacher found when she showed them how to play synthesisers.

Similarly, Taylor (1988), a teacher at Claremont School near Bristol, tried *Compose* with a class of physically-disabled children aged 8–10 years. Their disabilities include motor impairment of one or both hands, poor sight and cognitive difficulties of keeping rhythm and sequencing.

MUSIC MAKING WITH *COMPOSE* AT CLAREMONT SCHOOL

My class was lucky enough to have a weekly music lesson from one of Avon's leading advisory teachers, to whom they owe their interest and enthusiasm. Their ability to participate actively is limited and has consisted chiefly of singing and using untuned percussion, which they enjoyed to some extent. It left much to be desired in performance satisfaction and in overall control by the children of what they were attempting.

The children were all familiar with the BBC computer (we have one for the class's sole use) and when I introduced *Compose* most of them quickly learned how to use the program's facilities. Initially I tried it with the whole class of nine children. They were enthusiastic from the start, deciding whether phrases were beginning, middle or finishing tunes, tapping the rhythm where possible, fitting in words or sounds with the same rhythm, adjusting the speed and discussing the results. Collectively, they put phrases together, recorded and amplified the results, adding words, untuned percussion accompaniment and, where applicable, hand chimes and/or chime bar on the pentatonic scale.

From then on, small groups or individuals spent all their free time (and some class time) working on the program. They discussed and made up songs, fitted accompaniments and performed to anyone who would listen. Their music advisory teacher gave enthusiastic help and support in suggesting further uses of the program and by writing piano accompaniments for the children's compositions. The modified program using one or two switch entry has made *Compose* available to even the very severely physically-disabled children, to their great joy.

I feel that *Compose* has provided opportunities for this group of children to experience music making and performing which would otherwise be denied them, and being a non-specialist music enthusiast myself, even I can join in the fun.

From Cleveland, Stansfield (1991) reports that computer-related technology for teaching music has been introduced into many schools and is used successfully by pupils with special needs.

MUSIC AND COMPUTERS MEET SPECIAL NEEDS IN CLEVELAND SCHOOLS

The music IT advisory teacher is based at Gillbrook School, a comprehensive for children aged 11–16, in which special needs children work alongside the others and enjoy succeeding in a non-verbal activity. The school has an exceptionally well equipped music centre, used for in-service training of teachers as well as by the children.

Sarah Metcalfe School, another comprehensive, has an unusually high proportion of special needs pupils, including 42 with Statements. The music teacher is very enthusiastic and has acquired a music laboratory with 8 assorted computers and synthesisers. The special needs pupils work in a small group with him and a support teacher, using the same equipment as the others to explore sounds and sequences, and to make their own music, using *Compose*.

Tollesby, a secondary school for pupils with learning difficulties, has a long musical tradition. When the school was larger, before many pupils were integrated into mainstream schools nearby, the whole school was involved each year in a musical production. This sort of event is no longer feasible, but the children now have access to a well-equipped synthesiser laboratory, with an electric guitar and 6 Yamaha machines which include a sound sampler, voice banks, voice editor and drum pad. The children can mix their efforts on a Porta Two High Speed Ministudio with a Phillips MIDI system and record the results on tape. They can also try playing a large synthesiser, the electric guitar and the drum machine. Among the children aged 11–14, the least able group has regular classes in this laboratory with the music teacher, who has support from another musical teacher. All the children work individually or in pairs to produce music for a theme. This may be mood music or theme music for a film. The whole group listens to each contribution. Some pieces are mixed, if appropriate, with the Ministudio.

It is clear from these examples that some specialised equipment may be necessary. For example, a MIDI (Musical Instrument Digital Interface) transfers data from a computer to an instrument (or microphone) and vice versa. It is either an interface card or an external box, produced to match a particular model of computer. With a MIDI, the music teacher can choose a number of different timbres, depending on the synthesiser in use. Synthesisers are sound-producing units which control pitch, volume, duration and timbre, thus simulating sounds of instruments or even creating new sounds. Many have a piano-type keyboard. A tone generator is a specialised synthesiser, without a keyboard. A sound mixer controls volume and coordinates signals from two or more sources. A sequencer controls and sequences signals produced by a synthesiser. Digital sequencers can store pitches and rhythm patterns from a source such as a synthesiser.

Music as a vehicle for broader aims

At Clarendon School, Hampton, the aims were wider than using information technology to give pupils with moderate learning difficulties access to successful experience of musical creation and composition. The staff wanted to attract the interest of a nearby mainstream school by giving ordinary pupils a chance to enhance their musical skills within Clarendon, thus improving opportunities for integration of Clarendon's pupils and the others, as Mansfield (1991) describes. At the same time, the staff hoped to realise the musical talents of their pupils. The shared curriculum planning and teaching would be beneficial to staff from all the schools. As teachers of music without having been trained to teach it, they would enhance their professional development in their field while gaining confidence in how to give access to the music curriculum to all pupils, ordinary and special.

ACCESSING THE MUSIC CURRICULUM AT CLARENDON – WITH INTEGRATION

Many children at Clarendon and at the mainstream school seemed to be very keen, and were uninhibited about musical expression of all forms. We were amazed at their ability to concentrate and coordinate brain and limbs in complicated percussion rhythms, though the children themselves did not consider these to be 'real music'. They wanted to play keyboards, recorders, guitar and drums. Some pupils were motivated enough to spend their own time learning something of the language of music and the skills necessary to create it. They begged to be taught more, and constantly wanted access to the instruments and to the new high-tech music sequencer.

We really had to get a professional musician, because none of us were specifically trained to teach music or to use the 24-track recording and sequencing equipment. We lacked confidence in our ability to meet the pupils' musical needs. We needed a trained musician, a composer and keyboard player who could teach pupils at very different levels how to use the electronic equipment. Through a friend of the school we were fortunate to obtain the help of Sandy Lowenthal, an ex-music teacher and professional composer and performer. Initially, he helped voluntarily, but later funds for a two-year project came from the Performing Rights Society's Composers in Education Project and the Arts Council.

The 24-track equipment was purchased as part of our TVEI project, to assist pupils in accessing the music curriculum. Our intention was to capitalise on the good work they had already done on rhythm and pitch. We bought a Yamaha DX7 keyboard, its basic instrument range supplemented with sound cartridges for special effects, and a Roland MT32 multi-timbrel device to enhance the range and quality of sounds and to enable the 24 tracks to store the widest possible range of instrument sounds. We linked these to an Atari 1040 computer, with a high resolution Atari monochrome screen. The software, chosen with the help of the Gateway Recording Studio based at Kingston Polytechnic, is the *Pro 24* system.

At first, the children eagerly used the equipment to experiment with sounds. Motorcycles raced down the street, birds tweeted and bombs exploded. Sounds of the tropical jungle came next. With Sandy's help, some children became skilful enough to paint pictures in sound. They created a musical scene by overlaying different sounds on the tracks and synchronising the effects. Older pupils wanted to emulate Christmas carols and assembly songs, and went to great pains to recreate, note by note, their favourite jingles, adding percussion and speeding up their final compositions. Five verses posed no problems: with the computer they could repeat and copy phrases, cut and paste, and edit until they were satisfied.

The pupils' interest in music and IT became frenetic. Some pupils learned how to read musical notation and transcribed songs into the sequencer, note by note. Others preferred the 'play-by-ear method' and practised until they had perfected chords and small sections of melody. These sounds were then linked into a complete composition and recorded directly onto a tape, using Clarendon's tape deck, and played back through its amplifier. The children thus had high quality recordings to take home for parents to hear, plus copies stored for inclusion in their Records of Achievement.

Two pupils bought themselves keyboards, computers and sequencing software, and practised at home. In due course, they gave live performances on the school piano and the Yamaha keyboard, without having been taught more than the basic notes. Other pupils learned how to take the equipment apart and re-assemble it in the school hall for concerts. Some pupils used the high quality recording to enhance their own singing – much better than the poor piano accompaniment supplied by our headteacher! This activity culminated in a Christmas concert at which much of the music for the choir was recorded on and played through the sequencer by a previously non-musical pupil. The sense of achievement was electric for all the children involved.

The mainstream school staff became very interested when two of their pupils took the equipment home for a few days over half-term and completed the composition element of their GCSE in Music. Both were awarded 90% in their final exam. We agreed that the equipment should be moved temporarily to that school. Sandy Lowenthal began instructing its staff and pupils. Classes from the special school were timetabled into the ordinary Year 8 music classes.

By January 1991, links with the mainstream school had grown to include an integrated activity each day of the week, with joint music lessons in Years 8–11. A side-effect has been integration links in Design Technology, Mathematics, Art, Child Development and Home Economics for individual pupils and groups from Clarendon. When the project formally ends, staff will have acquired sufficient skills and knowledge to continue with confidence the joint musical and other activities.

Incidentally, *Pro12* can make life easier for children and teachers than *Pro24*. It has only twelve recording tracks, but pupils seldom want more than eight. Its simpler set of editing procedures and screen display may suit some with learning difficulties better than *Pro24*.

Music to deaf ears

Fawkes (1988) reports how computers are used to teach musical appreciation and skills at the Mary Hare Grammar School for the Deaf, near Newbury. His methods of teaching music to deaf children include developing a strong rhythmic sense through bodily movement, followed by gradually harnessing this sense to playing first percussion and then pitched instruments. He introduced some of his students to an IBM PC linked to a MIDI SAS Piano, with a suite of programs providing a musical Keyboard Fundamentals course.

KEYBOARD SKILLS AND THEORY: JANET TRIES ON HER OWN

Janet is a fifth former with severe hearing loss, who plays the recorder very well. Janet wanted to know something about keyboard playing and more music theory before she left school. Her notes after using Lesson 1 read 'Learnt first five notes by ear and a bit by fingering. Learnt to be able to recognise the notes by listening, before could only do it by reading the notes. Good for learning keys on the keyboard.' Janet discovered that by using her residual hearing through her hearing aids more acutely, she could distinguish the pitch of notes more accurately than before. In her recorder playing, she had, it seems, relied more on her ability to read the notation on the score than on actually listening to her maximum ability.

After Lessons 2 and 3, Janet wrote: 'Helps to learn the keyboard and makes me distinguish the notes. (I) always get E and F wrong and D and C. Have to keep repeating the time and play keyboard with it to get the right notes and then remember them! Is this cheating?' Such frequent practice, far from being cheating, is highly desirable, but only a computer would have the time and patience to provide it. Janet's problems of distinguishing the difference in pitch between neighbouring notes, particularly semi-tones, were only to be expected because of her hearing problems. She did not completely succeed in overcoming them, but at least she had gained access to another part of the curriculum.

Many of Fawkes' students used the system, to which he connected a powerful amplifier to enable more children to hear the programs' quieter kinds of sounds, such as the rhythmic 'clicks' in exercises on note values. The software was not written with deaf children in mind.

Music composition for blind students

The study of music often requires preparation of scores using conventional staff notation. For a blind person this is impossible without help. One method that has been adopted is to compose music in braille on a manual embosser which can then be passed to a sighted person to transcribe into a print score. Although this achieves the end result, it is restrictive in terms of independence and the amount of time involved.

TALKING MUSIC

Recent research at the Open University has applied established techniques of screen reading (see Chapter 5) to the needs of blind composers, to provide facilities similar to a talking wordprocessor but with letters and words replaced by notes and groups of notes. Figure 11.1 is an example of what one blind composer has achieved. There is nothing unusual about the score. It appears to be like any other score which would only reveal its uniquness when played. It illustrates how computer technology has provided independence and equality: the fact that the score was produced by a blind person is completely disguised.

Music therapists in the United States

In the US, a new group of professionals is being trained in music therapy, much of it computer-based. Sutin (1989) stresses that there are very few professionals who are knowledgeable about both music technology and the needs of disabled students. The technology is available, the students are needy, but more teachers must be trained. Krout (1987), a leader in this quite new field, says:

With learning disabled and behaviourally handicapped students you have about 30 seconds before the student decides whether or not a program is cool. They've typically had a lot of frustration and failure in their academic subjects and are very sensitive to the possibility of it in music. If they don't hear something that sounds good right away when they first try the program, the easiest way for them to deal with their perceived failure is just to turn it off. Letting the students start with the pre-programmed songs is the best way for them to begin with successful, enjoyable sessions and to lead to interest in more complex and creative programs.

In New Jersey, the Matheny School for 75 physically-disabled students has four music therapists. Music therapy includes relaxation training, creative expression, group participation and socialisation, leisure skills and computer music. There are two Apple IIgs computers, one linked to a Casio CZ1000 synthesiser, the other to a Yamaha Sequencer. Augmentative communication devices and adaptive inputs make these accessible to most of the students. Sutin (1989) describes a typical session:

MUSIC THERAPY FOR PHYSICALLY-DISABLED PUPILS: TWO US EXAMPLES

Linda Lemmerman, a music therapist at the school, is teaching JL, who is 18 and has cerebral palsy. Onto the computer she loads *Music Construction Set*, a composition program that displays a blank music staff and a selection of music notation symbols. JL has an adaptive input, a tracking ball, that enables him to choose the symbols, write tunes and play them back. He can move the ball and click its two switches with his headpointer, when he is in the right position in his wheelchair and the ball is also positioned properly. He selects a symbol, drags it to the place he wants it to be and drops it. In a short while, he has a ten-note tune, and plays it before saving it for further work next time.

NS arrives next, and Linda introduces her to *Instant Keyboard Fun*, with which she can play about 27 different children's tunes, such as 'Jingle Bells'. The words appear on the screen: next to them are capital letters indicating the melody notes. On the keyboard, three octaves are labelled with letters too: those in the octave below middle C have a short underline, those in the octave above have a line above them. NS uses the knuckles of her right hand to press the right keys. A correctly-chosen key is highlighted in green, a wrong one in red. The tune only continues to play when she hits the right ones. At the end of the tune, the computer tells her the percentage of correct presses. To press computer keys, she has a keyguard and a wrist pointer.

Music programs not written specifically for disabled students, may be valuable to them all the same. For example, Sutin (1990) reports on *Music Shapes* and *Instant Music*, which enable students to compose and play music without learning staff

Figure 11.1 - A sample of music from a blind composer

notation but incorporating pitch, rhythm and form. In using *Music Shapes* students move through a 'house', starting in the foyer, where they can choose one from seven boxes, Pitch, Time, Sound, Wave, Flips, Shelves and Save. Pitch leads to the Pitch Room, where they choose pitches for a sequence of seven tones (a 'shape' or tune) and play and/or store the tune. The Time Room deals with duration, Sound with timbre, Wave with harmonics and intensity. In Shelves they find a way of assembling the shapes into a composition and playing it. There are some pre-programmed tunes to give them the idea. *Instant Music* limits student creativity by providing pre-programmed tunes only. For each, students can change volume, tempo and instrumentation. By using the mouse, they can improvise to some extent. In *Music Studio* they can use either staff notation or paintbox. With the latter, they choose a colour to represent an instrument and paint a 'music picture' on the staff, using a long or short box to control duration. Again, there are pre-programmed tunes as examples to copy.

Music teachers wishing to use computer programs to help students with special educational needs usually have to rely, as Krout (1987) points out, on personal experience in deciding whether a particular program is suitable. Attractive screen graphics are often valuable in holding students' attention, but the level of complexity should suit the individual. Children with learning difficulties can be distracted by extraneous graphics, text, blinks and beeps. The program's method of responding to learners' mistakes may be very important. Some programs provide feedback through graphics (happy face), text or sounds only when correct answers are given. Others respond to mistakes as well. Programs which make music use it as their feedback, but do not necessarily indicate when mistakes are made and what they are. Novices, in particular, may be unaware of their errors.

Summary

This chapter provided examples of computer-based technology giving access to the music curriculum to children and adults with learning difficulties. These instances of good practice include work with learners with physical, sensory and cognitive difficulties. All can benefit. This is a field in which rapid advances can be expected as the technology comes down in price. Music teachers and others should quickly master the techniques.

12   Work Skills

Literacy, an essential work skill

In our earlier chapters on reading and writing we wrote mainly about children. For adults, being able to read and write is very important. Literacy is possibly the most essential work skill. Being able to complete written tasks is a matter of attitude as well as skill, and computers can help, as Wood (1990a) reports:

SUCCESS AT LAST!

Mark is 17 yrs old and joined the Multiskills Course at Derby College straight from a local special school. His numeracy and literacy are adequate, but in them and everything else he rarely attains the level of which he is capable. Mark is shy, has a very poor self image, and is totally lacking in self confidence. Perhaps Mark is also lazy, but it is difficult to assess exactly what is laziness and what is lack of confidence.

When given any task he stops before each new step and sit quietly waiting for a member of staff or another student to take him through it. Working with computers, it was a standing joke among the students that Mark never finished in the allotted time. He was intimidated by the technology, and was too 'frightened' to do anything other than enter text on his own. He would sit waiting for other students to tell him which keys to press next. All too often, just before the end of the lesson he would 'accidentally' knock the BREAK key, losing what little he had achieved.

For Mark's first attempt at using *Pendown*, I asked him to write about his time at college. He was much less intimidated by this program than by *Wordwise* and his confidence began to increase. As a result, he began to work faster and concentrate more. As the quantity of work increased, Mark became more and more enthused over his achievement. At this stage, the only thing he knew about the program was how to delete and insert. There was nothing to intimidate him, and he was free to concentrate on his writing.

After he had completed about twenty lines – an epic for Mark – I showed him how to use the dictionary facility. Once it had been pointed out to him that pressing the ESCAPE key at any time would take him back to his writing, no matter what sort of tangle he thought he had got himself into, his initial fears were overcome, and he began to use this facility with some confidence.

On its completion, Mark was delighted with his work. Because correcting on a wordprocessor is a positive rather than a negative process, he was happy to go through it correcting mistakes and making it as perfect as possible. When this was done, I took him step by step through saving, printing the title in large fonts and printing the rest of his work. Although simple, this for Mark was a very involved process. On obtaining the printout, I told him that this copy was mine, and if he wanted one for himself, he would have to repeat the process again. Mark's desire for a record of his work overcame his fear of the computer, and after very little hesitation (when it became clear that no one was going to help him) he went ahead and produced his own copy.

Successful completion of this work represented a real breakthrough for Mark. For the first time he had finished a piece of work almost totally by himself of which he was extremely proud. The quality of the printout helped considerably. His concept of his own ability enormously increased and manifested itself throughout all his work at college. He began to ask to go to the computer to do some writing, confident of his own ability to produce results. To my knowledge, this was the first time Mark had ever asked to do anything.

Learning about computerised databases

Accessing databases and computerised library listings for industrial and commercial purposes can be a valuable work skill. We found several examples of older children with special needs being taught to create and search such databases. Teachers often introduce computerised databases to extend teaching of mathematical topics, but like wordprocessing programs they can be used across the curriculum, particularly to sort and display information. Database programs usually include software for generating bar and pie charts, which help learners to identify trends and relationships as well as teaching them additional work skills.

At Boxmoor House School, Howard (1991) found that databases were particularly successful in motivating older boys with emotional difficulties to explore mathematical topics. It would have been difficult for them to achieve work of such quality without the computer. The boys collected information, organised it into fields, entered it as data into the *Quest* database program and then carried out their analyses, often using *Junior Ecosoft* for drawing charts. Some needed help in setting up fields in *Quest*, but could enter, sort and print out the data fairly easily.

THE CARS DATABASE

Matthew was not a very productive worker and needed to be motivated. He did have a strong interest in cars, however, and decided he would construct a database to compare the performances of 30 different cars. He spent a lot of time digging in motoring magazines for the figures. With a little help at first in setting up the database, for which he chose the fields, he was soon entering records and correcting his errors without difficulty.

Once the database was complete, he sorted the data to obtain lists of cars rank ordered by engine capacity, top speed, acceleration and fuel consumption. The next stage was to choose a field, top speed, to compare with the others. He sorted the records and obtained lists of capacity, fuel consumption and acceleration, relative to top speed.

Matthew found the lists of numbers difficult to interpret, so he transferred the data into bar charts and by studying these he drew three conclusions. If the top speed of a car is higher, then it is probably of higher engine capacity, uses more fuel, and has better acceleration, though only up to a certain point. He noticed some irregularities which I encouraged him to explain. Throughout the project, Matthew was able to prove to others and, perhaps more importantly, to himself, that he was capable of producing work of a high standard.

NAME	COUNTRY	ARMAMENT	SPEED	RANGE	WEIGHT	DATE	CREW
CENTURION	U.K.	105mm	34.6km/h	190km	51820kg	1949	4
T-62	U.S.S.R.	115mm	45.5km/h	450km	40000kg	1963	4
TYPE 61	Japan	90mm	45km/h	200km	35000kg	1962	4
MERKAVA 1	Israel	105mm	45km/h	500km	58000kg	1978	4
T-54/T-55	U.S.S.R.	100mm	48km/h	400km	36000kg	1950	4
M484A5	U.S.A.	105mm	48km/h	463km	48989kg	1952	4
M.60	U.S.A.	105mm	48km/h	500km	48987kg	1960	4
CHIEFTAIN FV4 201	U.K.	120mm	48km/h	450km	55000kg	1967	4
STRIDSVAGN (S) 103	Sweden	105mm	50km/h	390km	39000kg	1966	3
TYPE 74	Japan	105mm	53km/h	300km	38000kg	1973	4
PZ 68	Switzerland	105mm	55km/h	300km	39700kg	1971	4
Vickers	U.K.	105mm	56km/h	480km	38600kg	1965	4
CHALLENGER	U.K.	120mm	56km/h		60000kg	1984	4
AMX 32	France	105mm	65km/h	530km	38000kg	1979	4
AMX 30	France	105mm	65km/h	600km	36000kg	1967	4
LEOPARD 1	W.Germany	105mm	65km/h	600km	40000kg	1965	4
OF-40	Italy	105mm	65km/h	600km	43000kg	N.A.	4
LEOPARD 2	W.Germany	120mm	68km/h	500km	55000kg	1980	4
ABRAMS XM1	U.S.A.	105mm	72.4km/h	450km	53390kg	1980	4
T-64 & T-72	U.S.S.R.	125mm	80km/h	500km	41000kg	1972	3

Figure 12.1 - Jason looked critically at armoured fighting vehicles

THE TANKS DATABASE

Another boy, Jason, was very interested in armoured fighting vehicles. Normally he was not a very productive or neat worker, but he became enthusiastic about this project and took great trouble to present his work well.

He had to obtain a complete set of data for each type of vehicle, for each record, and his search took him to many different sources such as books and magazines, including those in the local public library. Without the facilities offered by the computer, Jason would have found very daunting the task of sorting, listing and plotting his information. Instead, he fed the data into *Quest*, and soon produced a table of results (see Fig. 12.1) and related charts. He discussed the reasons for similarities and differences in these, and looked more deeply and critically at data on armoured fighting vehicles than he would usually be expected to.

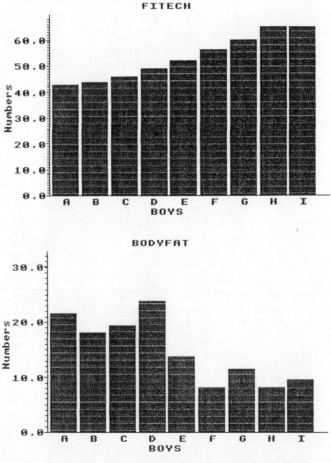

Figure 12.2 - The four with the most bodyfat were the least fit!

THE PHYSICAL EDUCATION DATABASE

During their physical education sessions, nine Year 10 boys measured their height, weight, span, heartrate and amount of bodyfat. They entered the data into *Quest* and sorted it to obtain rank order lists for each of these attributes. From these, with *Junior Ecosoft* they generated two charts, FITECH and BODY-FAT, on fitness and bodyfat (see Fig. 12.2). The boys could easily understand from the charts that the four with most bodyfat were the least fit. Discussion of the charts led to renewed enthusiasm to keep fit and watch their diet!

PAUL'S PIE CHART

Paul, in Year 10, had little confidence in his own ability and easily became disheartened. His teachers found him hard to motivate. He was interested in motor bikes, not much else. Fortunately, the boys collected old newspapers each week and among these was 'Motor Cycle International'. I asked him to look for the specifications of over 100 different motor cycle models, to analyse the distribution of the number of cylinders they had. This task appealed to him, though he needed some encouragement to keep at it.

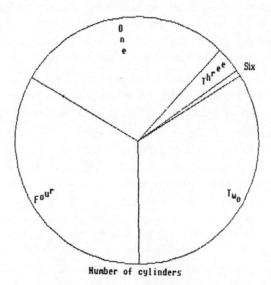

Pie chart showing the distribution of the number of cylinders motor bikes have

Figure 12.3 - Paul's pie chart for 100 different motorcycles

When it came to displaying the results, Paul's poor mathematical and manipulative skills presented difficulties and he wanted to give up. Instead, he found he could manage *Junior Ecosoft* quite easily. He entered his data and obtained a pie chart (see Fig. 12.3), which he was able to interpret. It turned out to be a useful and presentable piece of work, and he rightly saw it as quite an achievement.

Mansfield (1991) describes two interesting projects at a special school for children with moderate learning difficulties. The second had an immediate and direct impact at work for one pupil:

SEARCHING THE *DOMESDAY DISC*

As part of the school's information technology awareness work in the Leavers' Programme, our pupils looked into how data was stored on and retrieved from interactive videodiscs. We placed a BBC Master, with the laserdisc player and the *Domesday Disc*, in the front entrance of the school. On it was a sign saying 'Please Touch'. We did not expect the pupils to find it easy to access the system, but by lunchtime on the first day, two had mastered the software sufficiently to show it to six others. After two days the whole of the upper school of 40 pupils could use the equipment to some degree. Without instruction, they had discovered how to access the second side of the two discs so that they could interrogate the computer about their home town.

We moved the equipment to the Leavers' Room, and asked the children to complete various search tasks. At the end of a fortnight we tested every pupil, and almost all could find photographs of their own and other towns in the UK on the disc. Their geographical skills and understanding had improved.

The Leavers were given the *Ecodisc*, which allows them to explore the environment of a real nature reserve in Dorset. They can examine the flora and fauna and call up essential information. A video guide asks them to manage the reserve by making decisions regarding activities in it. Their decision-making is converted into realistic outcomes illustrated by video and computer graphs. We found that they soon learned how to change their actions to achieve greater productivity of the reserve or to please the fishermen and sailors. Almost incidentally, they learned to estimate, measure, read a map, identify a wide range of wildlife and understand information presented in graphs and charts. There was a speedy and enormous increase in their environmental knowledge.

The pupils were motivated by having access to such interesting data and they persevered in their co-operative problem-solving. The teachers, however, felt vulnerable in their role as facilitators because they were less able to measure outcomes against their own inputs. They were also less capable and more tentative than many pupils when using the equipment: they had to ask pupils to help them in setting it up and conducting searches for others. Pupils showed remarkable initiative with the equipment.

CREATING YOUR OWN DATABASE

We invited pupils to prepare a questionnaire for staff to answer about their cars. What make of car? Colour, number of doors, engine size, fuel consumption, and so on?

The pupils entered the data into the *Grasshopper* database program. They were shown how to interrogate the database and produce various graphs and charts. To our surprise, pupils who had been unable to understand graphs gained sudden insight into them by using the database they had created.

The final convincer came later. One of the pupils, Mark, was sent on a two-week work experience placement at Euro-Quik-Fit. He was on his own when a customer came in wanting an exhaust for his ageing Vauxhall. With great confidence Mark tapped the request into the store's computer and located the correct part. Afterwards, the mechanic expressed surprise at Mark's initiative and how quickly he had mastered the firm's database.

Spreading spreadsheets across the curriculum

Spreadsheets are programs for organising numerical data. Columns and rows of figures can be entered and manipulated. By applying formulae, calculations can be performed. Bar charts, pie charts and scattergrams can usually be produced direct from the data. Spreadsheets are widely used by industry, commerce and government for planning, statistics and accounting.

Howard (1991), again teaching older children with emotional and behavioural problems at Boxmoor House School, introduces spreadsheets across the curriculum, thereby equipping his pupils with skills of potential value in the workplace:

COSTING CORNFLAKES IN HEMEL HEMPSTEAD

When *Grasshopper* was introduced into Boxmoor House School, the children rapidly rated it as second only to the wordprocessing programs in its usefulness! It was soon helping them to manipulate numbers and perform repetitive calculations. They could readily check their entries from the screen or printouts. They found it easy to understand the display, and liked generating bar charts and scattergrams, presenting their results in pictorial form.

Of course, they needed to understand what they were doing. To construct the formulae, they had to be familiar with the relationships between sets of data, in terms of basic arithmetical operations. They had to learn the peculiarities of the computer, such as substituting * for x when multiplying. Actually, I think these emphasised, reinforced, even introduced certain concepts.

Soon some pupils could use *Grasshopper* on their own, others with a little help, especially with initial layout and constructing the formulae. Generally, they had few difficulties in transferring their knowledge to subsequent exercises.

A small group of Year 11 boys toured the town's major food stores collecting data on the brand, size and price of packets of cornflakes. They had to find the most economical brands and packet sizes, and identify any trends in the relationship between price and quantity, using the unit cost per 100g of corn-flakes.

With information to hand, the boys organised it with the spreadsheet. The concept of unit cost was new to them, but once they understood it they constructed a formula and carried out the calculations via the spreadsheet. They rank ordered the calculated values and put them into a bar chart comparing unit cost and a scattergram showing unit cost against quantity. Then they successfully determined the trends and drew conclusions. This is what they wrote:

> The results show the cheapest buy
> to be a 500g Sunblest packet(13.4p
> per 100g) from Gateway. The
> dearest, also from Gateway, a 250g
> Kellogg's packet(30p per 100g).
> Stores own brands are cheaper than
> Kellogg's.
> The scattergram shows that in
> general larger packets have a
> cheaper unit cost.
> The bar chart shows there is not a
> lot of difference between the unit
> costs for 750g and 500g packets.
> There is more difference and the
> unit costs are much higher for the
> smaller 375g and 250g packets.
> There is not much difference in
> taste. People often buy brands when
> there is a special offer or free gift.
>
> By Paul L.
> Chris and
> Paul Q.

The boys at Howard's school also used spreadsheets in science lessons when handling the results of experiments. For example, pupils investigating the density of materials gained time to study a wider range of materials, because the spreadsheet speeded up calculations and presentation of their results. They were better motivated, too, and showed improved concentration.

Even in physical education, spreadsheets came into play, according to Howard.

THE SERGEANT JUMP: A SPREADSHEET-BASED STUDY

Our Year 10 and 11 boys investigated whether there was any relationship between the height jumped and the pupil's weight. They fed data into the spreadsheet and were keen to see their results on bar chart and scattergram. Each compared his performance against the others'. They used the scattergram (see Fig. 12.4) to identify an optimum weight for achieving the highest jump.

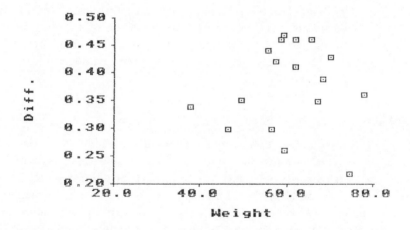

Scattergram of Diff. and Weight showing that boys with greatest Diff. value weigh between about 55 & 65 kg.

*Figure 12.4 - **The sergeant jump***

Computer aided drawing

According to Brown and others (1989), out of 12 working people in the US, one is disabled. A similar figure applies in the UK. Some physically-disabled people are remarkably successful in learning to use a computer aided drawing or designing system. Without full use of their limbs, they can operate the system to produce drawings and designs of the same high quality as able-bodied workers. Brown and others (1989) mention the case of Robert, still at college, and Scott (1989) reports another US example from New Jersey.

COMPUTER-AIDED DRAWING FOR PHYSICALLY-DISABLED ADULTS

Robert, a Californian college student, is a quadriplegic with no functional use of his hands. He learned to use *MindReader*, a predicting wordprocessing program which doubled his writing speed and improved his accuracy too. He then learned to use a computer-assisted design (CAD) program, and says he can now draw plans more easily and faster than when he had full use of his arms and hands. He is learning architectural drafting using the CAD program, and expects to acquire a marketable skill.

At Morris County Community College in New Jersey, physically-disabled students successfully learn computer-aided drawing. Out of the College's 15 workstations for drawing, five are reserved for these students, each of whom has adaptive devices as required, such as a puff-and-sip switch or head pointer. One student with cerebral palsy invented a replacement for the mouse: it has two wheels, one for horizontal cursor movement, the other for vertical, and he can spin them with his head pointer. Disabled students from this course have gone on to study for engineering degrees or moved into computer-related careers.

Control technology

It seems unlikely that many learners with cognitive difficulties can understand modern office and factory automation, a possibly important work 'skill'. Despite this, they can be introduced to control technology. Drage (1990) describes how computer-based control technology is taught at St. John's School, Bedford, which serves 3–19 year-old children with severe learning difficulties. The school's IT coordinator, Myles Pilling, wanted to contribute to the theme of Moving, being studied by all the children, and chose machines as his focus.

INTRODUCING CHILDREN WITH SPECIAL NEEDS TO CONTROL TECHNOLOGY

The method included a challenge (one short sentence), a problem-solving activity, a record of the results usually with *Folio* for wordprocessing or by diagrams and drawings, and lastly an exhibition of the challenges and results with the materials the children had used. Here are two typical challenges:

Robots

1 Make a robot come towards you using either Micro-Mike or a joystick.

2 Make the robot knock down a tower of bricks.

3 Help the robot find its home.

4 Make the robot draw a straight line, a zigzag and a square.

Equipment: BBC computer, floor turtle, nudge/trundle, joystick, Micro-Mike.

Control Technology

1 Make the Lego buggy move the board. Find the correct number to do it.

2 Find a use for a light bulb and an electric motor.

3 Design a fairground ride using Lego lights and motor. Make the light signal when it's stopped. Make the ride safe by keeping the speed low using the Wait command.

*Equipment: BBC computer, Primary Control Box, **Contact**, leads, light bulb, electric motor, light sensor, Lego buggy, Lego Technic.*

How did it turn out? The middle age group (7–13 years old) looked at control with the Lego buggy. One group discussed the reasons why the wheels turned and subsequently examined the cogs and gearing system. Using *Contact,* the commands Switchon and Switchoff were introduced in the context of how a light switch works.

Then a prepared program with a one letter title (only one key press required) was made and the group asked to alter the number on the Wait command which gives a pause. A game was established where the buggy had to be driven across the table or through the buggy park.

In a school where pupils find the logical thinking processes in understanding scientific concepts very difficult indeed, a great deal of stimulating and worthwhile work is going on.

Teaching problem-solving skills useful in the workplace?

Problem-solving skills are in demand in the workplace. Buckland (1991) studied the problem-solving skills of children with moderate learning difficulties. In particular, she evaluated the benefits to them of learning to solve problems using Logo and turtles (see Chapter 2 for details of her earlier work in this field).

CHILDREN IN GLEVUM LEARN PROBLEM-SOLVING WITH LOGO

If they are to learn problem-solving skills, children with learning difficulties often require extra guidance, and their teachers need a more detailed teaching strategy than is necessary with ordinary children. Such children find it hard to read, write, predict, reflect, estimate or evaluate. They lack confidence as they approach problems and expect the solutions to be difficult for them. Because they continually experience failure in learning, they develop a deep-rooted sense of inferiority and of being rejected. They have a poor self-image.

It must be wrong for teachers to reinforce in these children their negative feelings about their own worth, yet without alternative teaching strategies, teachers are likely to do so. What are these alternatives? First, they build on individual children's strengths. Second, because success is motivating, they build on success, breaking the pattern of failure and promoting a positive attitude. Third, they are challenging, stretching individual children as much as possible without risking failure and taking them to the highest possible level of problem-solving that they can achieve.

My study of problem-solving with Logo and turtles showed that very early on the children were keen to take control and devise programs. They were capable of doing so. Working mostly in pairs, they identified tasks for themselves, thus showing they could set problems. They worked with sustained interest for longer than the teachers expected. They planned, programmed (and debugged their programs) and solved their problems. Their recordings, designs and listings were of good quality. When they made mistakes, they accepted this momentary failure as a positive experience from which they could learn, because they were working under conditions where they believed they could succeed. By looking at their designs and listings, they could explain what they had done and perhaps where they had gone wrong. They were able to do this away from the computer, thus displaying their abstract reasoning abilities.

Above all, the children were proud of their achievements. They had proved they could adopt good work habits. They had revealed, to the teachers and to each other, skills that had gone unnoticed before. They had shown that they could take control of computers and solve problems with them.

Buckland's findings are all the more interesting when we compare them with the results of Krendle and Lieberman's (1988) comprehensive literature review on Logo for problem solving. They see no carryover for children in general from Logo to other kinds of problem solving. Another view comes from Mathinos (1990). Working succesfully with disabled children as well as the others, she shows that Logo gives them the chance to practice and reinforce problem-solving skills they already have. After surveying the research again, Keller (1990) says that children benefit most from Logo when they use it in structured lessons and when the teacher asks good questions. Or, as Riedl (1991) puts it: good results with Logo come from good teaching. Buckland's work seems to be successful for this reason. We must leave open the question of whether learning problem-solving at school with Logo has any impact on their abilities to solve problems at work: how could anyone prove such a link, anyway?

Learning other work-related skills

More direct access to work-related skills is needed. From Cleveland, Stansfield (1991) provides a set of examples of older children with special needs practising work skills with computers to help them.

RUNNING A CAFE BY COMPUTER, AND OTHER STORIES

At Catcote School, the older pupils, aged 15–16, run a cafe in the school with help from a teacher and outreach lecturer from the local FE College. They make their own food to sell and are taking on outside catering commissions for the Mother and Toddler Group and private parties. They have just begun to use *Datacard/Datasweet* to compile a reference system for the recipes they use. It contains data on ingredients and methods, and will be valuable to pupils who join the enterprise next year. They have also started to use *Poster* to make posters and display work.

Ormesby School is a mainstream comprehensive which has among its pupils some with physical and sensory disabilities (including blind children, and some with language and learning difficulties). In some cases, the degree of handicap is severe. A badge-making enterprise was set up by a group of Year 11 pupils, some of whom had physical disabilities. Andrew is small and frail and has cerebral palsy. He is quite able intellectually and likes using his Z88 laptop computer for written work in school and an Archimedes at home. He and two friends produced the artwork for the badges, with *ProArtisan*. To make the actual badges, physical strength is needed and was provided by other pupils, including one who has a language disability and hearing loss. Another pupil, Rebecca, set up an accounts system with *Pipedream*, an integrated package. The group designed invoices and set up a stock control system. In its first year, the enterprise was run by this group. This year, Year 10 children with learning difficulties are running it as part of a curriculum enrichment project. They design the badges with *Poster*, the choice of their teacher, who felt unable to devote the time needed to learn how to use *ProArtisan*. Recently Sharon, Kerry and Toni worked very hard to meet the deadline for an order for more than 200 badges for a local Trade Union event.

At Tollesby School, a secondary school for children with learning difficulties, pupils aged 14–16 help to run several enterprise schemes, all involving use of computers. For example, they run a tuckshop, keeping all records and accounts on a BBC computer. In horticulture, they use the computer to record price lists, write labels (with *Folio*) and keep stock lists with *View*. With the help of enterprise worksheets produced with Acorn DTP, they design logos, prepare labels and write letters. Various children have started small enterprises to do with framing pictures, or making jam or Christmas decorations. They write company reports and letters of application for jobs, all on the computer.

Tollesby is an inner city school, and has about 30 percent EBD pupils. Literacy levels have declined recently and teachers have too many non-readers. Yet these pupils will persevere for much longer periods with wordprocessing than with handwritten class work, and are less likely to tear up their work or lose their tempers when on the computer. With an eye to the world of work, Tollesby pupils wordprocess their own statements of their achievements and interests in the formal Record of Achievement which they, like all other Cleveland pupils, receive on leaving school. Their teacher only helps with spelling.

A broad approach to computerised work skills

At the Rumney College of Technology in South Glamorgan, young adults with learning difficulties take a work skills course that includes use of computers, as Jones (1990) describes:

WORK SKILLS: A COMPUTER WORKSHOP AT A COLLEGE OF FURTHER EDUCATION

Rumney College's Computer Workshop course is aimed at improving students' employment prospects. It includes work skills with particular emphasis on use of new technology and training in computer skills. Computers are used to teach literacy and numeracy and to give training in wordprocessing, database management and desktop publishing. The emphasis on employment skills is maintained by a continuous programme of work visits and work experience.

The curriculum includes computer work related as far as possible to real jobs: wordprocessing of letters and reports, desktop publishing of promotional material, leaflets and newsletters for the College and other organizations, spreadsheet production of accounts for the workshop and cooperative companies employing students from it, database management of student and course records, and of the College video and software libraries, and so on. As far as possible the work is graded to cater for a range of student abilities or is broken down into tasks so that students with different needs can work as a group. Although specific employment skills cannot always be covered within the time and resources available, the new technology does help to counteract effects of the 'handicapped' labelling. As one employer remarked, 'This person is handicapped and yet he's learning something that I don't understand?'.

The step-by-step approach of the College's training is successful in convincing employers that people with learning difficulties can make a full and useful contribution to the work force. The Computer Workshop has concentrated on greater independence through employment for people with learning difficulties but there is always a risk that students' raised expectations of getting jobs will ultimately be frustrated.

Associated with work are knowledge and skills such as those needed to travel to and from the place of work. The Special Needs Unit at Northbrook College of Design and Technology produced an interactive videodisc for adults aged 16–25 with learning difficulties (Millerchip, 1988). The aim was to produce a disc to help with problems associated with getting to and from work. The videodisc simulates transport problems such as coping with familiar and unfamiliar surroundings, map reading, timetables, using buses and related activities. It employs a game-type storyline, which can be played at different levels depending on individual needs.

Summary

Defining work skills is a controversial matter, particularly for individuals with special needs. Is it a waste of time teaching general problem-solving skills, say, that could be valuable at work for such individuals? We focussed in this chapter on examples of access to work-related skills that can be enhanced through using computers. First we dealt with teaching basic literacy. We went on to computerised databases, spreadsheets and computer aided drawing. Knowing something about control technology can be useful in the workplace, and we gave one example involving children with severe learning difficulties. Teaching problem-solving skills, a controversial area, came next followed by miscellaneous examples from Cleveland. We ended with an example of good practice in a broad programme to teach computer-based work skills.

13 Social and Life Skills

Teaching social and life skills

Social and life skills are those needed by people to cope with everyday demands. To a considerable extent in our culture, children pick them up through home and school, often without any formal teaching. Many children and adults with learning difficulties cannot do so, for various reasons. Schools and colleges therefore initiate programmes to help them. Computers give them access to this curriculum too.

For example, as many physically- and sensorily-disabled learners testify, computer technology helps to give them a sense of self-worth. For the majority, it enables them to use systems designed for able-bodied people and to carry out tasks to the same standard as able-bodied people do. It also gives them a feeling of independence, because they can carry out these tasks for themselves, with little or no help from others. Acquiring social and life skills is made easier for them. Haigh (1991), who has worked for many years with children with learning difficulties, is very positive about how the technology can help develop their social and life skills.

DEVELOPING SOCIAL SKILLS WITH THE HELP OF COMPUTERS

Computers can provide a stimulating setting for developing social skills. This is especially true when children use a computer to create a microworld they can explore. Safely in such a world, children who are failing can make a new start, be creative and test their ideas with their peers. Examples of such programs are *Logo*, *Contact*, *Image* and *Compose*. Adventure games, which also offer a kind of microworld for exploration, usually call for skills and knowledge beyond that of slow learners of an age appropriate to the content.

Social skills are developed when groups of children share and solve problems together. The programs generate opportunities for discussion: individual children advance ideas for evaluation by the others.

The computer gives children chances to improve their first attempts, and to appraise each others' work, which they soon learn to do in a constructive way. Because the computer enables children to produce work of a high standard of presentation, they are proud of their results and want to share and discuss with others what they have done. Among the best programs for developing social skills are those for simple desk-top publishing. Children need plenty of time to experiment with their text, graphics and presentation.

Mansfield (1991) takes a slightly different but also very positive line, suggesting that computer-based learning can be part of a strategy to give pupils with moderate learning difficulties an experience of success, in a new subject where they have had no experience of failure. This was one of the ideas raised repeatedly by teachers during short courses run by the National Council for Educational Technology (1990). They stressed that learning a language, a skill usually associated with bright pupils, boosted such children's self-confidence. Mansfield provides an example of good practice:

FRENCH LANGUAGE AND CULTURE FOR OLDER CHILDREN

To the surprise of some people, we decided to introduce a modern languages project into our school for pupils with moderate learning difficulties, in Richmond-upon-Thames, Surrey. We wanted to give our final-year (Year 11) children access to French through an experience of French culture, and hoped to use French as a focus for cross-curricular teaching. By using information technology in various forms, we thought we could make French language and culture accessible to pupils across a wide range of ability. At the same time, we would stimulate integration of these pupils with those in mainstream schools. If the project went well, it would be a possible model for other schools to emulate.

The children started with taped French music because we felt that they would learn language more readily through music and rhythm. They soon knew the French words for Frère Jacque, without yet understanding them. They moved on from music to an interactive videodisc, *Cette Ville* (IBIS), which enabled them to explore the French language, visits the shops in a typical French town, use francs to buy French food, yet remain detached and not feel self-conscious. They made responses in English through the keyboard. If they made mistakes, they knew they could return to the 'patisserie' and try again.

The children worked in twos and threes and quickly learned about some the differences between England and France. Using the disc, they listened to good spoken French set in the context of a real French town. They soon began to mimic and repeat the French words they were hearing. Confidence and motivation built up: they were eager to learn more.

In other classes, the French experience was extended into Technology, where pupils discussed what methods of construction had been used to build the Eiffel Tower. They attempted to construct a model with rolled paper tubes to prove the strength of the structure.

In 1990, the culmination of the French module came in several activities. Year 10 pupils took a trip to Boulogne. Year 11 went to stay in Dieppe for a short time. Year 8 visited the Channel Tunnel exhibition. There was an afternoon of boules for all pupils. For the final afternoon of the module, the children ate French food in a simulated French cafe staffed by pupils from a local public school.

This rich mixture of computer-based and practical work has enhanced our pupils' awareness of the French language and culture. They can recognise elements of the language and are prepared to attempt to communicate without fear of failure.

Some schools have introduced computers into Personal and Social Education, or Health and Physical Education. For example, Stansfield (1991) says that in Basselton School, Cleveland, computers are used in Personal and Social Education for all Year 8 pupils. *Town* is the basis for lessons on conflict resolution. *Health Data* and files about drugs and smoking, prepared with *Touch Explorer Plus*, provide a factual foundation for discussions. Computers, plus the Concept Keyboard and suitable software, provide an environment in which factual information can be imparted to all regardless of their reading level, thus encouraging reasoned debate.

On quite a different tack, Beste (1990) offers instances of symbol-using programs being helpful to learners with special needs in acquiring life skills:

INCREASING INDEPENDENCE BY USING SYMBOLS

At Whittlesea School in Harrow, students with severe learning difficulties are using Rebus symbols to interact with the community. The teachers want to increase the older students' independence when shopping. One teacher prepares and prints out a menu card from *Using Rebus II*. Students use the Concept Keyboard, with overlays of symbols, to 'write' their shopping lists on the screen. When they have finished, the lists are printed and each symbol is cut out. The slips of paper go into the students' wallets, which they take on the shopping trip to remind them of what they need when they see the shop assistant. Back at the school afterwards, each student follows a Rebus recipe to prepare the snack.

Adult students at Beaumont Further Education College in Lancaster – financed by the Spastics Society – are helped towards independence by a pack called Surviving with Symbols. It contains three floppy discs of *Using Rebus II* files, together with related Concept Keyboard overlays, designed 'to help students maintain their personal care routines'. Using the program, students with poor memories compile a checklist of routines to be followed. Others compile shopping lists for items such as toothpaste and tissues, as needed. Still others record the routines they have completed.

Beaumont College has produced another pack, Washing Symbols, to help students to organise their own laundry. The symbols are not Rebus, but those found on clothes and washing machines for selecting the right washing programme. For this pack, four programs were adapted: *Touch Explorer* and *What's That Picture?* for symbol-to-symbol matching, *Concept Keyboard Match*, for word-to-symbol matching, and *Prompt/Writer* for early writing. All of these accept Concept Keyboard inputs. Output can be through a speech synthesiser for non-readers.

Social and life skills for hearing-impaired learners

A hearing-impaired child needs practice, preferably in a safe environment, in coping with a variety of situations he or she is likely to encounter. Pinder (1990), working in the Hearing Impaired Unit at Darrick Wood Senior School, a comprehensive, describes how she uses *Town* in a Life Skills course to help a Year 9 girl with partial hearing and additional learning problems. *Town* simulates a journey from home to town to meet friends at a prearranged time. En route the player, who has some money, has to make decisions in response to incidents built into the simulation. Afterwards, the program can print a questionnaire about the journey and a summary of what happened.

ANN'S ADVENTURES IN TOWN

Ann enjoys using the computer for fairly easy maths programs, but not as much when introduced to language-orientated ones, such as *Developing Tray*. She is beginning to grasp the ideas behind adventure games and found the frog in *Lost Frog*, part of *Adventures*.

Ann tends to respond impulsively to problems. The first time she used *Town* she arrived too early to meet her friends and, when given a choice of what to do with her spare time, decided to go home at once. When asked why she didn't meet her friends, she declared the program silly, packed up the computer and got on with other work in silence.

The next day, she asked whether she could use *Town* again. This time, she succeeded in meeting her friends and was pleased. She had in fact taken her printout home and independently reasoned out alternative responses.

Since then, we have spent time discussing the two print-outs and answering the questions in full sentences, with reasons for her actions. Previously, she would have reverted to her stock phrases, 'I did it because I did it' or 'I just did', which can be very frustrating for the teacher who has spent up to 20 minutes getting her to put together more logical verbal responses.

Town has worksheets which provide a wealth of ideas and stimuli for associated activities. Ann and I have looked at the town plan to plot the best route. She rides a bike, so the sheet on road signs has proved very valuable, together with the Highway Code, which has led to discussions about safety. Two sheets on the empty house are being used by Ann's audiology teacher, to improve her expressive language. Useful words are recorded in her audiology book and on the ARROW tape recorder, which helps her to learn from hearing her own voice.

Pinder also describes how another teacher at her school used *Home* with two Year 8 girls. One is partially deaf, the other severely so, although she has some hearing at high frequencies. They are from totally different home backgrounds and have had contrasting experiences of schooling.

A STRING OF SAUSAGES AND A DOG!

We set up a video camera to record the girls' sessions on their own with *Home*, which encourages children to explore the consequences of their decisions. The main character in the 'play' comes home from shopping, only to be faced with various situations demanding decisions. The choices made by the players eventually affect whether the parents in the play allow them an evening out at a party.

The two girls tackled the program enthusiastically, stopping to discuss the reasons for their choices. Afterwards, we printed out a record of their decisions and the final outcome, and we used this in discussion work for several weeks. It led to debate about listening to other people's point of view, the consequences of various actions, the responsibilities of parents and children, and matters of living at home such as meal planning, pocket money, time-keeping and respect for others. The girls assured me that somewhere in the program I would find a string of sausages and a dog! Much more important, they both started to write a 'play' based on what had happened to them.

Finally, Pinder says that another program, *Electricity in the Home* proved surprisingly valuable, in the hands of a colleague, for a profoundly deaf Year 11 girl. It is in two parts, *Meters* and *Consumption*. Pinder introduced it as part of a Maths for Life course specially devised for this child, who cannot cope with GCSE Mathematics.

THROWING LIGHT ON ELECTRICITY FOR KATHY

Kathy had just been learning that electricity isn't free but has to be paid for. We were agonising over the next step: How much is electricity? The arrival of *Electricity in the Home* was a godsend.

First we had to make sure Kathy knew the names of the various household appliances depicted in the program, something not to be taken for granted in a profoundly deaf pupil. Then we started on *Meters*: you can switch on 1–3 appliances, out of 15 in the program, and see the power rating in watts on a simulated meter. Kathy watched the movement of the needle as each appliance or combination of appliances was switched on or off. Kathy found the worksheets quite straightforward, and could answer some of the questions unaided, using skills such as estimation, simple addition, subtraction and multiplication.

The *Consumption* program moves on to how much electricity costs. Kathy had been introduced earlier to the idea of electrical units. The beauty of this program was that she could actually see the cost increasing over the period required, say, to boil a kettle. Using the worksheet, she could then work out the cost of making breakfast.

The program had got her off to a good start. We made some more worksheets to reinforce the concepts and to include the idea of payment, because Kathy still seemed to have quite naive ideas about just how much electricity is used in a home per day or per week.

Children with emotional difficulties must learn social and life skills

Howard (1991b), a teacher at Boxmoor House School for children with emotional and behavioural difficulties, makes the important point that rather than accommodate pupils' disabilities, schools like his endeavour to change their pupils' condition. He says the use of computers in schools like Boxmoor House should be considered because they encourage such children to want to be involved in the learning situation, develop their ability to manage social situations in and out of school, and help them to understand, come to terms with and deal with their emotions.

These children can experience success, Howard says, based on increased stimulation and motivation, and improve their self-images through use of content-specific software or framework programs tailored to their needs, or general purpose software. The trouble is that such children do not usually respond well to a planned and prescriptive strategy of remedial teaching. They have often experienced failure in their previous school. Their teacher may have to take some unconventional steps before starting remediation. For example, computer-based adventure games provide a less formal, less threatening setting for developing basic skills, says Howard. In playing these games, the children also have chances to learn to work together, something which they find particularly difficult.

Games only take the children part of the way, however, and using general purpose software may be the next step. They can learn to use wordprocessing and desktop publishing programs, databases, spreadsheets and graphics programs.

This software is valuable to them in subjects across the curriculum. They learn information handling, logical thinking and creativity. The children are enabled to do what they could not do otherwise, within the curriculum. They are stimulated and motivated.

Howard also stresses the role computers can play in behaviour assessment and monitoring. Apart from straightforward uses such as teachers wordprocessing their behaviour assessment sheets and care plans for individual pupils, he also suggests a computer-based assessment scheme. Ideally, this would contain a bank of descriptors from which the teacher would draw in making a new assessment or modifying an old one. Assessments would be held on disk and periodically scored via the keyboard. Alternatively, a spreadsheet can serve in recording incidents of behaviour. In special schools with a highly structured behaviour management policy, perhaps based on a token economy, it can be invaluable in keeping accurate records that can be easily analysed to identify areas of improvement or continuing difficulty. Teachers could recall incidents by date and the pupil's name.

Similarly, computers and their software can be useful to children with emotional difficulties in preparing personal profiles for individual pupils. This helps them to 'own' their learning and behaviour goals and to participate in assessing their own performance. Records of achievement can include pupils' wordprocessed comments on their own work. Why bother with wordprocessing? The computer offers a pleasing format into which the children enter their remarks, after which the whole is printed out clearly for teachers, parents and others to see.

There is simulation software dealing with human relationships. Some programs may be threatening because they demand too much reading, at too high a level. Teachers must provide support then. If available, a screen reader producing synthesised speech may help. The chief value of working through these simulations and role-plays is often in the discussion they engender. Howard believes that programs currently available tend to be too detached and impersonal for his pupils, however, and the consequences remote and inconsistent. He would prefer to use programs which simulate a misdemeanour and its consequences for the miscreant, together with alternative acceptable ways to behave. These reinforce school or society's rules. Or he would like to use programs which present conflict scenarios, based on actual events and made as lifelike as possible. These could even be authored by teachers and children working together with the help of a branching program structure that would let them propose and depict various outcomes.

Teaching social and life skills to young adults

Vincent (1990) reports several examples from Further Education, of computers helping young adults with learning difficulties to master social and life skills. Let the teachers speak for themselves. First, Jenkins, Kavanagh and Morgan (1990):

BRIDGEND COLLEGE OF TECHNOLOGY HELPS RICARDO

At Bridgend College of Technology we have an ACCESS Centre founded on the expertise and experience of staff from the college's information technology and special needs sections.

Ricardo is a full-time day student in the special needs section, with moderate learning difficulties, together with social, emotional and behaviour problems. He is attending a Social Development Course. As noted on his entry to the course, Ricardo needs to be motivated and stimulated towards achieving his educational potential, to practise basic concepts and processes, such as numbers, colour, time, matching, conservation and ordering, and to gain experience of social situations, relationships and skills. His teachers had found that information technology was valuable in meeting such needs, and computers are used extensively on this particular course.

Using the Centre twice a week gives Ricardo access to a much wider range of hardware and software than in the special needs section. Both Ricardo and his special needs tutor benefit from the expertise of the Centre's information technology staff. Going to the Centre, which is based in the college's Management Block, greatly enhances his self-image as a useful and worthwhile member of the college community.

The Life Skills course at Frome College of Further Education, says Morrison (1990), is for 16–19 year olds with severe learning difficulties. They use two BBC computers with Concept Keyboards, AMX mice and a Microvitec touch screen. They also have access to the college's Nimbus network, on which they can use a graphics package with colour printer.

COMPUTERS IN FROME COLLEGE'S LIFE SKILLS COURSE

Our students bring computers into a wide range of their activities. We have software to support most areas of the curriculum. Some programs we bought and some we developed for individual students once specific needs were identified – for example, in social sight vocabulary. The students wordprocess their written work, including a regular Newsletter. They value highly being able to do this, and are strongly motivated. Their literacy skills develop through use of the keyboard and by scanning the menu or instructions on screen. They gain confidence from success on the computers, not least because of the 'age appropriate' aspect of modern technology. There is kudos in being able to cope, like their mainstream peers, with equipment that puzzles many of their parents.

Peter is a good example of a student whose achievement of learning objectives is promoted by work on computers. He joined us at 16 with problems of poor co-ordination and a very short concentration span. His work presentation was very poor so his self-esteem and tolerance of any activity were low. Peter discovered with the graphics program that however many mistakes he made he could try again and the only picture printed out was the one he was satisfied with. Repeated practice improved his hand-eye co-ordination and he began doing some excellent graphics work. Once his printouts were mounted for display, Peter had a much stronger reason to try to write captions neatly, without spoiling the effect of his work. We saw a transfer of skill across to his written work and freehand drawing.

Slaven (1990) discusses his college's link course, 'Going to College', designed for students with severe learning difficulties attending Social Activity Centres.

CARMARTHENSHIRE COLLEGE OF TECHNOLOGY AND ART USES COMPUTERS

This course demonstrates the full potential of computers in giving access to the curriculum and helping students to achieve their learning objectives. Software such as *Front Page Extra* encourages group work, in which discussion helps students to recall their visit experiences, leading with maximum ease to a pleasant-looking written report. Our students vary in ability: the more able can use the keyboard while the others give ideas for content. When students cannot cope with keyboard skills, our trainees in placement help them, applying in a real situation skills acquired during their own course. This approach contributed to the learning of staff, students and trainees.

The Concept Keyboard helps students unable to use the conventional keyboard to formulate sentences and recognise words. They use it with our overlays to help with use of the college canteen and in awareness exercises in support of the curriculum. We have some good software, such as *Supermarket*, *Shopping* and *Camping*, which we use often in preparation for a visit or activity. Packages like these are a great help especially when staff are teaching many courses and lack technician support or time to make their own overlays. The possibilities are endless especially with *Touch Explorer* which further extends use of the Concept Keyboard.

Lisa is a second year student following our Youth Training Scheme caring course. She uses *View* to plan, prepare and submit written work. Lisa's interest, developed in school, was carried into college. She maintains her spelling has improved because the computer has helped her to structure words. She likes handing in a neat report, and saves time when she wants to change paragraphs and sentences without rewriting the whole thing. The computer helps her to plan her assignments, and because it is fun the task becomes less of a chore. In her placement she helps clients to write letters and notices, using the wordprocessor. Lisa hopes to learn more about using the Concept Keyboard to help her client group and she may progress to a course offering a wordprocessing or IT qualification.

Finally, Harvey (1990) has this to say about computer-based activities for students with severe learning difficulties at his Somerset college:

LIVING SKILLS AT SOMERSET COLLEGE OF ARTS AND TECHNOLOGY

Full-time 16–19 year olds with severe learning difficulties joined the College community in 1988, after local reorganisation of school-based provision. Permanent staff were appointed and, after some in-house INSET focussed on content-free software, introduced computers across the curriculum. The students have the whole college as a resource, including BBC computers, with Concept Keyboards, video digitiser, assorted mice and printers. Our choice of software was influenced by the National Council for Educational Technology's research on information technology for students with learning difficulties in Further Education.

Computers enable students to engage in activities appropriate to their age, ones they can identify as similar to those they see 'mainstream' students undertaking. The daily living skills curriculum includes social skills, communication and numeracy, and the students surveyed local shops to identify each one's function as a retail outlet. With staff help they videorecorded the shop names, frontages, and common social sight signs. On returning to the classroom the students capture the video pictures through the digitiser with *Image*. The most able ones can independently use camera and software, and help other students in producing an exciting visual image, a record of their learning activities. This success enhances their self esteem.

Summary

In this chapter, by citing a range of examples, we reviewed good practice in using computers to teach social and life skills. From what the teachers say, it is clear that some very deliberately set out to teach these skills, while others prefer to incorporate them within broader programmes that are aimed at boosting confidence. Children and young adults respond positively to these opportunities.

Part 4

Policy and Practice

14 Assessing Individuals' Needs

Matching computers to individuals

There is little doubt that computers can enable individuals to overcome learning difficulties arising from a wide range of handicapping conditions. Numerous examples exist of learners who have gained access to parts of the curriculum that were previously denied to them or who have achieved progress that would not have been possible without the use of this technology. This success is not universal, however, and other individuals have not realised their expectations. Many have abandoned the computer as a device with which to overcome their learning difficulties.

Why should the use of a computer or other new technology device be associated with both success and failure? This can be true even when individuals' needs are the same. The answer to this question requires an appreciation of the factors associated with the matching of the technology to needs, and the taking of actions that can bring about this match. Unfortunately, this appreciation has not existed on many occasions in the past decade or more when governments, charities, organisations and others have sought to provide individuals with computers and other equipment to meet particular needs.

The situation is often exacerbated by the fact that a 'solution' appears to have been provided but, in reality, the solution is only superficially successful. This is the story of a student we shall call Ann.

RIGHT PROBLEM, WRONG SOLUTION: ANN'S STORY

Ann, aged 12, is unable to write as a result of an accident which left her almost completely paralysed. Her speech is very restricted and to participate in any classroom learning situation she requires the constant presence of an assistant. Through a charitable donation it became possible for equipment to be purchased that could assist in overcoming the many communication problems Ann experienced. In particular, providing an aid to writing was considered the prime objective.

In due course a computer and a printer were purchased, plus an alternative to the keyboard, a head mounted device that could, with minimal movement, be used to select characters on the computer screen for entry into a wordprocessor. To a casual observer the results appeared impressive: a pupil who could only move her head slightly was producing printed text with total independence. In reality, Ann was using technology that was both inefficient and frustrating, for numerous reasons. Characters and words presented for selection on the screen did not match either her curriculum needs or her vocabulary. No attempt had been made to optimize the rate of scanning between the characters and words from which she was selecting. Attention to these factors immediately yielded a five-fold increase in typing speeds. Subsequently, a different alternative to the keyboard proved to be more appropriate which yielded an even more efficient method of writing.

Stansfield (1991) underlines the importance of suiting the equipment to the pupil. She tells how David, a Year 11 pupil at Ormesby School in Cleveland, eventually found the right equipment for him. With proper assessment at the start, David could probably have avoided this story of trial-and-error.

DAVID FINDS OUT WHAT HE NEEDS

David, aged 17, has cerebral palsy but can move around on his own, with a rolator. He started to use a Typestar 90, an electronic typewriter, but soon progressed to a Tandy 102 laptop microcomputer. He also tried the Tandy WP2 and Sinclair Z88, but found the Tandy 102 had larger screen print and more positive keyboard keys, as well as enabling him to print direct from it. He can speak, but uses a Lightwriter as a communication aid to clarify words and speed up conversation.

David undertook his work experience at the Middlesbrough Information Technology Education Centre, where he worked at wordprocessing and desktop publishing. There, the instructors tried to get him to use a trackerball, but he preferred to struggle with a mouse confined by a framework to a limited area, so that he could be like the others. His teacher then fitted the trackerball to the most popular computer, the Archimedes with a hard disk: all pupils, including David, use it now.

Matching computers to individuals' needs is more difficult than it seems and has been neglected. This is true where government has provided equipment on a national scale and where funds have been raised by charities for a particular individual. The situation has been redressed through setting up centres that provide professional advice and support, such as the Federation of ACCESS Centres, the CALL Centre, the ACE Centre, FACCT and, in the US, the Trace Center.

When low cost microcomputers and other microprocessor devices became available, Odor (1982) suggested greater use of this technology for specialised communication aids and computer aided learning. He wrote that whereas earlier technology suffered from problems of limitations, with microcomputers we might have trouble coping with too much potential. He suggested a three-dimensional 'problem space'. Communication aids, for example, could be considered in terms of the wide range needed for particular combinations of handicaps and abilities; in terms of the curriculum area, age, difficulty level, and style of computer aided learning; and in terms of support in the forms of information, delivery, training and maintenance. This three dimensional approach illustrates the complexity of the problem. In identifying a solution for an individual, there are many factors to take into account.

Although focussed on communication aids, Odor's problem space model has helped to raise awareness of the need for a professional and multidisciplinary approach to matching computer applications to needs of individuals with learning difficulties. Experience has proved that the kinds of 'support' needed change: matching of technology to need is not undertaken once and for all. Rather, it should be done repeatedly as the individual learner acquires new knowledge and skills, as technology improves, and as the learner's environment alters, including curriculum changes. In addition, there will be periods when other support is required, such as training.

Assessment

In Chapter 1, we set provision of and support for computers and other equipment in the context of changes in the UK brought about by the Warnock Committee. The subsequent guide to the Warnock Report (Department of Education and Science, 1978) introduced the wider concept of special education, with the distinction removed between special education and remedial education. It assumed that up to 20 percent of children might need special educational help at some stage during their school career. It recognised that a special educational need might take various forms. Some learners would need means of access to the curriculum, through, for example, special equipment or specialised teaching techniques. Others would need a modified curriculum or particular attention to the social structure and emotional climate in which education was taking place. To protect the interests of children with severe, complex or long-term disabilities, the Committee recommended a system of recording each child's profile of needs and a statement about the special provision required. It recognised that effective record-keeping for all children would greatly assist in early identification of special needs. The Committee proposed that there should be five stages of assessment for children at school, and that a child's needs should be assessed at one or more of these stages as appropriate. Postlethwaite and Hackney (1988) summarise one Local Education Authority's guidelines for this five-stage process:

GUIDELINES FOR ASSESSMENT

At Stage 1 the head and school-based teachers, with parents where possible, are the only people involved. Observation of the pupil, results of normal school tests and of classwork and so on, parental information and data from medical and other records should be used to decide on action, which should be classroom-based.

At Stage 2 visiting teachers (for example, for the hearing-impaired) may be involved as well. Results of more detailed classroom tests, plus the information already obtained in Stage 1, should be used to decide on further classroombased action, use of aids or special materials and possible modifications to the curriculum.

At Stage 3 special needs advisors, educational psychologists, school medical officers and social workers may be added to the assessment team. The team's aim is still to keep the pupil in the mainstream school. Parental involvement is essential.

At Stage 4, a full multi-professional assessment occurs, on the assumption that information gathered in the first three stages is inadequate for the purpose of agreeing action to meet the pupil's needs.

At Stage 5, assuming it is agreed that the LEA rather than the school must make provision for the pupil's needs, a statement is produced. This will include details of the nature of these needs, the educational provision the LEA deems appropriate to meet them, the school placement it considers appropriate and any non-educational provision the LEA or other local agencies should make.

The essence of good assessment of individuals' needs lies in assessors' capacity to identify strengths as well as weaknesses, and thereby to decide on the best kind of support, human and technological as appropriate, for them. On the one hand, assessment teams ought to understand the support already being provided by home and school or college . On the other, they should be clear about how home and school or college contribute to individuals' problems, and about the characteristics of the individuals themselves. Assessment should not be a single occurrence but a continuing process, based on sound records maintained by teachers and carers such as doctors and social workers. Teachers have a prominent role to play, because they are so closely involved in all educational activities, but their opinions must be set alongside those of other professionals. The parents and the children concerned must receive a fair hearing and their wishes must be taken fully into account.

The concept of special educational needs established by the Warnock Committee, and subsequent recommendations concerning assessment and record keeping provide a framework for provision of equipment and devices for individuals. This approach ensures that all relevant needs are considered together. Even so, the range and potential of new information technology is such that there are no simple solutions. To tackle the complex task of matching, numerous centres have emerged offering advice, assessment and training. We discuss some of these centres below, for children and/or adults.

Aids to Communication in Education (ACE) Centre

The ACE Centre was established in 1984 as part of the Microelectronics Education Programme in England and Wales. The Centre is sited at Ormerod School in Oxford, a school for physically- and multiply-handicapped children, many with communication problems. The Centre takes a multidisciplinary approach to assessment, reflected in the Centre's staffing which includes two teachers, an occupational therapist, a speech therapist, and a technician. Referrals may come from teachers, parents, advisers or others involved in the general assessment of an individual. Subsequent assessment may occur at the Centre, at school or at home, and may take up to a day to complete.

To provide a professional environment for assessment, the ACE Centre also engages in activities that provide access to essential resources for staff and others who contact the Centre. Information is gathered about aids to communication. For example, one publication covers switches and interfaces (ACE, 1987). Over 100 different switches, from simple lever switches to eye, mouth and tongue switches, might provide someone with an individualised means of accessing communication or learning aids that might otherwise be inaccessible. The publication considers the need for good seating and posture as an essential prerequisite to positioning switches on various parts of the anatomy. A complementary publication focuses on the importance of seating (Gray, 1988), and includes the story of a boy we shall call Michael, illustrating the relationship between seating, posture and the use of switches:

THE GIFT OF SPEECH THROUGH PROPER SEATING!

Michael was an athetoid cerebral palsied boy, aged 6, with no speech. When left on his own on the floor he writhed from one spasm to the next. It took him eight minutes to inch his way over a distance of four feet to reach a toy he was interested in. His lack of control meant that he was unable to manipulate the toy, although he did manage to knock against one particular area of an activity board with irregular arm movements from a lying position on the floor.

Early attempts at seating without pelvic stability, and with arms left totally free gave Michael very little improvement in his switch control. Michael was then seated in his padded Rifton seat. An angled wedge cushion was placed on the seat to break the extension spasm pattern, and side padding placed at pelvic height for stability. He had a footrest and a tray with a stabilising bar. In addition, Michael needed a gaiter on his left arm to maintain this stability, but he then showed that he was able to operate two switches – one with his left foot, and another with his right hand, and for the first time in his life he was able to use a speech synthesiser to talk to his mother.

How successful is ACE in assessing individuals' needs? Recent data are not available, but Lysley (1986) studied children who had been assessed at the ACE Centre for a communication aid, 1984–1986. Completed questionnaires came in for 54 of 72 children selected, providing data on items such as school, age, disability and how the implementation of the Centre's recommendation had been achieved, including sources of funding. Respondents were also invited to provide an evaluation of the recommended communication aid. As for the impact of an aid on a child's communication, there was an almost even spread of answers which covered the range of 'insignificantly' to 'significantly'. Lysley said that the euphoria over computers for special needs children had to be put into some sort of perspective by his data. Perhaps his results indicate just how long-term and complex is the whole process of matching a communication aid to a child's individual needs. Often teachers and therapists are inadequately prepared and experienced to realise the full potential of an aid. They cannot relate it directly or indirectly to other facets of the child's social and educational learning. When asked about the impact of a communication aid on a child's access to the curriculum, the largest percentage responded at the mean value between 'minimally' and 'considerably'. This result appears to reinforce the previous conclusion that the impact was modest rather than substantial.

Overall, the study confirmed that initial assessment of an individuals' needs for communication aids is only one component of long-term support that an individual requires to exploit fully any aid subsequently provided. Centres such as ACE face a dilemma: should they meet the large number of requests for an initial assessment or to provide longer term assessment and support for a smaller number of children. This dilemma is unlikely to be resolved until the expertise of teachers, parents and carers can be increased, through training. Only then will there be a local resource that can both meet the longer term need for support and identify when the referral to the specialist centre should be.

The Open University and the National Federation of ACCESS Centres

For more than 20 years the Open University has developed a range of services for its students with disabilities. In 1991, over 3000 students with disabilities were registered on courses within the undergraduate and associate programmes. There is wide spread recognition that students with disabilities can benefit from access to new technology to enable them to study and communicate independently. A formal rather than informal support service for so many students could not be provided on a national basis by the University's own specialist staff. The impetus which led to a pilot project with the National Federation of ACCESS Centres (NFAC – a consortium of resource centres based mainly in further education colleges) was provided by the University's decision in 1987 to adopt a Home Computing Policy. This decision marked a significant shift in the university's response to students with disabilities. Their need for access to new technology is now strongly related to courses which require them to use a personal computer in their own homes. Adoption of this policy with its clear educational objectives added further to the belief in the university that assessment, training and support should be provided on a professional basis in partnership with NFAC. A pilot project was established in October 1987:

- To provide a national assessment, resource and information base from which a service could be developed for Open University students with disabilities, especially those with complex sensory and motor difficulties.
- To recognize the need for a formal rather than informal level of service which would provide students with individual assessments, advice, hardware support and training.
- To act as consultants to regional and advisory staff.

During the 12 months of the pilot, 59 students were assessed and supplied with appropriate systems and adaptations. Although priority was given to students taking courses within the Home Computing Policy, the project was open to potential students considering taking such courses and to students for whom access to microcomputer-based study aids was essential to their independent communication. Assessments for study aids and study strategies provided an opportunity for OU students to discuss their difficulties and investigate possible solutions. The emphasis was on assessing their study situation, rather than the students, and on considering the range of options which might be appropriate. Where time allowed, initial instruction was also given in the use of equipment. Students on the scheme usually attended the nearest college-based ACCESS Centre for the day, unless this was prevented by mobility problems. Because of the difficulty of predicting in advance the full range of hardware and software that might be required, home based assessments were the exception. A range of solutions were investigated, evaluated and recommended to meet identified study difficulties. Each student received a draft report for discussion within three weeks of the assessment. Approval for adaptations was given soon after the report had been completed. In most cases, staff spent a further day installing equipment at the student's home and gave initial instruction on how to operate equipment and software. Students then had to familiarise themselves with systems and software in their own time. Telephone contact at the ACCESS Centres was available in case of difficulty and, for students on courses with home computing, the university's Help Desk was also available.

An evaluation of the scheme (Hales, 1991) indicated that students fully expected the initial assessment to suggest modifications to hardware and software which would meet their individual needs. It was equally clear, however, that training in use of the adapted computers fell far short of what was required.

The Communication Aids for Language and Learning (CALL) Centre

The CALL Centre has provided an assessment service for communication- or writing-impaired learners within Scotland for several years. Assessment is conducted over an extended period, normally in a person's learning setting. This process is integrated with case study research. Referrals are from agencies, schools, centres and individuals. After initial contact, the Centre gathers information including names of people who might form part of a team to give further advice and on-going support.

Prior to initial assessment, members of the team try to collect a wide range of information, to place the assessment in context. After it, they design practical exercises around interesting and motivating tasks that can provide further feedback during the assessment process. The team may lend equipment that provides further evidence. Up to 60 such assessments may be taking place in parallel over periods of up to six months. The longitudinal case study approach adopted by the CALL Centre is the basis for an effective assessment service for individuals and yields valuable information for the Centre's action research. This approach does result in smaller numbers of individuals being assessed, compared to centres that focus on initial assessment. The resulting quality of support is high, however, and provides for progressive devolution of responsibility to the local support, which is identified at an early stage.

Another interesting approach taken by the CALL Centre has been to put a 'task force' into a school or centre for up to two days per week for a complete term. This extends the opportunity of assessing an individual in their learning environment to assessing that environment in relation to staff needs and resources.

The case study approach at the CALL Centre has yielded a wealth of information now being shared with others involved with assessment. This is happening through a computer-based interactive training and information resource, Microtechnology and Disabled Learners (CALL Centre, 1991), funded by the TVEI Unit of the Training Agency. We shall refer to it as the CALL Resource, a combination of human expertise, case studies, catalogues, documents and computerised databases. It draws on the multidisciplinary team's extensive experience acquired in working with over 500 learners since 1980. It provides assessment, training, information and on-going support. The Resource's focus is the process of assessment, as the main prerequisite for successful use of communication aids and adaptations to computers. All of the material in the Resource is linked to this central theme. The CALL concept of what an assessment process should involve has encouraged production of a package that can be used at many different levels, ranging from support for assessment process itself, through the preparation of training materials for newcomers (either professional or carers) to hunting for information on a very tightly defined problem. Much of the Resource is accessed by a hypermedia system which enables the user to move quickly from one area to another, whilst retaining good control over the level of detail needed for the particular task in hand. It has facilities for notetaking, recording and printing.

The entry point to the CALL Resource's system is shown in Fig. 14.1 which offers a number of options. For example, the selection of 'A Learners Story' may be appropriate for a newcomer or for promoting discussion in a seminar as a case study is unfolded. More detailed case studies are presented by selecting 'Other Learners: Other Curricula'. In this case there are more detailed case studies which have another level of information, revealed by clicking on the small arrows within the text.

Users can access many more case studies, all drawn from experiences at the CALL Centre. Information is presented in the same sequence as was received during the individual assessments. This provides a realistic content for the resource rather than contrived examples which might not reflect the complexities that are often met during the assessment process. Additional links to databases and glossaries provide an interesting and innovative approach to assessment.

The TRACE Research and Development Center

Brandenburg (1987) describes how the Trace Center has two affiliated programs which provide evaluations, a term often used in the US interchangeably with assessments: the Communication Aids and System Clinic (CASC), and the Communication Development Program (CDP). It is worthwhile comparing these with British practice.

The CASC team includes communication specialists, a position seating specialist, and a communication aids specialist. Anyone may be referred to the team who does not use speech as a primary interaction mode, whose speech is not functional, who does not have a functional writing system, or who requires assistance in

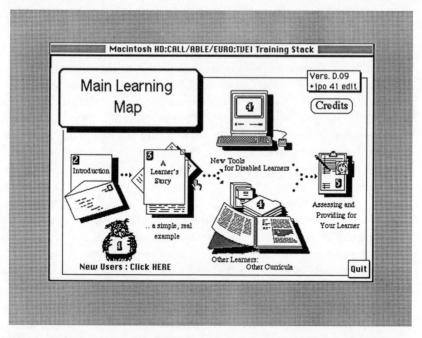

*Figure 14.1 - **Microtechnology and Disabled Learners: the CALL Resource***

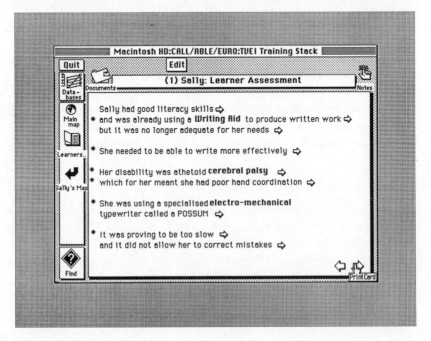

*Figure 14.2 - **Sally's assessment***

computer access. Referral leads to screening through written and verbal reports, then each case is reviewed by the team using a wide range of additional information about the individual. Evaluation may last from four to six hours and concentrates on positioning and seating, communication skills and needs, and communication aids and interfaces. Finally, implementation follows, which may include training, with follow-up to assess the need for re-evaluation. Brandenburg believes that evaluation is not simply recommending equipment, but rather the first critical step in planning for incorporation of assistive devices into an individual's environment. Such devices must be kept in perspective as tools, not solutions, giving teachers a chance to deal with disabilities and learning difficulties. At CASC, only a third of the initial evaluations result in recommendations for devices to be supplied. More often, recommendations focus on skill development and increased opportunities for interaction using low-tech, non-electronic devices such as communication boards.

Assessment as an ongoing activity

Assessment should not be considered to be a separate activity, but an on-going part of educational planning, and the importance of performance trials and diagnostic therapy should be emphasised. As for the scope of assessment, there still remain some aspects of special educational needs that are not covered. This is particularly true for individuals who have learning difficulties that arise from cognitive impairments. In these cases there may be significant scope for adaptation of software and curriculum materials associated with computers rather than the provision of communication aids or adaptation of equipment and devices.

Apart from initial assessment linked to Statements, pupils with learning difficulties can benefit from having a readable profile against which to measure their own progress. At Abbey Hill School, in Cleveland, teachers started to use *Profiling Package* with the school-leavers, to negotiate a report drawn from a databank of statements that would supplement the rather clinical *Annual Review* and provide a more readable record for parents. They now record progress and provide reports to parents with *Monitoring and Recording*: this program is content-free, so the school is able to enter a bank of comments or targets, which are displayed on the screen and become the basis for negotiating a report on the achievements and attitudes of each pupil's work record. The data can be presented in several ways, providing reports in 'parent-speak' or 'teacher-speak'.

Summary

There is a high degree of consistency among centres that have introduced assessment for people who might require a communication aid or a computer or other device adapted to meet their individual needs. Experiences and case studies clearly point to the need for a multidisciplinary approach set in the broadest context of environment, needs and abilities, and for the assessment process to take place over a long period if the full benefits of the provision of equipment and devices are to be realised. But there are still many children and adults who receive computers and other devices from various sources without any form of assessment. The main cause is lack of awareness amongst those who provide funding. Clearly this is not deliberate but the consequences can be serious for an individual, as examples in this chapter show.

15 Staff Development

A long story of neglect

As we said in earlier chapters, schools and colleges require a wide range of staff to help students with special needs. Among them are speech therapists, psychologists, counsellors, health workers, drivers and physiotherapists, as well as teachers, aides and other school-based staff. Introducing computer-related technology may well call for technicians, too. Each of these groups require initial training and in-service staff development activities. We focus here on the teachers.

Teachers deserve encouragement to build their confidence and skills in using computers across the curriculum to help learners with special educational needs. They must have time to evaluate new software and hardware, to update their files on individual children, to organise their teaching facilities and to keep in touch with local networks and hotlines through which they can exchange information on new software and good practice. Teachers also deserve proper training opportunities.

Unfortunately, the training of teachers for work in special education is a long story of neglect. Despite integration and mainstreaming of students in the 1980s, the vast majority of teachers at present in British and US classrooms did not learn about special education in their initial training. In Britain, not until the mid-1980s was the obligation laid on teacher training institutions to include special education in their courses: many have had difficulty in responding, but most young teachers now get an introduction to the field. In the US, no such general requirement exists. Not surprisingly, few teachers in either country can claim to have received initial training that included use of computers in special education.

This somewhat gloomy picture is brightened to some extent by recent in-service staff development activities, organised regionally or locally for teachers of students with special needs. The general goal of such in-service training is to fill gaps in initial training, or, more often, to bring staff up to date: in special education, 'We are all out of date' as Mittler (1990) puts it. A few of these activities have been aimed at enabling teachers to understand how computer-related technology can help their students: in US terms, the teachers are 'empowered' by this training (Male, 1988). In the UK, other workshops have looked at the National Curriculum and its implications – including the expectation that students aged 5–16 who have special needs will use computers for parts of their studies.

In a review of the use of information technology for special educational needs in schools, Her Majesty's Inspectors concluded (Department of Education and Science, 1990a):

> There is a need for continuing targeted in-service training of teachers (INSET) to extend good practice in use of IT in schools.

> INSET is needed in ordinary schools to develop awareness of the potential of IT to enhance the access of pupils with special educational needs to a broad curriculum, and to spread existing good practice.

Why is staff development still needed?

During the 1980s, the number of computers in education increased significantly. There is now an expectation that children and adults will have access to computers for a wide range of curriculum activities and individual needs that go far beyond their early use for programming and games. No longer are computers considered the sole province of the mathematics teacher or anyone with a singular interest in the technology. Although 'computer enthusiasts' can still be found in education, their influence has been considerably reduced as more teachers have become involved and the application of the technology has been extended across the curriculum. This devolution has been slow as it has required a major input in terms of staff development time and resources, aided by numerous local, regional and national developments.

In the future, even more staff development time and resources will be needed as there are different needs amongst teachers. Some have not yet used computers, some are at an early stage, and others have been involved for several years and their knowledge and skills need updating as new hardware and software emerge.

National intitiatives must be taken into account in considering the need for staff development. For example, a £4 million scheme was announced in July 1991 by the Department of Education and Science (DES) to provide schools in England and Wales with CD-ROM resources. This particular technology, when added to a computer, can be a valuable resource (see Chapters 5 and 7), but without appropriate training and resource materials for the teachers the hardware could be destined for a cupboard, labelled 'surplus to requirements - use unknown'. Such cupboards already exist! The DES has anticipated this problem: during 1991, the IT in Schools Unit at the DES funded the National Council for Educational Technology to identify

CD-ROM discs and curriculum materials which would form the basis of national advice that could be given to local education authority advisers and advisory teachers, to complement the later provision of the CD-ROM hardware and software. This is a good example of an integrated approach to technology provision and training. It draws on experiences of the 1980s which clearly indicated that providing technology without staff development was likely to lead to waste of the technology.

Some views on staff development

What do teachers and others in the field think about staff development? Wood (1990b) records the views of the coordinator of a project for slow learners in work preparation courses at Derby College of Further Education. He took a remarkably practical approach:

> Derby College was one of ten colleges involved in the overall project. Success of the project depended on the willingness of the staff to accept new ideas and to change their working practices. Under normal circumstances, staff development works best when those involved are themselves able to identify a particular need so that relevant projects can then be devised to resolve them. The very nature of this project meant that staff development was imposed. That so many demonstrated willingness and enthusiasm and were prepared to give up so much of their time, speaks volumes for their professionalism. There were those however who remained sceptical and unconvinced throughout.

> It was unrealistic to expect lecturers in individual subject areas to teach their students to be computer literate. Instead, each week every student took a 90-minute computer literacy class for which I was responsible. My aim was to familiarize the students with all the hardware, and over the year, to develop confidence and reasonable competence with *Pendown, Image, BCalc* and a database. This approach proved successful. Many lecturers who used the programs would not have done so had they had to teach the students how to use the programs themselves, either because they felt they did not have the time, because they lacked confidence in their own ability to teach the students, or a combination of both. Programs which were specific to a particular area I generally left to individual teachers. This caused no difficulties because most programs proved very user-friendly, and this, together with the increased computer awareness of the students, was usually sufficient to see them through.

> Although other lecturers were not involved in teaching computer literacy, they needed a good basic understanding of the hardware and all relevant software if they were to gain the maximum benefit from them and be able to help the students. To this end I set up staff workshops, but they were very poorly attended, probably because staff were expected to come in their own time. Some

lecturers involved were part-time, and consequently their time spent in college was very limited. The workload on staff was already heavy. Some staff were still unconvinced that the workshops were relevant for them. If these staff were to become more heavily involved, a different approach was obviously needed.

It was the enthusiasm and motivation of the students when working on the computer which impressed these lecturers most and convinced them of its value. In informal discussions with lecturers, I first identified a need in a particular subject area. I then searched for, and tested suitable software which would satisfy this need. Under the pretext of the project, I asked the lecturer involved if I could work with a small group of students in the class. During the project, this request was never once turned down. Once I began working with these students, it was usually only a matter of minutes before the lecturer came over to see what was taking place. Once his/her interest had been aroused, in most cases, the battle for acceptance had been won. As the benefits became obvious the lecturer spent more and more time looking on, and so learned to handle the program with the students. No words of mine could have demonstrated this as the students were able to do. After a few sessions, I was able to leave the lecturer with the group and move on to other areas, having first assured them that I would be instantly available should any minor crisis arise, giving them the confidence to continue. This approach was very time consuming, and I spent much of my secondment time working with classroom groups, but it was very successful. I was also able to involve many part time lecturers.

Computers have become so much an integral part of the Multiskills course that looking back, it is difficult to imagine how we ever coped without them. The students' motivation, enthusiasm and concentration span has greatly increased. They have become involved in work which without computers would have been beyond them, and the level of attainment in many areas has surprised and delighted everyone. Their success has given them new confidence in their own abilities. Overall, the project has added impetus and direction to the work of staff and students.

Similarly, Bangay (1990) notes that experience at Bury Metropolitan College led to the view that there needs to be a member of staff within each college with responsibility for computers and special needs, with time to co-ordinate staff development within the college and to take part in regional and national support network. It is not enough for developments to take place solely within the college. No one member of staff can possibly know or have the time to investigate new software and other developments whilst keeping up-to-date with educational reforms.

At the Isle of Wight CAT, at the time of Hitt's (1990) study, the special needs section was served by various mainstream tutors but no information technology lecturers. The majority of the staff came from basic or primary education. Their feelings about computers ranged from very sceptical interest to almost terror at the thought of using computers. The team leader was enthusiastic but with no experience or natural ability to draw on. Staff development had been very slow. Training days led by an interested mainstream colleague who 'knows a bit about BBC' did little to allay fears. He, like most so-called experts, seemed to speak a different language.

These views indicate some of the problems faced with staff development. Probably the most important is that, outside a relatively small proportion of teachers who have motivation and technological skills to take on the challenge of using computers in teaching, there is a much larger group who have neither motivation nor technological skills, and who remain sceptical about the value of computers in education. This is the realistic context for staff development. Staff development plans for individual teachers may have to vary considerably. Plans will need to take into account individual skills, needs of pupils and students, area of the curriculum, and whether support is to be drawn from local, regional or national resources. What is clear from our experiences is that teachers must not be put in a situation where a computer is delivered to a classroom together with only the technical manuals. This has happened on many occasions and in the absence of advice or support, teachers have sought to master the complexities of the hardware and software, and then tried to develop a teaching application. In these circumstances the potential for re-inventing the wheel is very high. At the very least, this approach usually leads to many hours of work for which there is little to show except frustration and disillusionment.

Two aspects of staff development particularly need to be considered in relation to learning difficulties and computers. They reflect current practice. The first is access to information; the second is training. They are not discrete, sequential activities but should be integrated over a long period of time.

Access to information

The starting point for the use of computers by children and adults with learning difficulties must be individual needs, as it should be for everyone who uses a computer. These needs can be very different and complex. Having identified a need, how does a teacher establish whether a computer can help with that need? In Chapter 14 we described assessment schemes and centres that have emerged for children and adults with physical disabilities and/or communication needs. Unfortunately, the majority of learners are not covered by assessment schemes: it is the teacher's responsibility to seek advice and support.

Providing information for teachers in English and Welsh schools was included within the original remit of the Microelectronics Education Programme established in 1982. Subsequently, this remit for special educational needs was carried out by the Microelectronics Education Support Unit (MESU) and then the National Council for Educational Technology (NCET). For seven years, four regional special education microelectronic resources centres (SEMERCs) took on this role and produced a range of newsletters and information sheets. These became a valuable resource for teachers as they included examples of good practice and experiences as well basic information about hardware and software. NCET produced a national newsletter (Special Update) and a series of information sheets (Briefing) following the ending of central funding for the SEMERCs in 1989. Many local education authorities joined together to fund regional centres to continue the provision of information and other staff development activities, though pressure on funding led to cutbacks in some parts of the UK.

Another source of information has been the Special Education Needs Database (SEND) which is hosted by the Scottish Council for Educational Technology (SCET) and made available via Prestel and CD-ROM. As this database expanded to meet the information needs of teachers in Scotland, and now the UK, case studies were included in addition to information about hardware, software and sources of advice. An interesting development was the allocation of pages within the database to schools and interest groups who could provide information on experiences in using information technology for special educational needs. Written by teachers for teachers this approach produced information that is realistic without raising expectations too high – which is one of the limitations of providing information about hardware and software in isolation.

In the US, the Trace Center provides information sheets and a reprint series for published papers. This service caters for a wide range of enquirers including those new to the area of information technology for people with disabilities. One reprint series on 'Commonly asked questions' includes 'I know someone who has a disability. How can a computer be useful to them?' (Trace Center, 1990). This paper surveys what can be achieved by the adaptation of computers, and points to other sources of information and professional advice. It concludes, 'In trying to determine whether a computer will help a given individual, it is important to first know exactly what it is that you would like the individual to do with the computer'. It reinforces the needs-led rather than the technology-led approach. Enquirers can obtain more detailed information through the ABLEDATA database which is distributed on CD-ROM for the full version. Interesting features on the disc include samples of speech from several speech synthesisers which enable comparisons in quality to be made without having to set up each device on a computer.

In the UK, in response to requests from teachers and advisers, NCET has developed several resource packs about different groups of learners. Each pack is prepared by a task group, identified and supported by NCET. The first is a set of materials representing current thinking about information technology and students with severe learning difficulties (Detheridge, 1990). It contains a set of newspaper style A4 pamphlets, each dealing with a specific topic and written by experienced teachers. The design of the pack allows for expansion and updating.

The CALL Resource (see Chapter 14) is another valuable source of information with its numerous case studies. In addition it includes a means of linking to databases such as SEND and ABLEDATA. The prospect of a single resource on a teacher's desk has come nearer through CD-ROM. It is already technically feasible to bring together on the one hand the means of assessing individual needs, and on the other a wide range of information about experiences, case studies and the availability of hardware and software.

Training

When computers were first used in education, there was little understanding as to how they might be used. They appeared to many teachers to offer a major step forward as they could be programmed for any individual application and the knowledge required to do this appeared to be modest. The reason for this was that the programming language BASIC was included with most computers. Little effort was required to write a program for applications such as the calculation of areas of rectangles, triangles and circles. This approach was reinforced by courses in computer literacy which often focused on BASIC programming. How many unfinished or inconsequential programs were produced in the 1970s and 80s will never be known. The experience was valuable for some teachers and a few programs were produced that had significant implications for people with disabilities and special educational needs.

Of course, the prospect of every teacher being trained as a programmer was neither realistic nor necessary. What training do teachers need? Can experiences help to determine the training needs for the future? What new developments are emerging that might assist? These questions all arise once it is accepted that computers have a role to play in helping children and adults with learning difficulties. Experiences that we have gathered suggest that several aspects of the use of computers can be identified where training is required (see Fig. 15.1).

Computer literacy training is still a requirement when teachers are new to computer technology. There are basic concepts to understand and a few skills to acquire. But these are minimal and do not include programming except for an awareness of what is involved. It is important that techniques associated with the management of storage devices are understood, together with methods of copying and backing-up programs and data. An appreciation of alternatives to keyboards and visual displays such as speech output and voice input is also appropriate for teachers of children and adults with special educational needs. Beyond computers, an awareness of other information technology devices and their use in education provides a broader context.

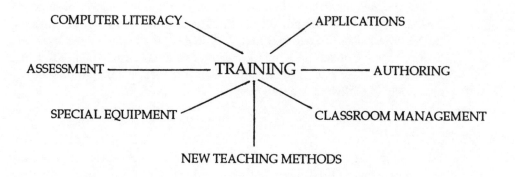

*Figure 15.1 - **What training do teachers need?***

Training in the use of **applications** (computer programs) is essential. This includes both the functional use of the programs and their application to learning difficulties and individual needs. An approach that has found favour is the use of a small number of powerful and flexible programs, plus curriculum materials, to provide effective support for learning. The content-free (framework) programs we have mentioned so often, such as wordprocessors, databases and spreadsheets, are particularly valuable. This approach is incorporated in a training pack (Garrett and Dyke, 1988) developed from courses within the Microelectronics Education Programme. The tutor's notes include examples of INSET courses together with an introduction to special educational needs software. Examples of support materials for use with content-free software make up the second book in the package together with a video that illustrates some of the software and devices described in the text. Two programs in particular are used in the training pack – *Touch Explorer* and *Prompt 3*. Descriptions of classroom applications of *Touch Explorer* include a tactile database, a story teller, and a builder of language and concepts. All of the ideas work with a Concept Keyboard. This is also true for the introductory wordprocessor, *Prompt 3*. The book on support materials includes nearly 100 ideas for using the wordprocessor, with examples of overlays.

One of the features of SEMERC residential courses was the bringing together of special education coordinators and advisers from groups of local education authorities to develop INSET plans for the following year. In a report on the 1987 course (Redbridge SEMERC, 1987), 17 of the 23 participants chose to use the time to develop some aspect of the use of content-free software in their plans. This is not an unusual statistic in the UK where using content-free software for a wide range of special educational needs is widespread and successful.

Grants for Education Support and Training (GEST), a DES funding scheme for local education authorities, includes the provision of communication aids for children for a period of three years (1991–94). This has immediate implications for training in **assessment**. We described the work of the ACE Centre in Chapter 14 but this new phase of funding requires a wider awareness of the need for assessment and training. The evolution of ACE Centre training illustrates the impact of increasing numbers of children who will be using communication aids and the support that is required. In earlier years the ACE Centre concentrated on individual assessments and awareness raising through open days. Current plans include Centre-based training days and INSET for individuals, specialised regional courses and outreach training.

Training in the use of **authoring** software on a computer will be needed as multi-media applications are developed. The bringing together of text, still and moving images, and sound creates new opportunities to use computers for children and adults with learning difficulties. It will build on the success of content-free software and the use of the Concept Keyboard by teachers to design imaginative overlays that can be motivating and help overcome learning difficulties. This has been demonstrated by technologies such as laser vision (interactive video) but the techniques for producing the discs are at present beyond the scope of most teachers. This is likely to change as software is developed for commercial multi-media applications that could readily be used in teaching, and the availability of low cost, high capacity storage devices.

For the foreseeable future there will be a need for teachers to be trained in using **specialised equipment** for children and adults with physical and sensory disabilities. This may be braille transcription software for blind people or communication systems for deaf people. Whatever the device or system, teachers will be needed to be trained in their functional use and their application to learning difficulties. There are also training needs for the students.

The **classroom management** of computers presents further training needs. One of the outcomes of the widespread availability of low-cost information technology devices is that many people have personal devices. It is not inconceivable in the near future (indeed there are examples now) that every student in a special school or college has personal use of or access to a computer to help overcome learning difficulties. In terms of hardware and software this results in a very large increase in resource levels in classrooms. Experiences indicate that teachers are having difficulty in managing these resources.

Examples do exist of the successful integration of information technology devices into the classroom. Initially, the use of a closed circuit television (CCTV) in a middle school classroom for one partially sighted boy was not successful as he became isolated in one corner where the equipment was sited. Subsequently (by accident rather than through training), the CCTV was used by other pupils to magnify samples of leaves which had to be drawn. The status of the pupil increased significantly as he was the only person who could operate the CCTV, and his involvement in joint work with other pupils also increased.

The increased use of computers in the classroom can lead to the use of new **teaching methods**. For example, in Chapter 4 we described access to text by students with physical disabilities using hypermedia. As course material, books and assignments can be provided through this medium, it is necessary to consider alternative teaching methods: it may be more feasible to introduce self-paced learning where a complete course is available on one high capacity CD-ROM.

Not all teachers take advantage of training opportunities. This may be because of competing demands on their time or lack of awareness of the need for training. One local education authority introduced a novel incentive scheme. In Bedford-shire, an IT support centre adopted a policy of not releasing software to teachers unless they had participated in a training programme which included functional use of the software and how it might be used within the curriculum. There is no doubt that this policy leads to savings in time for teachers (beyond the amount invested in training) and improved standards in the application of software. A further benefit is that teachers from various schools come together for a common purpose during the training course which provides an opportunity for subsequent exchange of experiences through interest or user groups.

Summary

Staff development is a crucial factor when computers are used for learning diffi-culties. This includes both the provision of information (particularly experiences of other teachers and case studies) and training in the functional use of the technology and its application to individual needs. The value of using a small number of content-free programs lies in mimimising the training required and maximising the opportunities to overcome learning difficulties. Training initiatives to date have been inadequate.

16 The Next Decade: Changes Still Needed

Looking back to look forward

It often helps to look back before looking forward. When personal computers first became available in the 1970s, there was no collective policy on how they might be used for or by individuals with disabilities and special educational needs. Among the first to notice that this new information technology device had a great deal to offer were teachers and carers working with people with physical and sensory disabilities. An exciting period of innovation followed as developers tried to exploit the potential of computers and related microelectronic devices. Early successes included adding speech output to computers, thus providing specialised facilities such as 'talking calculators' for blind people, and replacing computer keyboards by switches to provide a writing facility for severely physically-disabled people. These worthwhile developments were usually associated with individuals or small organizations, who worked in relative isolation to meet the specific needs of a few individuals.

This pioneering work in the 1970s demonstrated that computers and other microtechnology had an important role to play for many people with special needs. In some ways this was a surprise, because the companies that made the original investment in such things as the development of wordprocessing programs for computers had solely commercial motives in mind: the potential market in commerce and industry was huge. Doubtless they were pleased that the same programs were exploited, often without any adaptation, in education, employment and in the home by many people with disabilities and special educational needs. Some authorities might even argue that the introduction of computers into commerce and industry has yielded only marginal benefits, whereas for learners with difficulties, computers have given a new dimension to their lives, as shown by examples in this book.

How many have benefitted from the use of computers? That is not easy to determine. Data exist on how many computers have been provided in mainstream and special education, but not on the benefits gained. Only detailed evaluation, which seldom occurs, could tell that story. It is easier to look at the potential. Hundreds of thousands of individuals *might* benefit because they have special educational needs: these include the 2 percent (approximately) of children within the UK who have Statements or records of need, a further 18 percent of all children, identified by Warnock as requiring some form of special educational provision during their school career, and the 35,000 students in further and higher education (Stowell,1987) who need similar provision.

The fact is that only a minority of these individuals have had access to computers, and success has not been universal. Many learners who have been provided with computers and other devices have not had their needs met. These needs are diverse and complex. They may also change as individuals move between different stages of education and are engaged in training and employment. Computers and other microelectronic devices add further complexity, which is why, as we discussed in Chapter 14, better assessment of individual needs is essential. But what are the other factors associated with success and failure? Some of them are indicated in Fig. 16.1. We can illustrate the interplay of these factors through the experiences of David, one individual who, over a period of ten years, met success, failure and frustration in using computers to meet his needs. Although other learners will not

Figure 16.1 - The individual and new information technology

have the same needs and experiences as David, for them the implications of using this new technology are likely to be similar.

FROM FRUSTRATION TO REALISATION

David lost his sight over 20 years ago. This resulted in the loss of his job in the printing industry. To open up the prospects of a new career, in 1982 David registered as a student with the Open University. At first, his access to course material was solely through audio recordings on standard cassettes, a reasonably satisfactory alternative for printed text but not for diagrams and pictures.

Difficulties of learning at a distance soon emerged when he found he needed to correspond with the University and produce written work for tutors. For some courses, David also needed access to computers.

To help meet these needs, a charitable organisation provided him with a computer and speech synthesiser. His expectations were immediately raised. Unfortunately, at that time, individual assessments were not carried out with the inevitable consequence that his needs were not met. The whole person approach was not adopted. David did persevere with the computer and after a year was able to listen to individual characters being spoken from the screen, a very tedious process but, in relative terms, successful for him as he had only his own circumstances to judge progress by.

David's progress was suddenly accelerated by getting a new computer and speech software, together with a 'talking wordprocessor' and 'talking BASIC'. Immediately he had the means of producing printed text both for letters and written material such as essays for tutors. In one of his first letters to the University in 1983 he wrote 'this is the first time for 13 years that I have been able to write independently'. He now had access to information and was able to find out about other developments.

The computer proved to be valuable to David beyond his immediate study needs. He developed an interest in computer games and produced the equivalent of space invaders and many others that could be used by blind people by a combination of speech and sounds that represented the usual screen displays. In turn, he established a 'talking magazine' for distribution on audio cassettes which provided many other people with access to information. Above all, he integrated the computer into his life. He used the computer almost as frequently as a sighted person would use a pen and paper. It is this integration that has been a key factor with David, and with many other people.

In progressing to graduation, David's choice of courses that made up his degree profile was extended by having the use of a computer. In particular, he was able to follow courses with a computing element. Although by no means fully achieved, his access to the curriculum was considerably enhanced.

After graduation, David sought employment. His first job was to provide a technical advice service by telephone to blind people, and other users, concerning the devices and software produced by Dolphin Systems for Disabled People. Subsequently, he was appointed as an administrator at the Open University where he now works. His demands on the technology to meet his needs have increased significantly. His workstation now has talking versions of several programs that are needed within his work as well as a wordprocessor and electronic mail. He has a scanner to capture printed documents which he then reads within the wordprocessor. The skills that David has acquired over several years have proved to be invaluable. It is also interesting to note that many people who read David's electronic mail or who receive printed memoranda are unaware that he is blind – this equalising effect of new technology is an important factor for him in developing professional relationships within the University.

David's computer at home has also undergone a transition. He has added to it a CD-ROM player so that he can 'read' discs with a speech output. The first was *Microsoft Bookshelf* which gave him access to a full version of a dictionary for the first time since he lost his sight. Recently, through combining CD technology, hypertext retrieval software and screenreading software, David has gained access to all the 1990 articles from the 'Times' and 'Sunday Times'. This is an example of bringing resources together.

This story has to end with a concern for the future. Most new commercial software is being produced with a graphical user interface (GUI) such as *Windows* 3 for IBM compatible computers. Although sighted users get an easier-to-use interface with graphics, icons and pointers, blind people face considerably greater difficulties. David may be at an even greater disadvantage than before in accessing computers by *Windows* 3 – an example of a paradox of new technology.

Two factors that this story does not highlight are continuity and training. The continuity factor arises when someone moves within education (such as school to college, or college to university) or from education to employment. The need for the same or different technology may arise but the source of provision may not be the same. In either circumstance, the person is vulnerable if technology is withdrawn and has to be replaced on transition. For this reason, the provision of technology that is independent of the stage in a person's life is clearly desirable.

David's story does not highlight the need for training people like him in how to use computers and other microelectronic devices. The training he got is disguised by his long term links with projects and individuals who provided support over several years, and by his use of training and reference materials made accessible through screen reading software on his computer. For many, training – or lack of it – is likely to cause most difficulties once a computer is provided even when the computer is the most appropriate choice. Learners must acquire skills in both the use of enabling technology and computer applications if their broader needs are to be met.

Access to the curriculum

When computers are used by children and adults with learning difficulties, the broad implications in Fig. 16.1 apply. We turn now to consider in more detail factors involved in access to the curriculum (see Fig. 16.2).

To get access to the curriculum with computers, first of all individuals have to get access to the computers. Without doubt, as we have shown, use of enabling technology to provide access to computers is widespread and diverse amongst children and adults with learning difficulties. The technology includes screen-readers for blind people, alternatives to keyboards (switches, speech input) for physically disabled people, and keyboards with overlays of pictures or words that match skills and language for individuals with cognitive difficulties. Enabling technology provides access to computer applications used in mainstream classes as well as in special education. It is the first factor to be considered in assuring success.

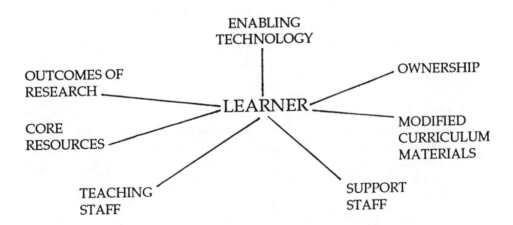

Figure 16.2 - Factors influencing access to the curriculum

A second factor, important for both teachers and learners when computers are used, is the feeling of ownership, gained through recognition of an individual's contribution to a program or application. Teachers feel they 'own' the overlays they create for the Concept Keyboard to meet specific needs. They like to be able to adapt the language and content of programs. They prefer content-free software that they can fit into their own teaching style or method, and often reject content-specific software that cannot be modified. Learners feel much the same way, as many of our examples show. They are delighted when they create something they can call their own. This seems to be a powerful reason for the success of teachers who bring into their classrooms software such as *HyperCard*, with which children can use hand scanners to capture pictures, and the sound input facilities to record speech and effects. The learners have an effective medium for developing their own stories with text supplemented by pictures, speech and sound.

Teachers are often overwhelmed by the diversity and complexity of computer software, however, particularly when computers are first introduced to meet special needs. This third factor was recognised in the 1980s by the Special Education Microelectronic Resource Centres (SEMERCs) in the UK when a core library of software was introduced. The idea of the core was to exploit the minimum number of software applications across the maximum number of curriculum areas. This approach led to widespread use of content-free software (such as wordprocessors) and the development of related curriculum materials, a fourth factor. Teachers had to be trained in the functional use of only a small number of programs.

Because not enough is yet known about how to provide access to the curriculum through computers, research continues. Outcomes of research, the fifth factor, must be taken into account in the context of the needs of children and adults with learning difficulties. Recent developments, as we have mentioned, include compact disc technologies and multi-media. Individually, or in combination, these developments could be applied to learning difficulties. Our earlier examples indicate the benefits of CD-ROM for blind learners who have been denied access to large reference works such as encyclopedias. For physically-disabled learners who do not have enough motor control to handle a book, having bookshelves on a disc that hosts text, moving and still images, with sound, is an inviting prospect now realisable. Other needs may be met soon. There are direct implications for learners of continued research.

Finally and most obviously, teaching and support staff are very important in giving learners with special needs access to the curriculum through computers. We discussed their training in Chapter 15.

At the start of the 1990s

To make the most of computers, it is important to formulate local, regional and national policies that can provide the supporting infrastructure and coordinate developments. Central governments in the UK and elsewhere have taken some initiatives, but not enough. Changes are still needed. But first, what is the current situation?

In 1990, as we mentioned in Chapter 1, Her Majesty's Inspectors declared that information technology was making a unique and valuable contribution to the learning of pupils with special educational needs, enriching their learning experiences and enhancing their access to a broad curriculum (Department of Education and Science, 1990a). The inspectors added, however, that further developments were crucially dependent on individual teachers, who needed more training, information, equipment and technical support. They listed four major constraints on the spread of good practice:

- Few teachers, and particularly headteachers, had yet received sufficient training, information or technical support.
- The availability of equipment varied from school to school and depended too much on the school's ability to raise private funds.
- Few LEA advisers and inspectors were sufficiently familiar with use of information technology for special educational needs.
- Local expertise was lacking in assessment of pupils needing information technology as an aid to communication or curricular access, and agreed systems were needed to pay for such aids.

Since the inspectors' survey, more training has been available, and almost all special schools have access to a suitable range of hardware and software. The number of LEA advise and inspectors familiar with computers and special needs has dropped sharply as central government funding has ended. At best, we can say that some progress has been made, but not enough.

With the aim of helping students with special educational needs in further education the Further Education Unit and the Open University searched for local, regional and national initiatives concerning new information technology (Vincent, 1990). The study was within an OECD programme 'Supporting Active Life for Young People with Disabilities'. The researchers tried to chronicle the experiences of teachers, advisers and others who provide support for students using computers and other microelectronic devices, and of students themselves. They drew some conclusions worth summarising here:

- The new technology can give students with disabilities and special educational needs a wider choice of courses and enhanced educational and employment opportunities. This is broadly true for all aspects of disability and special educational needs, but the new technology cannot provide enablement, access or opportunities without proper assessment and re-assessment of individuals' needs, training for students and their teachers and carers, information, advice and technical services.

- Because providing the technology, assessing and training students and others, and using the technology are complex activities, further education colleges need 'facilitators' with access to advice, experience and good practice. Students will then have opportunities that, in turn, can increase their independence.

- The new technology can enable students to acquire skills that match current and future requirements in employment. Many employers are still unaware of this.

- Staff training must be continued, particularly in how the new technology can meet individuals' needs. Students' expertise and experience should be recognised, because they have made significant contributions to staff development.

- After a decade of innovation and development, there is now a considerable body of experience and good practice in the further education sector. Dissemination of this knowledge is essential if duplication of effort is to be avoided.

The picture in the US is similar. Blackhurst and others (1989) reviewed barriers to using computer technology in special education. The equipment barriers they list are common to all classrooms. Implementation barriers include lack of planning, finance and human resources. Teacher training in this field is inadequate, whether initial or in-service. Anti-technology attitudes and traditional ways of organising classroom teaching are barriers to be overcome through further training. Possibly teachers in special education are more receptive to the technology than many of their colleagues because they are accustomed to assistive devices, commonly use a wide range of techniques and in many cases belong to support networks interested in computers.

Where next?

There is no doubt that information technology in general and computers in particular are helping to overcome the learning difficulties of children and adults. In many cases, the technology has provided new or enhanced access to the curriculum. There has been considerable progress since the 1970s, but more remains to be done. We conclude by offering some pointers to the future. They are based on the experiences drawn together in this book. We highlight the users of the technology, their teachers and the support required to make effective use of the technology.

Individual learners

First, consider the users, the individual learners. We have stressed throughout this book that the provision of a computer or similar technological device must be led by need. Assessment is a mechanism for this and should be available to everyone. For those who have learning and communication difficulties that arise from physical disabilities there are centres where professional multi-disciplinary assessment can be provided. In the UK, learners can go to centres such as ACE, FACCT, NFAC and CALL. Clearly this provision must continue. Learners with sensory disabilities are less well supported by suitable assessment centres, and those with cognitive and emotional difficulties have very few opportunities at all. The picture in the US is similar, with excellent provision in some states and for some forms of disability, but less elsewhere.

Overall, the scale of the problem is daunting: huge numbers of learners could be involved. This is why development of materials such as the CALL Resource (Chapter 14) must continue, to extend knowledge and skills to teachers and others so that they can participate in the assessment process.

We must also ask who takes responsibility when individuals transfer between different stages in education, and between education and employment? This is a major challenge to local and national government: formal divisions between health, social services, education and employment mitigate against integrating provision and support for new technology devices for children and adults with special needs. At present an individual is likely to have to go through a similar assessment process every time he or she moves between educational establishments and/or employment.

Enabling technology should be person-centred rather than circumstantial as at present. To achieve this, collaboration between government departments, including co-funding, must become commonplace. This will be a radical change because local and national government developments are mostly related to budgets. For example, although the DES initiative to provide funds for communication aids is generally considered welcome and necessary, its restriction to schools is more related to the mechanism for GEST (Grants for Education Support and Training) than a reflection of need. If the DES IT in Schools Unit became the IT in Education Unit and took on the responsibility for further, higher and adult education then a complementary strategy might emerge. The concept of an IT for Life Unit seems to be too far from reality at the moment.

Teachers

The implications of using computers to help children and adults with learning difficulties are significant for teachers as well as the learners. How can teachers be helped in future? Can the valuable resources already produced by organisations and individuals be brought to the finger tips of teachers? Much has been done through national and regional schemes and initiatives, but more must be done until every teacher has immediate access to the resources when needed.

Observations in the classroom suggest that at present only some of these resources find their way to teachers' desks. Sources of materials, advice and information can be quite numerous, but these resources are not likely to reach teachers in a coherent and comprehensive form. We think every teacher ought to have better access to such resources.

The National Council for Educational Technology has gone some way to meeting this desirable objective through producing briefing sheets and curriculum resource packs (see Chapter 15). The Council brings together groups of teachers who have a common interest. Each group contributes to the development of targetted curriculum materials (see, for example, Detheridge, 1990). This approach provides a framework for many to contribute to a national resource which is then widely disseminated in a common format. Cooperation with a national organisation leads to some consistency. It also helps to avoid replication of effort and ensures that the products are widely advertised.

Developments in Scotland, however, have had a different emphasis compared with the rest of the UK. Scotland now has considerable expertise in centres that support learners with physical and sensory disabilities, and in many cases also provide assessment in relation to communication aids, computers and other new technology. Support for children and adults with cognitive and emotional difficulties is not as well developed. One reason for this is that the equivalent to the SEMERCs in England and Wales did not emerge. The SEMERCs were proactive in supporting the use of content-free software for special educational needs, but similar support was lacking in Scotland. In addition, without a national programme in Scotland there has been no equivalent role for the Scottish Council for Educational Technology (SCET) to that of NCET (previously MESU) in England and Wales. We feel that teachers have probably been the losers.

Networking

All the expertise needed cannot reside in one place, that is clear. The diversity and complexity of learning difficulties and the range of technology are too great. Research, development, training, assessment and modified curriculum materials needed by, say, a blind student does not exhaust the list of support that he or she requires. For this reason specialist centres have emerged. It is inconceivable that every school or college could replicate these centres. It would be ineffective if they did. In Chapter 14 we described how the Open University draws upon the National Federation of ACCESS Centres (NFAC) to provide support for disabled students using computers rather than developing yet another centre. The Federation has set an example in the Further Education sector by promoting the concept of networking, the sharing of experience and expertise. The group of colleges within NFAC is a valuable regional network, not supported through a national programme as the SEMERCs were. The sharing within NFAC grew out of a clear need rather than as a result of direct funding. Within the colleges, networks vary: examples of good practice are commonest when departments such as information technology and special needs can work closely together, just as networks between schoolteachers yield benefits. Creation of groups associated with particular learning difficulties or areas of the curriculum can also be beneficial. These groups are usually voluntary, without access to funds. Many fail to prosper, which is unfortunate because such sharing of knowledge and experience is vital. Modest sums to foster this type of activity can have significant returns.

National organisations have a crucial part to play in networking, not least in providing information and advice, and in disseminating good practice. Better coordination between organisations would reduce duplication of effort, particularly regarding information and computerised databases. The potential for wasting resources in the creation of databases is very high and frequently realised. We do not suggest there should be just one database for the whole of the special education sector, but the scope for networking and collaboration must be recognised, to the benefit of information seekers who often need quality rather than quantity. An important step towards raising quality is a £3 million three-year project recently announced by the Department of Health in the UK. This will rationalise the provision of much information, including that about education, for people with disabilities through establishing local information federations with links to national providers.

Networking must be made effective. It can bring essential resources into the classroom. Teachers will be helped to exploit computers for children and adults with learning difficulties. These learners will have better access to the curriculum. To policy-makers, the issues appear not nearly as urgent as they seem to the teachers and learners. The stones in the river do not know how hot it is out on the hill.

Software Directory

Program	Computer(s)	Publisher or Supplier in UK or US
Acorn DTP	Arc	Acorn Computers, Cambridge Techno Pk, 645 Newmarket Rd, Cambridge CB5 8PD
Adaptive Firmware Card	ApII	Adaptive Peripherals, 4529 Bagley Avenue N, Seattle, WA 98103
Adventures	N	ILECC, John Ruskin St, London SE5 0PQ
Annual Review	BBC	NCET, Science Park, Coventry CV4 7EZ (with Leeds LEA)
Bank	BBC	Microspecial, William Collins plc, Westerhill Road, Glasgow G64 2QT, and Hill MacGibbon Ltd, St Bartholomew House, 92 Fleet St, London EC4Y 1DH
BCalc	BBC	Gemini Marketing, 18a Littleham Road, Exmouth, Devon EX8 2QG
Beeb-Bliss	BBC	Blissymbolics Communication Resource Centre (UK), S Glamorgan Institute of Higher Education, Western Ave, Llandaff, Cardiff CF2 2YB
Bliss-Apple	ApII	MECC, 3490 Lexington Ave N, St Paul, MN 55126
Bliss News	BBC	Blissymbolics, as above
Bliss Snap	BBC	Blissymbolics, as above
Bliss Synrel	BBC	Blissymbolics, as above
Blob 1 and 2	BBC/M, N, Arc	Widgit Software, 102 Radford Rd, Leamington Spa, Warcs CV31 1LF
Bookshelf (CD-ROM)	PC	Microsoft, as below
Brimble Hill Suites	BBC	*Blue File, NorthWest SEMERC, Fitton Hill CDC, Rosary Rd, Oldham OL8 2QE
Bubble Dialogue	Mac	University of Ulster, School of Education, Coleraine BT52 1SA
Cette Ville (videodisc)	IBIS	
CloseView	Mac	Apple Computer, 6 Roundwood Ave, Stockley Park, Uxbridge
Coins	BBC	Microspecial, as above

Collage	N	BECC/MUSE, PO Box 43, Houghton-on-the-Hill, Leicester LE7 9GX
Compact Suite	BBC, N	BIMH & ILECC, Wolverhampton Rd, Kidderminster, Worcs DY10 3PP
Complete Speller, The	BBC/M, N	Northern Micromedia, Resources Centre, Coach Ln, Newcastle-upon-Tyne NE7 7XA
Compose	BBC/M, N, Arc	ESP, 75 Beechdale Rd, Bilborough, Nottingham NG8 3AE
Concept Keyboard Match	BBC	Blue File, as above
Contact	BBC/M	RESOURCE, off Coventry Grove,Exeter Rd Doncaster DN2 4PY
Count With Blob	BBC/M, N, Arc	Widgit, as above
Crackit	PC	School of Education, Southampton University SO9 5NH, or NCET as above
Crossword Call-up	BBC/M, Arc, N	Northern Micromedia, as above
Dart	BBC/M, Arc	The Advisory Unit, Endymion Rd,Hatfield AL10 8AU
Datacard/Datasweet	Arc	Kudliansoft
Datashow		NCET, as above
Decision Maker	Mac	Kinko's Academic Courseware Exchange 255 W Stanley Ave, Ventura, CA 93002
Degas Elite	Atari 1040	
Developing Tray	BBC/M, N	ILECC, as above
Domesday Disc	BBCM	Cumana Ltd, Pines Trdg Estate, Broad St, Guildford GU3 3BH
Dragon Dictate	PC	Dragon Systems, 90 Bridge St, Newton, MA 02158
Early Fingers	BBC	Blue File, as above
Easy Type	BBC	Sherston Software, Swan Barton, Sherston, Malmesbury SN16 0LH
Ecodisc	BBCM	Cumana Ltd, as above
Electricity in the Home	BBC/M, Arc	Blue File, as above
Exploratory Play	Apple IIe	Peal Software, 5000 N Parkway, #105 Calabasas, CA 91302
Facemaker	BBC	esm Ltd, Abbeygate House, East Rd, Cambridge CB1 1DB
Fairy Tales/ Christmas Tales	BBC	Blue File, as above

Fantasy Island	BBC	Tressell Publications, Lower Ground Floor, 70 Grand Parade, Brighton BN2 2JA
Floor Robots (1 and 2)	BBC/M	Blue File, as above
Folio	BBC, Arc	esm Ltd, as above
From Pictures to Words	BBC, N, Arc	Widgit , as above
Front Page Extra	BBC/M	Newman College & MAPE, Genners Lane, Bartley Green, Birmingham B32 3NT
Fun Phonics	BBC/M	PAVIC Publications, Sheffield City Polytechnic, 36 Colegiate Cres, Sheffield 2BP
Ghost Hunt	BBC	
Going Places	BBC/M	Widgit Software, as above
Graded Mazes	BBC/M	David Haigh, The Park Special School, Lowfield Lane, Wakefield WF2 8SX
Grammatik III	PC	Reference Software, 330 Townsend St, Suite 123, San Francisco, CA 94107
Grass	BBC/M, Arc, N	Newman College, as above
Grasshopper	BBC/M, Arc, N	Newman College, as above
Handiword	PC	
Healthdata	BBC, Arc, N, PC	Healthdata, 21 Vicar's Cl., London E9 7HT
Home	BBC/M	Northern Micromedia, as above
Hyperbook	Mac	Longman Logotron, Dales Brewery, Gwydir St, Cambridge CB1 2LJ
HyperCard	Mac	Apple Computer, as above
Image	BBC/M	Homerton College, Hills Rd, Cambridge CB2 2PH
Instant Keyboard Fun	ApIIe/gs	Electronic Courseware Systems, 1210 Lancaster Dr, Champaign, IL 61821
Instant Music	ApIIe, Amiga	Electronic Arts, phone 415 572 2787
Junior Ecosoft	BBC	Advisory Unit, as above
Keys	BBC	Abbey Hill School, Cleveland
Keyworks	Mac	Apple Computer, as above
MacDraw	Mac	Apple Computer, as above
Macintalk	Mac	Apple Computer, as above
McGee	ApIIe, Mac	Lawrence Productions, 1800 S. 35th St, Galesburg, MI 49053
Mallory Manor	BBC/M, N	Newman College & MAPE, as above
Mazer	BBC	Blue File, as above
Mazes	BBC	Blue File, as above
MicroSoft Works	Mac, PC	MicroSoft Ltd, Excel House, 40 De Montfort Rd, Reading RG1 8LP

MindReader	PC	Brown Bag Software, 2155 South Bascom Ave., Campbell, CA 95008
M/Mazer	BBC	Blue File, as above
Monitoring and Recording	Arc	Kenrick and Jefferson
Mouse Perfect	Mac	Apple Computer, as above
Move It	N	MUSE, as above
Moving In	BBC/M, Arc	Blue File, as above
Music Construction Set	AplIe, PC	Electronic Arts
Music Shapes	AplIe/gs	Music Systems for Learning, 311 East 38th Street, Suite 20C, New York, NY 10016
Music Studio	AplIgs, PC	Activision, phone 415 329 0500
Outspoken	Mac	Apple Computer, as above
Paintbox	N	
PAL	PC	Scetlander, 74 Victoria Crescent Rd, Glasgow G12 9JN
PALSTAR	PC	Scetlander, as above
Pendown	BBC/ M, Arc, PC	Longman Logotron, as above
Phases 2	Arc	NorthWest SEMERC, as above
Picture Play	BBC/M	Blue File, as above
Podd	BBC	esm Ltd, as above
Poster	Arc	4 Mation, Linden Lea, Rock Park, Barnstaple EX32 9AQ
Print Shop, The	AplIe, Atari	Broderbund Software, 17 Paul Drive, San Rafael, CA 94903
Pro12	Atari	Steinberg, c/o Evenlode Soundworks, The Studio, Church St, Stonesfield OX7 2PS
Pro24	Atari	Steinberg, as above
ProArtisan	Arc	Clares, 98 Middlewich Rd, Rudheath CW9 7DA
Profiling Package	BBC	Mick Ellis
Prompt3 (see next entry)	BBC	
Prompt/Writer	BBC/M, N	NCET, as above
Quest	BBC	Advisory Unit, Endymion Road, Hatfield AL10 8AU
Quest Paint	BBCM	Watford Electronics, 250 Lower High Street, Watford WD1 2AN
Read Right Away		
Representational Play		Peal Software, as above
AplIe		

Scenario Designer	BBC/M, N, Arc	Blue File, as above
Scenarios	BBC/M, Arc	Blue File, as above
Soundspace	BBC	Hybrid Technology
Speedwriter	Arc	Le Computer
Spider	BBC	
Stylus	BBC/M, N	Newman College & MAPE, as above
Stylus	Arc	Northern Micromedia, as above
StoryMaker	Mac	University of Ulster, as above
Superart	BBC/M	Watford Electronics, as above
Superpaint	Mac	
Switch On	BBC/M, Arc	Brilliant Computing, PO Box 142, Bradford BD9 5NF
Switch On Travel	BBC/M, Arc	Brilliant Computing, as above
Talking Keys	Mac	
TIG	BBC/M	Blue File, as above
Time	BBC	Abbey Hill School, Cleveland
Touch and Learn	BBC/M	Dudley College (Homer & Chapman)
Touch Explorer Plus	BBC/M, Arc, N	NCET, as above
Touch Explorer Plus Prompt/Writer	N, Arc	RESOURCE, as above
Touch Games 1 and 2	BBC/M, Arc	Brilliant Computing, as above
Touching Sound	BBC/M, Arc	NCET, as above
Town	BBC, N	Northern Micromedia, as above
Turbo Lightning	PC	Borland International, 1700 Green Hill Rd, Scotts Valley, CA 95066
Typing Tutor IV	PC	
Using Pictures	BBC/M	Widgit, as above
Using Rebus	BBC	Blue File, as above
Using Rebus II	BBC/M	Blue File, as above
Ventura Publisher	PC	
View	BBC	Acorn Computers, as above
Viewbook	BBC/M	Information Education
Voice Navigator	Mac	Articulate Systems
What's That Picture?	BBC/M	Blue File, as above
Windows 3	PC	Microsoft, as above
Word Attack	ApplIe	Davidson Software, 3135 Kashiwa, Torrance, CA 90505

Word	Mac, PC	Microsoft, as above
Word Perfect	PC	
Wordstar	Mac, PC	
WordSwopper	Mac	University of Ulster, as above
Wordweb		
Write This Way	ApII, Mac	Interactive Learning Materials, PO Box S, Croton Lake Road, Katonah, NY 10536

*Blue File programs are freely copiable for educational purposes within the UK

Interactive Video Dictionary is a product of the Scottish Interactive Technology Centre, Moray House College, Holyrood Road, Edinburgh EH8 8AQ, from which details can be obtained of hardware required.

Key

A	Acorn BBC A3000
ApII	Apple II
Arc	Acorn Archimedes
BBC	Acorn BBC or BBC+
BBCM	Acorn BBC Master 128
BBC/M	Acorn BBC or BBC+ or Acorn BBC Master 128
Mac	Apple Macintosh
N	Research Machines Nimbus
PC	IBM Personal Computer or compatible

The directory includes only those programs mentioned in our book. We have done our best to ensure that information given is accurate, but this is a rapidly changing area. We apologise that no further details are included about a few programs. In the UK, the National Council for Educational Technology (Bailey and others, 1990) recently published a software catalogue for teachers of pupils with severe learning difficulties. In the US, teachers of children with special needs generally use programs for the Apple II range and Macintosh computers. A principal distributor is Don Johnston Development Equipment Inc, PO Box 639, 1000 North Rand Rd, Bdg 115, Wauconda, IL 60064.

References

ACE Centre (1987) Switches and Interfaces. Edition 2. Oxford: The Centre.

Bangay, B. (1990) Bury Metropolitan College. In Vincent, T. (ed) *New Technology, Disability and Special Educational Needs: Some Case Studies in Further Education.* Coventry, UK: Empathy Ltd, Hereward College of Further Education.

Beeson, C. (1988) Manchester SEMERC's Special Needs in Mainstream Project. In Johnston, J. and Buckland, M. (eds) *Ten Teachers' Accounts of Using Micros with Children with Special Educational Needs.* Bristol: Bristol SEMERC.

Behrmann, M. (1985) *Handbook of Microcomputers in Special Education.* Windsor: NFER-Nelson.

Behrmann, M. (1988) *Integrating Computers Into the Curriculum: A Handbook for Special Educators.* Boston: College-Hill Press.

Bell, J. (1991) Personal communication.

Beste, R. (1990) Using symbols – can the computer help. In Detheridge, T. (ed) (1990) *Technology in Support of the National Curriculum for Children with Severe Learning Difficulties: a Resource Pack.* Coventry: National Council for Educational Technology.

Biklen, D. (1990) Communication unbound: autism and praxis. *Harvard Educational Review*, 60, 3.

Blackhurst, A. E. and others (1989) *Advancing Technology Use: Barriers to Research Utilization.* Reston, Virginia: Center for Special Education Technology.

Boyce, A.J. and Turfus, S.J. (1990) Doncaster College for the Deaf. In Vincent, T. (ed) *New Technology, Disability and Special Educational Needs: Some Case Studies in Further Education.* Coventry, UK: Empathy Ltd, Hereward College of Further Education.

Brandenburg, S. (1987) *Overview: Evaluation/Assessment Defined and in Relation to P.L. 94–142 and P.L. 99–457.* Madison, Wisconsin: University of Wisconsin-Madison, Trace Research and Development Center Report.

Brightman, A. (1989) Challenging the myth of disability. *Educom*, Winter.

Brown, C. and others (1989) *Computer Access in Higher Education for Students with Disabilities: A Practical Guide to the Selection and Use of Adapted Computer Technology.* Second edition. Sacramento: California Community Colleges.

Buckland, M. (1988) Logo, the floor turtle and children with special educational needs. Unpublished MPhil thesis, Council for National Academic Awards.

Buckland, M. (1991) Personal communication.

Butterworth, I. (1991) Personal communication.

CALL Centre (1991) *Microtechnology and Disabled Learners: An Interactive Training and Information Resource.* Edinburgh: The Centre.

Cartwright, G. P. (1984) Computer applications in special education. In Walker, D. and Hess, R. (eds) *Instructional Software: Principles and Perspectives for Design and Use.* Belmont, California: Wadsworth.

Coleman, C.L. (1988) Computer recognition of the speech of adults with cerebral palsy. Paper presented at the Fifth Biennial International Conference on Augmentative and Alternative Communication, Anaheim, October. Quoted in Lahm, E. (1989) *Technology with Low Incidence Populations: Promoting Access to Education and Learning.* Reston, Virginia: Council for Exceptional Children.

Crossley, R. and McDonald, A. (1980) *Annie's Coming Out.* New York: Penguin.

Dando, Helen (1991) Personal communication.

Daniels, H. and Ware, J. (eds) (1990) *Special Educational Needs and the National Curriculum: the Impact of the Education Reform Act.* London: Kogan Page.

Davidson, J., Coles, D., Noyes, P. and Terrell, C. (1991) Using computer-delivered natural speech to assist in the teaching of reading. *British Journal of Educational Technology*, 22, 2.

Dean, M. (1990) Pupils take over the production of resources. *PrintRun* (Newsletter of the Bristol SEMERC), Summer.

Department of Education and Science (1978) *Special Educational Needs.* Report of the Committee of Enquiry into the Education of Handicapped

Children and Young People (The Warnock Report). London: HMSO.

Department of Education and Science (1989a) *From Policy to Practice*. London: The Department.

Department of Education and Science (1989b) *Information Technology from 5 to 16: Curriculum Matters 15*. London: HMSO.

Department of Education and Science (1989c) *English in the National Curriculum: Key Stage 1 Orders*. London: The Department.

Department of Education and Science (1989d) *English for Ages 5–16: Consultation Report, Key Stages 2/3/4*. London: The Department.

Department of Education and Science (1990a) *Education Observed: Information Technology and Special Educational Needs in Schools*. London: HMSO.

Department of Education and Science (1990b). *English in the National Curriculum: Key Stages 2/3/4 Orders*. London: The Department.

Department of Education and Science (1991a). *Survey of Information Technology in Schools*. Statistical Bulletin 11/91. Darlington: The Department's Analytical Services Branch.

Department of Education and Science (1991b) *Survey of Information Technology in Initial Teacher Training*. Statistical Bulletin 12/91. Darlington: The Department's Analytical Services Branch.

Detheridge, T. (ed) (1990) *Technology in Support of the National Curriculum for Children with Severe Learning Difficulties: a Resource Pack*. Coventry: National Council for Educational Technology.

Detheridge, T. and Hopkins, C. (1990) Switch control. In Detheridge, T. (ed) *Technology in Support of the National Curriculum for Students with Severe Learning Difficulties: a Resource Pack*. Coventry: National Council for Educational Technology.

Disdier, A. (1988) Has technology overlooked the autistic? *TECH-NJ* (Journal of the Department of Special Education, Trenton State College, New Jersey), 1, 1.

Drage, C. (1990) Taking control. *Educational Computing and Technology*, 11, 7, November.

Edwards, A.D.N. (1991) *Speech Synthesis: Technology and Disabled People*. London: Chapman.

FACCT (1989) Personal communication.

Fawkes, W.G. (1988) Using the IBM PC to teach music to deaf children. In Barnetson, P. (ed) *IBM Personal Computing in Schools*. London: Kogan Page.

Fenwick, J.T. (1991) Write This Way. *TECH-NJ* (Journal of the Department of Special Education, Trenton State College, New Jersey), 3, 2.

Fowler, P. (1988) *IT Helps: Information Technology for FE Students with Special Needs*. Cambridge: Foister and Jagg.

Garrett, J. and Dyke, B. (1988) *Microelectronics and pupils with special educational needs – support material for the in-service training of teachers*. Manchester: Manchester University Press.

Goldenberg, E.P. (1979) *Special Technology for Special Children*. Baltimore: University Park Press.

Goldenberg, E.P. and others (1984) *Computers, Education and Special Needs* Reading: Addison-Wesley.

Goodwin, M.S. and Goodwin, T.C. (1969) In a dark mirror. *Mental Hygiene*, 53.

Gray, C. (1988) *The Importance of Correct Seating*. Occasional paper. Oxford: ACE Centre.

Green, S. (1990) A study of the application of microcomputers to aid language development in children with autism and related communication difficulties. Unpublished PhD thesis, CNAA/Sunderland Polytechnic.

Griffiths, A. and others (1989) *Computers/IT and the Hearing Impaired Child*. Bristol: National Council for Educational Technology.

Hagen, D. (1984) *Microcomputer Resource Book for Special Education*. Reston, Virginia: Reston Publishing.

Haigh, D. (1990) Developing thinking skills. In Detheridge, T. (ed) *Technology in Support of the National Curriculum for Students with Severe Learning Difficulties: a Resource Pack*. Coventry: National Council for Educational Technology.

Haigh, D. (1991) Personal communication.

Hales, G. (1991) *An Evaluation of the Open University/National Federation of ACCESS Centres*. Project on information technology as an aid to study for Open University students with disabilities. Student Research Centre Report No.39. Milton Keynes: Institute of Educational Technology, The Open University.

Hameyer, U. and Waldow, J. (1987) *Using the Computer in Special Education: Current Approaches and Practices in the Federal Republic of Germany*. Kiel: IPN, Kiel University.

Harvey, D. (1990) Students with severe learning difficulties. In Vincent, T. (ed) *New Technology, Disability and Special Educational Needs: Some Case Studies in Further Education*. Coventry, UK: Empathy Ltd, Hereward College of Further Education.

Hawkridge, D., Vincent, T. and Hales, G. (1985) *New Information Technology in the Education of Disabled Children and Adults*. London and San Diego: Croom Helm and College-Hill Press.

Hitt, P. (1990) Isle of Wight College of Arts and Technology. In Vincent, T. (ed) *New Technology, Disability and Special Educational Needs: Some Case Studies in Further Education*. Coventry, UK: Empathy Ltd., Hereward College of Further Education.

Holliday, P. (1987) Personal communication.

Homer, A. (1990) Personal communication.

Hope, M. (ed) (1986) *The Magic of the Micro: A Resource for Children with Learning Difficulties*. London: Council for Educational Technology.

Hope, M.H. (1987) *Micros for Children with Special Needs*. London: Souvenir Press.

Howard, W. (1991a) *Using Information Technology to Support Pupils with Challenging Behaviour*. Coventry: National Council for Educational Technology.

Howard, W. (1991b) IT and EBD: Looking forward. Hemel Hempstead: Boxmoor House School, mimeo.

James, J. (1988) A project on crime detection using Mallory Manor. In Johnston, J. and Buckland, M. (eds) *Ten Teachers' Accounts of Using Micros with Children with Special Educational Needs*. Bristol: Bristol SEMERC.

James, V.J. and Eyland, E.P. (1991) Australian network provides language, literature and coaching for hearing-impaired students. *British Journal of Educational Technology*, 22, 2.

Jarvis, C. (1988) Work to be proud of: achieving success with wordprocessors. In Johnston, J. and Buckland, M. (eds) *Ten Teachers' Accounts of Using Micros with Children with Special Educational Needs*. Bristol: Bristol SEMERC.

Jenkins, J.P., Kavanagh, M. and Morgan, J.W. (1990) Case study: learning difficulties and behavioural problems. In Vincent, T. (ed) *New Technology, Disability and Special Educational Needs: Some Case Studies in Further Education*. Coventry, UK: Empathy Ltd, Hereward College of Further Education.

Jones, C. (1990) Computer workshop for young people with learning difficulties. In Vincent, T. (ed) *New Technology, Disability and Special Educational Needs: Some Case Studies in Further Education*. Coventry, UK: Empathy Ltd, Hereward College of Further Education.

Jones, C.F.G. (1989) Electronic blackboards or microworlds? *British Journal of Special Education*, 16, 2.

Jones, C. and Morgan, H. (1990) Nimbus' graphics programs prove popular with children with severe learning difficulties. *PrintRun* (Newletter of the Bristol SEMERC), Summer.

Kanner, L. (1943) Autistic disturbances of affective contact. *Nervous Child*, 2.

Kanner, L. (1971) Follow-up study of eleven autistic children originally reported in 1943. *Journal of Autism and Childhood Schizophrenia*, 1, 2.

Karnes, L. (1990) An introduction to dyslexia, diagnosis and treatment. In Hales, G. (ed) *Meeting Points in Dyslexia*. Proceedings of the first International Conference of the British Dyslexia Association, Bath. Reading: The Association.

Keller, J.K. (1990) Characteristics of Logo instruction promoting transfer for learning: a research review. *Journal of Research on Computing in Education*, 23, 1.

Kelly, V. (1988) Using the IBM PC to help children with learning difficulties. In Barnetson, P. (ed) *IBM Personal Computing in Schools*. London: Kogan Page.

Kelly, V (1990) Appropriate help for secondary school students with specific learning difficulties. In Hales, G. (ed) *Meeting Points in Dyslexia*. Proceedings of the first International Conference of the British Dyslexia Association, Bath. Reading: The Association.

Klein, C. (1990) Learning support: a different slant of teaching adult dyslexics. In Hales, G. (ed) *Meeting*

Points in Dyslexia. Proceedings of the first International Conference of the British Dyslexia Association, Bath. Reading: The Association.

Krendle, K.A. and Lieberman, D.A. (1988) Computers and learning: a review of recent research. *Journal of Educational Computing Research*, 4, 4.

Krout, R. (1987) Evaluating software for music therapy applications. *Journal of Music Therapy*, 24, 4.

Lahm, E. (1989) *Technology with Low Incidence Populations: Promoting Access to Education and Learning*. Reston, Virginia: Council for Exceptional Children.

Lewis, P. (1990) Logo, the Floor Turtle and Greenfield Special School. *PrintRun* (Newsletter of the Bristol SEMERC), Summer.

Luebben, A.J. and Oeth, R.B. (1990) Alternate input access: a comparison of keyboard emulating interfaces. *Closing the Gap*, 9, 2.

Lysley, A.G. (1986) *ACE Centre Assessments (1984–1986)*. Report submitted for the Special Diploma in Educational Studies, University of Oxford.

McMahon, H. and O'Neill, B. (1989) *Language Development, Hypermedia and Dialogue Tools*. Coleraine: Faculty of Education, University of Ulster.

Male, M. (1988) *Special Magic: Computers, Classroom Strategies and Exceptional Students*. Mountain View, CA: Mayfield Publishing.

Mansfield, J. (1991) Personal communication.

Margolies, B. (1990) Attention deficit and the Macintosh. *Macintosh Lab Monitor*, Winter.

Marsh, J. (1990) An individual experience. In Vincent, T. (ed) *New Technology, Disability and Special Educational Needs: Some Case Studies in Further Education*. Coventry, UK: Empathy Ltd, Hereward College of Further Education.

Masland, R. (1990) Neurological aspects of dyslexia. In Hales, G. (ed) *Meeting Points in Dyslexia*. Proceedings of the first International Conference of the British Dyslexia Association, Bath. Reading: The Association.

Mathinos, D.A. (1990) Logo programming and the refinement of problem-solving skills in disabled and non-disabled children. *Journal of Educational Computing Research*, 6, 4.

Megarry, J. (1989) Signing on. *Times Educational Supplement*, June 16.

Meng, B. (1990) With a little help from my Mac. *Macworld*, September.

Meyers, L. (1986) *Programs for Early Acquisition of Language*. Calabasas, California: Peal Software.

Middleton, T. (1990) Trends in the use of technologies by handicapped persons in the United States. Paper read at the Second International Conference on Computers for Handicapped Persons, University of Zurich, December.

Miles, T. (1990) Towards an overall theory of dyslexia. In Hales, G. (ed) *Meeting Points in Dyslexia*. Proceedings of the first International Conference of the British Dyslexia Association, Bath. Reading: The Association

Millerchip, J. (1988) Northbrook College Interactive Video Project. *Video Disc Newsletter* (University of London Audio-Visual Centre), 17.

Mittler, P. (1990) Foreword. In Montgomery, D. *Children with Learning Difficulties*. London: Cassell Educational.

Morgan, A. (1990) Computer aided art and design in Ysgol Cefn Glas. *PrintRun* (Newsletter of the Bristol SEMERC), Summer.

Morgan, Ann (1991) Personal communication.

Morocco, C.C. and Neuman, S.B. (1986) Word processing and the acquisition of writing strategies. *Journal of Learning Disabilities*, 19, 4.

Morrison, C. (1990) Social and life skills. In Vincent, T. (ed) *New Technology, Disability and Special Educational Needs: Some Case Studies in Further Education*. Coventry, UK: Empathy Ltd, Hereward College of Further Education.

National Council for Educational Technology (1990). *Languages for All: IT in Modern Languages Learning for Children with Special Educational Needs*. Coventry: The Council.

National Council for Educational Technology (1991). *The IT Needs of Hearing-Impaired Pupils and their Teachers. Information Sheets 1 and 2*. Coventry: The Council.

National Curriculum Council (1989a) *A Curriculum for All*. York: The Council.

National Curriculum Council (1989b) *Consultation Report: English*. York: The Council.

National Curriculum Council (1990) *Non-Statutory Guidance: Information Technology Capability*. York: The Council.

Newell, A.F., Booth, L. and Beattie, W. (1991) Predictive text entry with PAL and children with learning difficulties. *British Journal of Educational Technology*, 22, 1.

Nolan, M. (1990) After years of silence, a child communicates. *The Post-Standard* (Syracuse, New York), September 3.

Odor, P. (1982) Microcomputers and disabled people. *International Journal of Man-Machine Studies*, 17, 1.

Odor, J.P. and Buultjens, M. (1987) *The Raised Diagram Toolkit*. Research Note RN5. Edinburgh: CALL Centre.

Paveley, S. (1990) Profound and multiple learning difficulties. In Detheridge, T. (ed) *Technology in Support of the National Curriculum for Students with Severe Learning Difficulties*. Coventry: National Council for Educational Technology.

Pester, K. (1988) Meeting special educational needs in the primary classroom. In Johnston, J. and Buckland, M. (eds) *Ten Teachers' Accounts of Using Micros with Children with Special Educational Needs*. Bristol: Bristol SEMERC.

Pester, K. (1991) Personal communication.

Pinder, S. (1990) Information technology and its use at Darrick Wood Hearing Impaired Unit. Bromley: Darrick Wood Senior School, London Borough of Bromley, mimeo.

Postlethwaite, K. and Hackney, A. (1988) *Organising the School's Response*. Basingstoke: Macmillan Education.

Pratt, J. and Richards, J. (1990) Extending Maths topic work with Touch Explorer Plus. *PrintRun* (Newsletter of the Bristol SEMERC), Summer.

Riedl, R. (1991) Research notes: Logo revisited. *The Catalyst*, 8, 2.

Rostron, A. and Sewell, D. (1985). *Microtechnology in Special Education*. London: Croom Helm.

Scott, N.G. (1990). An overview of software suitable for disabled postsecondary students. *Closing the Gap*, 9, 2.

Scott, W. (1989) Adapted CAD Program at County College. *TECH-NJ* (Journal of the Department of Special Education, Trenton State College, New Jersey), 1, 2.

Scott, W.C. and Viola, P. (1990) BASIC and beyond: computers motivate emotionally-disturbed teenagers. *TECH-NJ* (Journal of the Department of Special Education, Trenton State College, New Jersey), 2, 2.

Shenkle, A.M. (1989) Zack and the Mac. *TECH-NJ* (Journal of the Department of Special Education, Trenton State College, New Jersey), 2, 1.

Singleton, C. (ed) (1991) *Computers and Literacy Skills*. Hull: British Dyslexia Assocation Computer Resource Centre, University of Hull.

Skeffington, R. (1991) Personal communication.

Slater, A. (1991) *Literacy Project – Words in the Community: SPECCAL Course Project, 1989–90*. London: Inner London Educational Computing Centre.

Slaven, G.(1990) Social and life skills. In Vincent, T. (ed) *New Technology, Disability and Special Educational Needs: Some Case Studies in Further Education*. Coventry, UK: Empathy Ltd, Hereward College of Further Education.

Stansfield, J. (1988) Using AMX art for examination level work. In Johnston, J. and Buckland, M. (eds) *Ten Teachers' Accounts of Using Micros with Children with Special Educational Needs*. Bristol: Bristol SEMERC.

Stansfield, J. (1989) Talking computers. *Information Technology Special Educational Needs Newsletter (Cleveland)*, 2.

Stansfield, J. (1990) What's new? *Information Technology Special Educational Needs Newsletter (Cleveland)*, 6.

Stansfield, J. (1991) Personal communication.

Stowell, R. (1987) *Catching Up? Provision for Students with Special Educational Needs in Further and Higher Education*. London, National Bureau for Handicapped Students.

Sutin, M.S. (1989). Accessing the muse: music technology. *TECH-NJ* (Journal of the Department of Special Education, Trenton State College, New Jersey), 2, 1.

Sutin, M.S. (1990). Accessing the muse: music technology and the handicapped user. *Closing the Gap*, 9, 2.

Swezey, S. (1991) The facilitated communication controversy: truth or suggestion? *The Catalyst*, 8, 2.

Taber, F.M. (1983) *Microcomputers in Special Education: Selection and Decision-Making*. Reston, Virginia: Council for Exceptional Children.

Tanenhaus, J. (1990) What's new in special education software. *Closing the Gap*, 9, 2.

Taylor, J. (1988) Compose, a classroom report. In Johnston, J. and Buckland, M. (eds) *Ten Teachers' Accounts of Using Micros with Children with Special Educational Needs*. Bristol: Bristol SEMERC

Taylor, J. (1990) Aided communication. In Detheridge, T. (ed) *Technology in Support of the National Curriculum for Students with Severe Learning Difficulties*. Coventry: National Council for Educational Technology.

Trace Center (1990) *I Know Someone Who Has a Disability. How Can a Computer be Useful to Them?* Trace Reprint Series 'Commonly Asked Questions'. Madison, University of Wisconsin.

Vincent, T. (ed) (1990) *New Technology, Disability and Special Educational Needs: Some Case Studies in Further Education*. Coventry, UK: Empathy Ltd, Hereward College of Further Education.

Vincent, T. and Schofield, J. (1986) Information technology and braille examinations: an automated approach. *Programmed Learning and Educational Technology*, 23, 2.

Ware, J. (1990) The National Curriculum for pupils with severe learning difficulties. In Daniels, H. and Ware, J. (eds) *Special Educational Needs and the National Curriculum: the Impact of the Education Reform Act*. London: Kogan Page.

Watchman, W. (1990) A breakthrough for Luci! *Print-Run* (Newsletter of the Bristol SEMERC), Summer.

Wedell, K. (1990) Overview: The 1988 Act and current principles of special educational needs. In Daniels, H. and Ware, J. (eds) *Special Educational Needs and the National Curriculum: the Impact of the Education Reform Act*. London: Kogan Page.

Welchman, M. (1990) Experiences worldwide. In Hales, G. (ed) *Meeting Points in Dyslexia*. Proceedings of the first International Conference of the British Dyslexia Association, Bath. Reading: The Association.

Wilsher, C. (1990) Treatments for dyslexia: proven or unproven? In Hales, G. (ed) *Meeting Points in Dyslexia*. Proceedings of the first International Conference of the British Dyslexia Association, Bath. Reading: The Association.

Wood, A. (1990) Witches with everything. *Micro-Scope* (Newsletter of Newman College and Micros And Primary Education: Special Education Special Issue), Summer.

Wood, G. (1990a) Individual experiences. In Vincent, T. (ed) *New Technology, Disability and Special Educational Needs: Some Case Studies in Further Education*. Coventry, UK: Empathy Ltd, Hereward College of Further Education.

Wood, G. (1990b) Derby College of Further Education - the ESF/CET project. In Vincent, T. (ed) *New Technology, Disability and Special Educational Needs: Some Case Studies in Further Education*. Coventry, UK: Empathy Ltd, Hereward College of Further Education.

Index

References in italics indicate computer programs

236